THROUGH
JAMAICAN
LENSES

THROUGH JAMAICAN LENSES

A MEMOIR

FERN JUNE KHAN

UNIVERSITY PRESS OF MISSISSIPPI / JACKSON

The University Press of Mississippi is the scholarly publishing agency of
the Mississippi Institutions of Higher Learning: Alcorn State University,
Delta State University, Jackson State University, Mississippi State University,
Mississippi University for Women, Mississippi Valley State University,
University of Mississippi, and University of Southern Mississippi.

www.upress.state.ms.us

The University Press of Mississippi is a member
of the Association of University Presses.

Library of Congress Cataloging-in-Publication Data

Names: Khan, Fern June, author.
Title: Through Jamaican lenses : a memoir / Fern June Khan.
Description: Jackson : University Press of Mississippi, 2024. | Includes
bibliographical references.
Identifiers: LCCN 2024024450 (print) | LCCN 2024024451 (ebook) | ISBN
9781496852953 (hardback) | ISBN 9781496852946 (trade paperback) | ISBN
9781496852939 (epub) | ISBN 9781496852922 (epub) | ISBN 9781496852915
(pdf) | ISBN 9781496852908 (pdf)
Subjects: LCSH: Khan, Fern June. | Jamaican American women—Biography. |
Jamaican Americans—Biography. | Jamaica—Biography.
Classification: LCC CT368.K43 A3 2024 (print) | LCC CT368.K43 (ebook) |
DDC 973/.0496972920092 [B]—dc23/eng/20240611
LC record available at https://lccn.loc.gov/2024024450
LC ebook record available at https://lccn.loc.gov/2024024451

British Library Cataloging-in-Publication Data available

DEDICATED TO MY HUSBAND:

ISMAIL,
FROM THE MOMENT WE MET, WE KNEW
THERE WAS THE SUBTLE PROMISE OF A FUTURE TOGETHER.

CONTENTS

PREFACE

In 2006 my friend and colleague Dr. Richard Lieberman, professor and director of LaGuardia Community College's Archives, interviewed me for a curriculum that he was developing on immigration for the New York City Public Schools. After almost six hours of being interviewed and providing numerous original documents such as my original passport and letters, I was surprised at the number of stories that flooded my memory as we talked. Prior to the interviews, I did not believe that I had a compelling enough story, one worth sharing.

However, I have always enjoyed listening to, or reading stories like, *The 1,001 Arabian Nights*. I believe that some stories can have an amazing ability to transform lives, to inspire, or simply to bring nuggets of happiness, comfort, and sometimes relief, to the listener or reader. So, although my story may be similar to an immigrant story, it is my unique and personal story. My story is also a Jamaican story situated within a particular era in Jamaica's and, later, America's history.

During my growing-up years in the forties and fifties, Jamaica was still a British colony; George VI was the king of England until 1952; a governor appointed by King George was assigned to serve Jamaica every four years, unless his appointment lasted longer; the Jamaica Government Railway was the main source of distance travel; and speaking "good" English, also known as "the king's English" was an imperative among the rising middle classes.

In writing this narrative, my purpose was to share a balanced view of the Jamaica of my youth and how my early experiences—of feeling safe, close family relationships, having positive role models, and even developing healthy ways to cope with the social and economic challenges that also existed—have all contributed to shaping and strengthening my identity, my sense of self, as well as how those early experiences enabled me to not only adjust to new cultural and educational experiences in the United States but also to develop professionally and to thrive.

By the time Jamaica received its independence from Britain in August 1962, I had already left Jamaica, had just graduated from New York University. Queen Elizabeth had ascended the throne upon the death of King George, her father. The Jamaica Government Railway was no longer in operation. School headmasters were now called principals. And the island now used Jamaican dollars instead of the British sterling currency.

My childhood memories, more accessible from age four to seventeen (1943–1957) are set within the context of colonial Jamaica, prior to the emergence of the ska or reggae musical rhythms. During my youth many Jamaicans were already exposed to the music, performers, films, and literature from America and England, as well as to the stories of economic success from relatives and friends who had traveled abroad, whether as seasonal farm workers or as immigrants to Canada, America, or England. As a result, we had also acquired a global perspective.

Sharing my youthful perspective on Jamaica's music, food, idioms, or sayings, and the implications of color and class, is my contribution to the complex history and social tapestry that is the Jamaican story. Indeed, my memories of those developmental years in Jamaica are still alive with the fun times, Jamaican humor, and healthy relationships with adults and my peers.

Jamaicans are a colorful people; we relish good humor. The native language, patois, is bold, richly descriptive, precise, and humorous, with no words wasted. Jamaicans name a place or an object by the way they perceive that object; for example, the sole of one's foot is referred to as one's "foot bottom." Jamaican poetry and music have used patois effectively to express the feelings, attitudes, and experiences of the people. A composite of English, Spanish, and African languages, patois was developed by enslaved people to communicate among themselves, and on my visits to Jamaica, I have observed that speaking patois seems, in general, to be more acceptable today.

While my journey to and my lived experiences in America have been, indeed, remarkable and memorable, the early influences from my grounded Jamaican cultural and social background, my parents' love and their unshakeable belief in my ability, and the constant affirmations by relatives and friends provided the developmental context for an optimistic attitude, an internal joy, and laid the foundation for subsequent professional achievements in my adult years. In addition was my own quiet resolve and ambition to have a purpose in life and to always perform to the best of my ability.

My hope is that this narrative will not only add to the literary and educational genre but inspire and excite readers to recall their own stories, regardless of their geographic beginnings. In writing my story, I have been enriched by learning so much more about Jamaica's history and culture from books authored by Jamaicans, from their own perspectives, for example, Sherlock and Bennett, Basil K. Bryan, Rachael Manley, Jacqueline Bishop, George Meikle, and so many other writers, as well as by the compelling stories that I heard from African Americans whose impressive accomplishments and courageous actions were achieved despite extreme racial biases and barriers. My own knowledge of Jamaica's early history, especially its connection to slavery, emancipation, and the resulting social impact on Jamaica today, has increased. I was also able to acknowledge the individuals who have significantly influenced my personal and career growth by sharing our journey together.

From a foreign student at NYU in 1958 to a social worker to a higher education administrator, I have come to learn and appreciate the cultural and regional diversity within America. I have a better understanding of the complexity of local and distant environments, and a deeper appreciation for the human condition, nationally and internationally.

My story could fit within Caribbean studies, as a cross-disciplinary reference for sociology, immigration, higher education, education, multicultural education, and adolescent development. In addition, throughout the narrative, there are themes and ideas that could be expanded through, and inspire, further research. Any vernacular used in the narrative has been placed within quotation marks and/or defined within the context of the story.

Mine has been a rich and exciting journey that I am humbled to share with all who are interested, and I hope you find as much joy in reading my story as I found in writing it.

N.B. Throughout the chapters on Jamaica (chapters 1 through 7), the spelling of words is British English. Once the American phase begins, the spelling reverts to the American spelling of words.

THROUGH
JAMAICAN
LENSES

CHAPTER 1

GROWING UP IN RURAL JAMAICA, 1939–1945

I was four years old, standing back-to-back in a line of young children, each of us with a slate and slate pencil in our hands, ready to write letters that our teacher called out, c-a-t, m-a-t, r-a-t, etc. I eagerly awaited the teacher's voice to tell us what to do next. We then repeated the words in unison prior to writing them on our slates. My mother had taken me to this school, less than half a mile from my grandparents' home, because I was said to be a bright little girl. I therefore needed to learn how to read and write. There was no public transportation in rural Cornwall Mountain, so we all walked to wherever we had to go. My mother and grandmother would often talk about how they walked over five miles to church and back in Chichester, another community, on Sundays, so reaching distant places by walking was a given in Cornwall Mountain and other rural villages throughout the island. Walking was so much a part of life in the country that no thought was given to the feeling that "it's too far to walk."

I was in a new pink and white dress patterned with delicate flowers, and I had a pair of new shoes and socks as well as a small slate, which my mother carried in one hand while she held my hand with the other. As we walked toward the school, Mama told me that she, too, had attended that school as a little girl. When we finally arrived, I thought that the building looked really old, and I felt disappointed. Upon entering through the main door, we had to be careful where we walked, since some of the wooden flooring had become loose. I wasn't sure that I was going to enjoy this school and at first held on tightly to my mother's hand, until I noticed several young children waiting quietly on nearby benches. Looking at the children, I felt a bit apprehensive, since I didn't know any of them. I wondered where they were from and where they lived. With encouragement from Mama, I walked over to join the children. Then, with a sense of dismay, I also wondered, "What if they won't play with me? What if they don't like me?" My worried thoughts were interrupted by my teacher's voice as she introduced me, the newcomer, to the group and told us to stand up and form a line and to be ready for the next activity.

I do not recall my teacher's name, but I am sure that she lived in our community and was well respected. Teachers were well respected in Jamaica. What they didn't earn in salary was made up for by the respect they received. The building was on one level and was the only elementary school in the village; all the classes were on the same floor, with blackboards separating them, and there were children's voices everywhere. "Keep your voices down!" was a common refrain throughout the building.

I was born at home in rural Cornwall Mountain, Westmoreland, in 1939. Westmoreland was once home to many sugar estates, and I had heard my grandparents talk about the Frome estate as one of the parish's more famous sugar estates. Westmoreland is the westernmost of Jamaica's fourteen parishes, located on the southern part of the island. It is bordered by the parishes of Hanover, St James and St Elizabeth. In addition Jamaica has three counties, Cornwall, Middlesex, and Surrey, which I learned in school to rhyme with "Cornmeal, mixit and stir it!" Every situation, name, or event could erupt into a rhyme, a saying or an amused observation in Jamaica. That was and still is the innately humorous side of Jamaica and its people. There is humour in every aspect of life.

Until around age five, I lived with my mother, Auvril E. Mair; my grandparents William Rufus Mair and Sarah Richardson Mair; my sister Hope, then a baby; and a cousin, Roy, in the village, with many other relatives living throughout the community. I was the first female grandchild in my grandparents' household in five years, was the centre of attention for everyone, and felt very special. I had a happy childhood filled with loving parents, relatives, and neighbours.

Although my father, Egbert Gladstone Spence, visited me when he had time off, he worked with the Jamaica Government Railway and so lived wherever he was stationed. He had promised my grandfather that he would marry my mother, but that was not to be. My mother and I visited my father wherever he was stationed, so I grew quite close to him and was unconcerned that he didn't live with us. On those visits my father would take me around to introduce me to all his neighbours and friends, who expressed their pleasure at meeting me. My father was also born in Westmoreland, in another village, but grew up in Kingston from a young age.

The Mairs were an extended family like all the families in Cornwall Mountain. We lived in a large four-bedroom house surrounded by many acres of land owned by my grandfather, also known as Poop. Prior to his retirement, my grandfather held a significant government position as a bailiff/tax collector in the parish, which involved travelling to different parts of the parish. He was also a landowner, owning over sixty-six acres of land in and around the village, as well as a grocery shop that he had rented. I often accompanied Mum, my grandmother, to buy groceries from that shop. My grandfather had done well economically for his family.

We lived comfortably in our community, where the Mair family was well known. There was even a nearby village called Mair Hall, so named by Alexander Mair, the original Mair, who came from the town of Turriff, N.E. Scotland, in the mid-late eighteenth century, and settled there, three generations before my grandfather was born.[1] My grandfather was of the fourth generation of Mairs. His parents were William Alexander and Sarah Ann Mair, described as "both persons of color and free conditions." He was one of eight children born to William and Sarah Mair in Westmoreland. With each generation having seven or more children, the Mairs constituted a huge community, with cousins scattered throughout Westmoreland, and the adjoining parish of Hanover. My grandparents had eight children together, four boys and four girls, six of whom were of light to medium brown complexions, while two looked more Indian, with darker complexions and straight black hair. However, outsiders would often remark that the siblings all had "that Mair look."

My grandfather also had two older sons with his first wife, one of whom, Brother Lawrence, also lived in Cornwall Mountain with his wife, Cousin Amy, and their nine children. (Families were large in those days, and familial titles like "Brother" or "Cousin" were often used as titles of respect.) Brother Lawrence had his own business making pots and pans for household use, and I used to visit his family frequently and listen to him sing "I Love Miss Amy," his wife, as he worked. His children were very close to my grandmother. As adults, at least three of Cousin Amy's children lived with us in Kingston at various times; Beryl, the oldest daughter, owned a business in Savannah-la-Mar, Sadie was a nurse, Lola was among the first three policewomen to be trained and hired in Jamaica, in 1949, and Courtney was a policeman. Several other brothers migrated to England once they became adults.

Just like my mother, my grandmother, Mum, was the kindest and most gentle person ever, and I, and everyone else, really loved being around her. Mum was of average height and build, and was of a light brown, wheat complexion, with long, soft, wavy hair almost reaching her waist. Her hair was always parted in the middle and braided mostly in four long braids which she then coiled in two overlapping rows on her head. She had a gentle voice, was always cheerful and kind, and wore long cotton dresses, skirts, and an apron, as was the custom for older women living in rural areas. I have not looked into my grandmother's genealogy but believe she came from a background similar to my grandfather's. My grandmother's maiden name was Richardson, and she and my grandfather were both from the same parish, Westmoreland, looked alike, and were obviously of mixed-race heritage.

I loved to be near my mother and grandmother. They both had an aura of calm, and I always felt safe and special around them. I used to watch Mum as she churned butter from milk. She would then hand me a slice of bread covered with the newly churned butter, creamy, tasty, and filling. My happy reactions as I bit into the delicious treat gave her much pleasure, and even though I was young, we used those moments to truly share and to connect with each other. Those moments with my grandmother were delightful, fun, and full of laughter and good-natured teasing. She cooked delicious meals on coal stoves, used by almost every family in Jamaica. Those coal stoves were also used when ironing clothes. To iron my clothes, my mother would "catch up the fire," that is, light the coals with a match and then place three or four irons in upright positions with their tips touching, forming a conical shape. When the irons were very hot, she lifted one iron from the fire with a thick cloth holder, wiped the iron on a nearby piece of cloth, and the ironing of a garment that had been washed, starched, sprinkled with water and folded into a ball shape to remain damp, would begin. To whiten clothes, they would be first washed in soap and water and then laid out on stones or grass for the sun's hot rays to "bleach" them. The sun's rays worked as expected.

The kitchen and pantry were housed in a large building, unattached to, but about two feet behind the house, so we moved easily between the dining room and the kitchen. My grandfather, who was of a light complexion, was probably of average height. His initial height was hard to discern, since he was, when I knew him, much older and stooped over from a bent spine. He was probably in his late eighties or early nineties when I left Cornwall Mountain, but I think that he must have been quite handsome in his youth, given that he still looked handsome to me. I was too young to ask my grandfather about his lineage, and I regretted that I did not return to visit him before he died. My mother much later told me how much my grandfather loved and admired me, and how he always said that I would do well in life.

Stories from the Country

I enjoyed hearing many stories about my grandfather and his escapades, especially with ghosts. In Jamaican folk tales, our huge cotton trees were usually associated with ghosts, also called "duppies," reputed to inhabit or live near those trees. So returning from one of his tax-collecting trips in another town one night, he said that he encountered a "rolling calf," a kind of ghost, who blocked his way and would not let him continue his journey home. According to folk tales, "rolling calves" were fierce creatures who travelled along lonely country roads at nighttime. They were said to be in chains, which rattled and frightened their victims. My grandfather said that he made the appropriate sign to ward off the rolling calf, hitched his horse to a tree, and slept under a cotton tree until the next morning. According to one relative, that was his version of why he could not be home that night.

While I was still living with him, my grandfather hosted a team of so-called travelling magicians who had come to our village to perform. They needed a place to stay, and since we had one of the larger houses, he generously offered them to spend the night with us. We were excited to have these visitors who could perform magic, and I chatted a lot with them, since we didn't often have outside visitors. They ate dinner with us, and then we went to sleep. When we awoke the next morning and went to greet them, the "tricksters," also known as "Samfie Men," were nowhere to be seen. They had magically disappeared with my grandfather's cash and some items from the living room, including a lamp, and were never heard from again. Life in the country where neighbours knew so much about each other offered so many opportunities to gather storytelling material.

Behind my grandparents' house were several acres of land laden with a rich variety of fruit trees. My younger sister Hope, who grew up in Cornwall Mountain, has recalled with fondness the various fruit trees on our grandfather's property; there were plums, star-apples, grapefruits, oranges, and tangerines; guavas, avocados (known as "pears" in Jamaica), breadfruit, ackee, and cocoa trees. As a child I waited for a family member to open the dark brown cocoa pods to enjoy the sweet, creamy taste of their pulpy seeds before they were placed in the sun to dry. Then the seeds were pounded in a mortar, rolled into balls, and later brewed as delicious hot chocolate, the real chocolate. I can still recall the grainy but delicious taste of that special chocolate brew.

On one side of the house was a huge water tank, which provided water for our daily use. A few yards from the tank was the grove where the coconut trees were planted. I used to walk there while gathering almonds (children were told that bats brought the almonds at nighttime and left them), getting an adult to break the shells open with a stone, and then eating the elongated nuts. Life in Cornwall Mountain was a very happy one for me as a child and, later, for my younger sister, who lived there much longer than I did, surrounded by a warm, loving, and close-knit family and community.

The country environment provided sufficient opportunities to play, to explore in the bushes, to walk about, to simply observe nature, and to climb trees, although I wasn't much of a climber. I do not recall having toys but did not miss them, because there was always so much to do outside the house, to learn and use from the natural environment around us. I recall once creating a doll with a face using the young breadfruit "bulb," which was brown and elongated, and I played in and explored the wide-open and available spaces.

And then there were those frequent visits to our neighbours or just stopping by someone's house to say hello. I do not recall the planning of any activities for me or for my cousins, that is to say, playdates. Children accompanied their family members wherever they went or stayed home with relatives. I interacted comfortably with adults, whose main requirement of all children was an exhibition of good manners and being respectful to adults. These were important values among Jamaicans. I and other Jamaican children were raised on the aphorism "Manners maketh a man." We understood then that the word "man" included everyone. Moreover, adults had so many interesting stories to tell each other that I was always close by to listen and absorb these stories even when I wasn't supposed to be listening. "Children should be seen and not heard."

Living without Excess; the Healing Arts

Life in the country was also about knowing how to live without excess, since access to well-equipped haberdasheries[2] was not within easy reach. So women and men learned to sew, with some women becoming seamstresses to earn a living, while the men were tailors. In health situations, knowledge and use of herbal and home remedies was the norm. If a child was sick, there was always "bush tea," "fever grass tea," soursop leaf, or some other local herb for tea or home remedy to the rescue. To reduce a fever, children or adults would be "rubbed down" with the "bay rum" kept in every household; for burns or a cleanser, there was always "sinkle (or single) bible," or aloe. Likewise, if a woman was about to deliver a baby, the midwife lived nearby.

Midwives were critical in rural communities, since, in general, hospitals were in the towns, which were often miles away from the village communities, and many doctors lived in or near the towns. Those midwives learned their profession from older midwives, so the practice was based on observations and assisting more experienced midwives in their practice. The knowledge was passed on in the rural areas; they did not go to a school to learn midwifery.

In Cornwall Mountain, we lived in a community where families knew each other and relatives abounded. Diagonally across the street from our house lived Ms. Meg and her family the Russells, with whom the Mairs were related through various connections. Ms. Meg, of very light complexion and almost waist-length hair, was a very pleasant woman and close friends with my grandmother. Their house, a two-story wooden structure with a verandah on the top floor, was typical of some older houses in the Caribbean. Ms. Meg and her husband had several sons, one of whom, Lance, worked in Kingston at the famous Nathan's Department store, as a shoe salesman. Lance was my favourite in that family, and in my teens whenever I needed new shoes, I was assured of a discount from Lance, as well as one shilling for pocket money.

If the Russells had lived in the US, they would have been considered white. In Jamaica they saw themselves as Jamaicans who happened to be "light-skinned" Jamaicans, and I have personally known a few other light-skinned

Jamaicans who did not consider themselves white. However, there were other light-skinned Jamaicans who saw the many advantages that their skin colour afforded them and who took full advantage of the social status afforded by their appearance.

Variations in skin colour could create complexity and favouritism within Jamaican families, and there were stories that when some of those light-skinned Jamaicans migrated to Canada or America, they passed as being white, married into white families, and sometimes severed connections with their Jamaican relatives.

One day two young brothers, in their early teens, came to visit our community. My grandmother, a few other people, the two brothers, and I were in Ms. Meg's front yard, where she had a very tall coconut tree. Ms. Meg asked the older brother to pick some coconuts for her. The youth climbed the tree and picked a few coconuts. Ms. Meg was delighted but then requested that he again climb the tree, and, being obedient, he did. However, in picking the next group of coconuts, he slipped and fell to the ground, splitting his head. He died on the spot.

We were horrified! On learning what had happened, his poor family was devastated. The community was in shock. We all attended his funeral, my first one as a young child, and I remember the grief and sadness of the event and the talk that commenced afterwards. I had wondered why he had to die; he was so young, and I felt so sad for him and for his family. Everyone blamed Ms. Meg and talked about her being greedy. "If she had been satisfied with the first pick, this would never have happened!" Poor Ms. Meg. She was distraught and sorry about this fatality. The story surrounding this youth's untimely death stayed with me and other residents for many years.

I recall seeing the croton plant, with its variegated leaves, near his grave at the funeral. Since then, I have always associated this colourful plant with graveyards, especially in the Jamaican countryside. These plants were always near graves in the country. I avoided funerals for many years (the fact is that I really didn't know of anyone close to me who had died), until my lovely Aunt Bea passed away while I was in my late twenties and living in New York City. She was on vacation in Hawaii with her daughter, my cousin Gloria, and was having a fun time dancing when she collapsed and died. When I attended the viewing, she had the most beautiful smile on her face. I was fascinated and could hardly take my eyes off her face. It seemed almost radiant. Since then I have overcome my resistance to attending funerals and viewing the body.

There were no high schools in Cornwall Mountain. Prior to graduating from elementary school, students took a local exam called "First Year."³ My mother told me that she and her graduating class sat for the first-year exam and that only one girl passed. She was so disappointed. The story explaining this dramatic result is typical for Jamaicans and probably other Caribbean islanders, where belief in obeah, a powerful supernatural force, was often used to explain an otherwise difficult-to-understand occurrence. Seen as a spiritual and healing practice brought to the Caribbean by enslaved Africans, obeah is usually called on as one's personal instrument to help oneself or, more often, to hurt others. According to Frommer's *Jamaica*, "Obeah is a superstitious force that believers hold responsible for both good and evil."⁴

Mama explained that the mother of the girl who passed the exam had prepared a meal for the entire class. Everyone except this girl ate the food. Because she was the only one who did not eat the meal and she passed the exam, the village residents felt that her mother had placed "something" in the food to ensure there would be no competition for her daughter. The "something" may have been a potion of some sort with "special ingredients" received from a local obeah-man or obeah-woman at a cost. Sometimes, to protect a believer from harm or from evil, an obeah-man might give him or her something to wear or to keep in the house.

Obeah, also known as Myalism, is practised throughout the island. If someone suddenly became sick, physically or emotionally, or if sudden misfortune happened to a family, an individual, or a business, and there did not appear to be an immediate reasonable explanation for the condition, it was often felt that someone had "worked obeah" on the victims. Obeah was scary to me, since there were awful stories about individuals who had been negatively affected by the practice, and so when I arrived in NYC and no one talked about obeah, and there was a more psychological or sociological understanding of personal and emotional crises, I was quite relieved.

Obeah is not a common topic of daily conversations in New York City, or within academic environments unless the discipline is sociology/anthropology. However, visit any heavy concentration of Jamaican or Caribbean communities in New York City, and the belief in this practice is still very much alive. The late Samuel Selvon, author of *Trinidad*, and Jamaican sociologist Dr. Erna Brodber⁵ have been writing about cultural and religious practices like obeah to bring greater authenticity to obeah's existence as well as to the Caribbean novel form. Obeah is also noted in Violet Harrington Bryan's *Erna*

Brodber and Velma Pollard, a detailed, informative, and fascinating analysis of the sisters' writings that focuses on culture and place in rural Jamaica. Erna Brodber's concept of "spirit theft," where one steals another's spirit to strengthen the former's power, was illuminating, and I look forward to her future writings in this area. The obeahman is similar to the roots-man, or Dr. Buzzard, in South Carolina's Gullah culture. Whether in Jamaica or in the Sea Islands Gullah cultures, both groups of spiritualists have the capability of working on behalf of good or evil outcomes.

To pursue a career, students from rural areas like Cornwall Mountain wishing to teach, study nursing, or further their education had to take the second- and third-year examinations while they were in elementary school. The select few who desired to attend high school had to leave Cornwall Mountain for Montego Bay or Kingston, a major city and the island's capital respectively, where they would board with relatives or other adults, or attend any of the reputable boarding schools, like St Hilda's High School in St Ann's parish; Ferncourt; or Westwood High, founded in the 1800s, a top academic school preparing girls with a rounded education.

Jobs were few in Cornwall Mountain unless you were in the trades: tailor, shoemaker, seamstress, shopkeeper, blacksmith, "higgler"—chiefly women who sold ground provisions and other items and were effective negotiators—or postal workers. This lack of opportunity to advance pushed many young people, including my grandparents' two older daughters, Evelyn, known as Aunt Bea, and Dorothy, known as Aunt Dor, and later their two youngest daughters, Auvril and Juliet (there were four sisters in all), out of the rural area and pulled them to Kingston, the big city, and Jamaica's capital; that push-pull factor was fully at work. Aunt Bea soon left for the United States, where she married and was building her own life. Of my four uncles, Uncle Cyril had his own shop in Kingston before leaving for England. Uncle Lester, known as "Mass Cubie," worked in Cuba and on his return owned a small trucking business. Uncle Jackson, my favourite, drove a truck for Desnoes & Geddes, one of the large and well-known beverage companies in Kingston. He was very generous and always filled with good humour. Winston, the youngest of the sons, was a barber.

On arriving in Kingston, my mother and Aunt Juliet lived with their older sister, Dorothy, manager of a milk shop, a small but popular restaurant in Cross Roads, a commercial area adjacent to the residential area. Milk shops were common throughout the island, selling Jamaican patties, sodas, local pastries, and ice cream, and sometimes other food items. Over the years of living in Kingston, Mama, Aunt Dor, and I would often visit the home of Uncle Jackson and Ms. Goldie, his girlfriend of many years, in Kingston, where we were always welcomed and treated to sumptuous Sunday dinners of rice and peas, stewed or curried chicken, fried plantains, boiled flour dumplings, green bananas, or other delicious food items. The laughter and joviality that ensued was typical for the adult siblings, who were close and cared about each other. Uncle Jackson, who already had children, including my cousin Lurlene, with several former girlfriends, married Ms. Goldie much later in life. They had no children together.

CHAPTER 2

Living and Learning in Kingston

During the forties and fifties, I developed as a young adult, formed healthy relationships with adults and peers and was socialised into Jamaica's cultural norms and achievements. I developed pride in being a Jamaican, pride in our national leaders and our unique strengths as a country, relished our sense of humour, and absorbed the use of proverbs or sayings.

When my mother decided to leave Cornwall Mountain to join her two sisters in Kingston, I do not recall if she took me with her or whether I joined her at a later date. I know that I arrived in Kingston somewhere between ages five and six. My journey from Cornwall Mountain, a rural village, to Kingston, the huge and bustling city, was my first significant transition. Most behaviours that I knew from the country seemed not to matter much in Kingston, except having good manners. While the adults in the country were predictable and were known and trusted by my grandparents and therefore by me, this was not so in the city.

In addition, life in the city was very challenging for the Mair sisters and was very different from the comforts of the country. They now lived in rented apartments instead of a family house and were now on their own. In spite of the challenges, they managed to have a reasonably good life. Both my mother and Aunt Juliet were attractive young women and soon obtained jobs. Aunt Juliet had a sales position at the highly reputable Sangster's Book Store. I am sure that she was hired because of her light complexion and good looks. She also met and became friends with a member of the police constabulary. He had a high position and soon began visiting our family.

He once escorted my aunt to a dance at the Silver Slipper, a famous night club in Kingston. As they left our home, I was in awe of my aunt, who looked so stunningly beautiful in her long evening gown that I have never forgotten that moment. Although we liked him and he treated my aunt with respect and admiration, I much preferred the quiet, younger, dark-complexioned, good-looking, and kind maths teacher who wanted to marry her. But my aunt wanted to leave Jamaica, so she had little desire for a serious relationship. My mother worked for a short time at the Jamaican Tobacco Company but didn't like her job and soon left. In the meantime, both sisters had applied for visas to immigrate to the US. Only Aunt Juliet received the call from the American embassy.

Normally, if a relative was fortunate enough to obtain that coveted American visa, it was expected that that individual would, of course, support his or her family with regular cash contributions for the family's expenses. These remittances are key to Jamaica's economic wellbeing. Dr. Basil Bryan reports that "by 2010, remittances stood at US$2 billion, over 60% of which came from the United States, with the United Kingdom and Canada accounting for much of the remainder."[1] Family members were also expected to send home frequent or annual "barrels," with American clothing, shoes, dry goods, soaps, canned goods like corned beef or tuna fish, spaghetti, black pepper, pens and pencils, Avon cosmetics, and so on. What excitement in households when those barrels arrived! They were usually large, about four or five feet tall, since they had to hold enough goods to sustain families for six months to one year. My family was no different. Before leaving Jamaica, my Aunt Juliet promised to support us and to send as many goods from America as possible. The notice that a barrel was at the customs office awaiting our collection and payment was cause for celebration. Usually family friends and relatives knew of the barrel's arrival. This event warranted a visit and leaving with some of the much desired items. I was always excited to see what was in the barrel for me.

On one occasion I received two beautiful dresses, a subtly striped pink dress with a flared skirt and two inner side pockets, and a simply designed yellow dress with black trimmings. I was so excited that I could hardly wait to see how they would look on me. I tried them on immediately, and to my delight the fit was perfect! Among the other items for me was a red autograph book bound with a zipper. I was so proud of my autograph book and decided that only people special to me would be invited to write poems or greetings.

That autograph book with its many inspiring writings has provided quiet encouragement, during challenging and celebratory periods, throughout my developmental years.

Coming from a small community in the country, I had not yet met any devious individuals, so I was still in trust mode when meeting new people in Kingston. One unforgettable incident that taught me that not everyone is trustworthy happened when I was about age eight or nine and still in elementary school. My father, who after his marriage to my stepmother continued to play an active role in my life, and was now a stationmaster at the Albany Railway Station, in the parish of St Mary. He had sent money to my mother in Kingston to purchase shoes for me. I was usually very responsible and ran many errands successfully, including to the post office about a half mile from our house, so Mama sent me to get the registered letter.

I had just left the post office with the letter in my hand and was headed home when a slender woman with a friendly face approached me and innocently asked whether I had a registered letter. Since she seemed "respectable" (a commonly used descriptor in Jamaica meaning the individual was neat looking and therefore "socially acceptable") and was an adult, I said yes. Then she cautioned that I had to be very careful when carrying that kind of letter. When I concurred, she offered to hold the letter for me while she treated me to an icicle from a cart that was next to the curb where we were standing.

Foolishly and trusting, I handed her the letter and took the icicle. I really thought she was being so kind. It seemed like two seconds later when she handed the letter back to me, again told me to be careful, and left. Without even a glance at the envelope, I hurried home, gave the envelope to my mother and went outside to play. Within seconds, my mother appeared on the verandah, very upset, and inquired about the money. The envelope was empty. Why was the envelope opened? I couldn't believe what I was hearing, so I told her about this woman who had approached me.

I had never seen my mother so upset. She was always so even tempered and calm. But she declared that I would not be getting any new shoes. Recognizing that I was at fault, I resigned myself to no new shoes. However, from that day onward, my mother never had any reason to be so angry with me. I was now learning about the different kinds of people living in this big city and needed to be more careful and cautious. Even with this revelation, never having to seriously mistrust anyone previously, I still couldn't believe that someone who seemed so caring and decent could be so deceitful and dishonest. Yet she was; besides, she was obviously very skilled because every-thing happened so fast, without a trace of suspicion on my part.

That negative experience did not change my personality; I continued to relate positively to people I met. But I also became a keen and reflective observer of individuals and their behaviours, both expressive and nonex-pressive, in males and females alike. Because I continued to engage adults in conversations, I was often told by the adults, "You have an answer for everything! You are too ripe!" The word "ripe" in Jamaica implied that I acted too mature for a child.

I was now becoming accustomed to city life. I was also getting to know my aunts, who shared many stories with me, including some about my mother. Aunt Juliet and Mama were closer in age, so she and Mama grew up together as children. Aunt Juliet related how she often got my mother into trouble because Mama was so quiet and obedient, and when my grandfather caught and punished them, Mama took more of the whipping. She didn't run away like my aunt did.

Aunt Juliet and I grew very close; she was lots of fun, and she enjoyed our conversations. She was the only aunt who could comb my hair to please me: straight parts with three or four neat braids and ribbons at the end of the braids. Because of our close relationship, I often thought of writing a book entitled, *Every Child Should Have an Aunt*. My Aunt Dor's story was that she wanted to study nursing, which her father could readily afford; however, he told her that educating women was a waste of money; they would just get married and have children, "so it made no sense to waste money on educating girls." This attitude towards educating women was common throughout the island well into the 1930s and forties. I learned, however, that my grandfather provided financial assistance to a male relative who became a successful and notable businessman in Kingston. She regretted his decision regarding her career choice and actually neither married nor had children.

Instead, Aunt Dor became the elder who took care of her siblings and her relatives in Kingston until she passed away in her early eighties. Once when my mother was seeking employment, I suggested that she contact that same now well-off relative; she resisted, saying that she had her pride and wouldn't dream of approaching him. Her response didn't make any sense to me, since he was a relative even if we didn't know him, and I told her so. I felt that he would have been responsive, but my mother remained determined not to approach him or anyone else for help; yet she was always ready to help others. Being responsible for and helping my family was a value that I learned from my family and that has stayed with me over the years. It was therefore natural for me to fulfil my mother's dream to go to the States, when I was able to do so.

Although my grandfather left a will dated June 5, 1952, naming his eldest son as executor with clear instructions about the distribution of his land and significant cash for each of his children, my mother and her sisters did not see this will until much later in their adult lives. I doubt that any of them ever received a penny of their inheritance. My sisters, Hope and Philippa, and I, were fascinated to read his will, which we located some years ago. My grandfather's will stated the following: "I give my son Cyril one shop, Dwelling House and Three acres of Land at Cornwall Mtn. At Poltolock Mtn. eight acres of land. My son Cyril should take care of his mother until her death, He should give his brothers and sisters the sum of ten pounds 10.0.0 each." And then he listed the names of all his children. I knew that we had significant property in the country, but we had never heard of any income coming to my mother and her sisters. As a result, being very practical, I had little interest in owning property as I developed into adulthood.

Within a few weeks after my arrival in Kingston, my mother located a primary school near to our home, Miss Cooper's School, owned and operated by Miss Cooper, a gentle woman with a very kind demeanour, lovely and welcoming smile, dark complexion, and straight greying hair. The tuition was one shilling per week. Miss Cooper was Indian by background and had a slight foot impediment that caused her to walk with a limp. She lived with her mother in a modest house with a small garden in the front, facing the street, with its own gate. The one-room school building was behind her house, and there was a huge yard that served as the children's playground during recess. I made friends easily with my schoolmates and enjoyed playing games like hopscotch and Farmer in the Dell with them during recess.

The yard hosted a standpipe that provided water when we got thirsty from playing. I would hold my left hand under the pipe and drink as the cool and delicious water flowed into my cupped hand. In the classroom students sat on benches placed in rows and were grouped based on our ages. On initially entering the mixed-age classroom, I noticed two little girls looking at me. I overheard one of them whisper to her classmate, "What big eyes she has." I was introduced to the class, and during recess I met Gweneth Gray and Wynsome Hamilton, who lived in the same house, not far from me. We became friends but it was Wynsome who became my very best friend in childhood and throughout our adult years in New York City.

I left Miss Cooper's School to enrol in Half Way Tree Elementary School in first class. "Classes" were descriptors used in elementary schools, while "forms" were used in secondary schools in Jamaica. Half Way Tree School was considered to be "a good school," attracting students throughout Kingston and St Andrew, the neighbouring parish. I was delighted to enrol there, because my father was a graduate, and I was always eager to follow in my father's footsteps.

Growing up in Jamaica during the forties and fifties provided me with the courage, good humour, relationship skills, self-esteem, and capacity for empathy, kindness, and optimism necessary to live a good and meaningful life. I was always a happy and likeable child with an outgoing personality. As I grew older, I discovered that I liked the feeling of being useful and enjoyed being helpful when help was needed. I could also find a solution for almost every challenge; for example, if my family needed groceries but the funds from my aunt in the US had not yet arrived, I could get groceries on credit from any of the four grocery stores in my neighbourhood.

Even though I was eight or nine years old, the Chinese shop owners knew and trusted me. Among my habits while shopping was to always count the change received after paying for items. One day after purchasing "paradise plum" candies, known as "sweeties" in Jamaica, I found and returned the extra "thrupence" in my change to the shopkeeper. I was actually quite surprised at the overchange and wondered how he could have made such an error. He was quite pleased and happy to accept the coin, and I couldn't help wondering if he had been testing my honesty. Anyway, from that day on, I was always greeted with a friendly smile and words of welcome, an unusual behaviour from this particular shopkeeper.

I felt very secure and grounded in being a Jamaican during my elementary school years. Besides learning that Jamaica was the largest of the British West Indian islands, I learned many poems glorifying our island, written by Jamaicans of diverse ethnic backgrounds; for example, Claude McKay, a black Jamaican who later immigrated to America, wrote "Flame-Heart," in 1954, where he reminisces on what he has forgotten about Jamaica though he will always remember "the poinsettia's red, blood-red in warm December"; and Louise Bennett describes the cunning of Jamaican women, strong and long liberated, qualities unknown to the men, in her 1982 poem "Jamaican Oman."

Other poets include Una Marson, who wrote "Jamaica" in 1930, and Tom Redcam, whose Irish parents came to Jamaica in the 1700s and whose "My Beautiful Home" poem about Jamaica was written in 1929. Many of those poems speak to the beauty of the hills, its flora and fauna, the variety of birds, the setting sun, the people, the beautiful Caribbean sea, and the winds that blow in from the sea at night to cool the island. Those poems were taught in school, and I absorbed their direct and indirect messages: Jamaica was a special place, and though so many people were leaving the island, essentially for economic reasons, the majority planned to return one day. Jamaica also had its wealth of intellectuals. I was awed by the many extraordinary intellectuals, mostly men's voices, but also women like Misses Edith Walton James, Mary Morris Knibb, Gladys Longbridge, who later became Lady Bustamante, and others, dedicated to uplifting the lives of Jamaicans through political, educational, and economic means.

Among the leading intellectuals of that period, and they were numerous, especially poets and writers, was our premier, Norman Washington Manley, who was instrumental in the 1936 founding of the Jamaica Welfare Ltd, designed to help the poor in rural areas. It was the first community development nongovernmental organisation in the country, Notable too was Rev. Percival Gibson, a founder of Kingston College, a private school for boys, in 1925. Much later, there was a very famous and distinguished-looking Jamaican, the multi-talented author and brilliant scholar Dr. Rex Nettleford. Rex, with his beautiful black complexion, was also a dancer and choreographer. Famous for his erudition and eloquence, he—according to his obituary—earned fourteen honorary degrees and doctorates, and was a most captivating speaker. Once he began to speak, the listener was totally enraptured. I had that experience when I first heard him speak in New York City (NYC) at a Caribbean event on Park Avenue, and then again, at an informal luncheon that a group of us living in NYC planned in order to raise funds for Excelsior High School. He was gracious, humble, and so easy to connect with, one to one. Dr. Nettleford was also a prolific writer, a cultural, intellectual, and academic leader whose never-ending work included being advisor to five vice chancellors of the University of the West Indies (UWI). He became vice chancellor in 1998. Rex also received Jamaica's highest national honour, the Order of Merit. Following his death in 2010, the Rhodes Trust established the Rex Nettleford Prize in Cultural Studies at the UWI to preserve his legacy—a wonderful gesture for an outstanding citizen and a true Jamaican icon and hero. Simultaneously, I couldn't help wondering whether Cecil Rhodes, a wealthy, influential South African, a committed white supremist, had "turned over in his grave" at Rex's prize, even though Rex was not the first Black male to receive an award from the Rhodes Trust.

Because my Aunt Dor was an avid reader of our local newspapers, she talked about those Jamaican individuals frequently. I was aware of their names, and their national and international successes demonstrated that Jamaicans had the capacity to achieve locally as well as globally, a source of pride for me. Another factor that I understood and, I believed, was also understood by a segment of the population prior to independence, was the feeling of being in a safe space because we were British subjects and felt protected by the Crown.

Of course, I had not travelled outside of Jamaica then and so had no comparison. Jamaica was my whole world, and I was content. However, the reality was that, even then, despite the good nature of its people, daily living was, and continues today to be, economically very challenging for so many individuals, especially when an advanced education was lacking. Even so, I have seen some differences between the years of my growing up in Jamaica, and the experiences of young people living there today. And the differences are related to a complex of circumstances. Of these circumstances, personal safety was not an issue during my youth. Front gates and doors were often left open, and I walked confidently alone among all kinds of neighbourhoods.

We lived in the Cross Roads area, which was predominantly residential and was a safe area with a mix of upwardly mobile families as residents. Today, that once residential area is all commercial, and safety is a huge issue in many communities across the island. Houses are now iron-gated everywhere, even in the country areas. Iron bars are installed on all windows and doors, and even the shops and grocery stores are protected by metal bars and half-opened doors. No houses had bars anywhere during my youth. And then, there was the unavailability of jobs for most people, especially for women and the poor population, many of whom left the rural areas in search of employment in Kingston. The unemployment rate has worsened today with many Jamaicans experiencing severe economic hardships.

In my neighbourhood many residents owned their houses, while many families rented apartments from the owners. My family rented, but we remained within the same area even when we moved to a different address. And even if we weren't friends, I knew who lived in almost all the houses in my neighbourhood; over time I became friendly with a few of the more pleasant and welcoming families. My close friends and I were aware of class differences even then, easily recognizing those children who conveyed, subtly or directly, that they were of a higher social status. It was easy to determine whether or not they were putting on airs, and we either tolerated or avoided them. Their attitude could be based on any number of social factors, including education level, father's employment status, the private schools they attended, skin colour, ethnic identity, or other self-imposed factors. However, although we did not have much money, I have never felt deprived or like a minority individual in Jamaica. The word "minority" did not exist for us. We were Jamaicans regardless of social or economic status.

During my youth in Kingston, there was so much to see and do, and I was neither afraid nor worried about social barriers. There were Saturday-morning movies for children at the famous Carib Theatre featuring the Lone Ranger and Tonto, Hopalong Cassidy, Roy Rogers, Tarzan, and other themed series. Paying for one's ticket was the only criterion for admission to its movies for children; I was unaware of any discrimination based on class or colour and am sure there would have been an uproar were the latter to happen. On arriving at the theatre, I would see groups of excited but well-behaved children and teenagers waiting to purchase tickets. Once we entered the theatre, there was much anticipation as the light dimmed and the music familiar to us all heralded first the cartoons, and then the main feature. My good friend Wynsome and I would often be in the mix of young people inside that theatre.

Wynsome and I also attended Brownie meetings held on our church premises. She was so talented and could always follow the annual Maypole dance without missing a step, whereas I would often make a wrong turn. We played jacks on her front steps, but Wynsome was a skilled player and always won. We enjoyed pleasant walks in our neighbourhood to share the latest news.

Early on, I had quietly decided that Wynsome was my best friend even though there were four of us young girls who were good friends in our neighbourhood group. Although we all got along well, I secretly hoped that Wynsome would also choose me as her best friend, but this was not something we ever talked about over the years we knew each other. Communication was so easy between us; we understood each other, and because we also had different interests, we learned a great deal from each other.

Aunt Juliet and I would often walk to Cross Roads, the central business area where the shops, post office, banks, bakery, and other businesses were located, to buy the famous and tasty Bruce's patties; sometimes we would obtain a car ride to buy Slim Jims (a type of sundae) from Dairy Farmers, a popular ice cream parlour that was some distance from our home. In addition, car rides to the airport to see planes taking off or landing was entertainment for us and other families in the city. Those were simpler days. Returning many years later as an adult, I realised that there was so much more to see, learn about, and appreciate on the island, with its rich history and culture and amazing natural beauty of which I was only partly aware in my youth.

Among other memorable events during my formative years in Jamaica was the coming of Rediffusion to Jamaica in 1950. Rediffusion, a small radio box about fourteen inches wide and with only one station, was a technological innovation providing access to local and national news, and a diverse range of programs, including commentaries, music, sports events, and local stories for hundreds of Jamaicans. Families could rent this small box from Radio Jamaica and Rediffusion Network, the local radio station, for a modest monthly amount, and now could also listen to the then-popular love-story serial *Second Spring*, broadcast from the United States. My family, friends, and I would gather around the Rediffusion box on a Monday, or another specified evening, at 7:00 p.m. to listen to the latest instalment in this never-ending serial, and then offer our individual comments at the end of the program.

CHAPTER 3

CULTURAL, EDUCATIONAL, AND
RELIGIOUS EXPERIENCES

Jamaicans were proud of the famous Hope Gardens, a large and popular botanical garden frequented by schoolchildren, including my high school class, adults, young people in love, foreign visitors, scientists, and others. Hope Gardens rests on two hundred acres of a once-thriving sugar estate owned by Maj. Richard Hope, among the original English colonists who captured Jamaica in 1655. Now a public space owned by the government, the garden's orchid house displaying many rare species was extremely popular and attracted many plant scientists from abroad; so were the maze, where children experienced the thrill and fear of not finding their way out, and the fascinating fountain with "croaking frogs" and huge water lilies, in the centre of the garden. There is one photo of me in Hope Gardens, posing in the yellow dress, designed with one row of black lace in an apronlike pattern on the front. As teenagers, my friends and I loved receiving clothing from America. They just looked different, and we wore them with pride even though our dressmakers sewed beautiful dresses for us at modest costs. And as we observed other girls on the street, we always knew which clothes were from America.

The annual Christmas Pantomime at Kingston's famous Ward Theatre, where local talents like Ranny Williams and Louise Bennett performed in short plays and skits using the Jamaican patois, was eagerly anticipated by everyone because of its belly-laugh humour. The brilliant performances by these Jamaican artists often resulted in sold-out performances, leaving many disappointed individuals standing outside the theatre to hear the roar of applause reverberating from the rafters. Jamaicans were so proud of these artists and their enormous talents.

In the early 1950s, my Aunt Dor and I were among hundreds of spectators who lined the roadway to see Queen Elizabeth when she visited Jamaica. The excitement was palpable since Jamaica was still so much in love with the royal family. As the royal procession passed by us, I was struck by her youth and gracious demeanour. She was welcomed with a spectacular performance by the exemplary Jamaica Military Band in Kingston's famous park, the Race Course, and was reported to have enjoyed the celebrations.

I looked forward to Christmas, a joyful time when we drank our famous sorrel drink and ate fruit cake. My mother, Aunt Dor, and I would go shopping to purchase the "fruits": raisins, currants, prunes, and fruit rinds in the market. These fruits were then soaked in wine for months before baking or steaming the fruit-soaked "black" or rum cakes. Although quite delicious and mouth watering, it was advisable to eat small slices. And how can I forget our famous eggnog, always homemade, with vanilla and nutmeg, and with a little rum, which most adults would add before drinking? December 26 was Boxing Day, another national fun-filled holiday, where dance parties in homes were the norm.

These parties had adults and children dancing together. They were family events. I enjoyed dancing to calypsos, merengues, or the latest pop, rock-and-roll, and rhythm & blues tunes coming from the US throughout the year. Some of these artists, including the Platters, Nat King Cole, and LaVerne Baker, also visited and performed in Jamaica, and I attended several of their performances. I still have LaVerne Baker's signed photograph in my photo album, and Nat King Cole's autograph. Jamaicans were always excited to hear the music coming from the States, and to genuinely welcome the artists and learn about their lives.

We also had classical visiting artists, like Don Shirley and Philippa Schuyler, who performed in Jamaica in either 1946 or '47, and were very well received. Schuyler later became a reporter but died in a helicopter crash returning from Vietnam. Our Aunt Dor had read about Ms. Schuyler in the *Daily Gleaner*, liked what she read, and so named my second sister Phillippa when she was born.

As a young child, I was an avid reader and had a membership in the Half Way Tree public library. I would check out four or five books weekly and so became known to the librarian. My favourite series were Nancy Drew, Girl Detective; the Hardy Boys; the Bobbsey Twins; and a series about famous Americans: Clara Barton, girl nurse; George Washington, the boy who never told a lie; Abe Lincoln, the Hoosier schoolboy; and others. I was drawn to fairy tales and stories about the Middle East like *The 1,001 Arabian Nights*. The authors Emily Loring and Grace Livingston Hill were popular among some young girls, but I found the latter's stories a bit too righteous, unromantic, and hard to relate to.

I also loved reading stories about a comedic Jamaican boy from Chapelton who was always a challenge to his teacher, but none of my Jamaican friends or relatives now in the US seem to have heard of him or can remember his name, which was Newsy Wapps. His creator was Eddie Burke, who wrote *The Life and Times of a Jamaican Boy*, in the 1920s. I had actually received some of those early books from my Aunt Juliet, who worked at Sangster's Book Store on Harbour Street, but I left those books behind in Jamaica and never saw them again. Two other Jamaicans who wrote early on about identity in the thirties were Claude McKay and Una Marston, feminist, activist, writer, and producer of radio programs.

However, literature about Jamaica and the daily life of its people written by Jamaicans was very scarce during the forties and fifties. The closest to documenting and showcasing the everyday lives of Jamaicans using the local dialect was Louise Bennett, whose works appeared during the fifties. Plenty of writings existed about Jamaica by Englishmen and some Jamaicans, but these were primarily about its political, economic, historical, and some selected social themes; poems about Jamaica were numerous and often lyrical. The literature that I would have loved to read featured themes to which I could relate as a young person, relationships between and among the Jamaican people, the different and many ethnic and cultural groups in existence and their customs, love stories, and our day-to-day lived experiences. The oral tradition was prevalent among young adults, who loved to tell ghost and Anancy stories to children while seated on verandahs during night gatherings. That was always a scary but fun experience.

Even though I was only ten years old when Jamaican author Vic Reid's novel *New Day* was published in 1949, I remember the general excitement in Kingston that a local Jamaican had actually written a novel about Jamaicans. I and other Jamaicans rejoiced without even understanding the true and deeper implications of this event; Jamaicans could write novels about their own experiences! *New Day* was described as the first West Indian novel to be written using the Jamaican dialect, and "the first West Indian novel to be written throughout in a dialect form."[1] At last, Jamaica had its own local author. What a boost for us children, youth, and adults growing up in that period. It was the beginning of what my esteemed friend and colleague Joan Maynard, now deceased, the founder and former executive director of Brooklyn's Weeksville Cultural Centre, would many years later call "cultural vaccination," the importance of young children seeing themselves reflected in the everyday stories to which they were/are constantly exposed. Years later, authors like Roger Mais began to use Jamaican patois in their novels about the local people.

The University College of the West Indies (UC) was the only higher education institution during the fifties. In 1962 UC was renamed the University of the West Indies. By then the College of Technology formerly known as CAST and the Caribbean Maritime University preparing Caribbean students to work in the shipping industry were in existence. Acceptance to UC was very competitive and required passing a rigorous exam, so students took their academic work seriously and studied very hard. Undergraduates wore robes to classes until the sixties, when they rebelled against the red robes, and all liberal arts students were required to spend at least two weeks as student teachers in a high school. I was in high school when a young and very handsome Derek Walcott, an undergraduate from St Lucia, was assigned to my class to teach English literature. All the girls were thrilled to see and to talk with him; however, he was a serious scholar and did not easily engage in conversation.

Years later while an undergraduate at NYU, I again met Derek, who was visiting his Jamaican friend and journalist Jervis Anderson. I had met Jervis along with Jamaican Lebert (Sandy) Bethune, poet and filmmaker, while both were still students at NYU; Jervis was also a biographer for Bayard Rustin, organiser of the 1963 March on Washington, DC, and for A. Philip Randolph, founder of the Brotherhood of Sleeping Car Porters. He was also a staff writer at the *New Yorker* for years until his retirement. I was proud of Jervis's success and often wished we had kept in touch following graduation from NYU. Anyway, upon learning that Derek's play *Dream on Monkey Mountain* was being performed at Teachers College, I attended a performance. I found the theme to be complex, was glad that I had attended, and was proud of Derek as a successful playwright, a Caribbean professional and, later, a 1992 Nobel Prize winner in Literature.

Even though my enrollments in elementary and high school were distinct transitions for me, those Jamaican school experiences were quite positive. Over the years, I have realised how quickly and easily I adjust to new situations. Perhaps I was always ready and waiting for a new experience without ever consciously verbalising this. In both schools I developed excellent relationships with my teachers and related well with my classmates. In addition, there was so much to learn and to discover in both elementary and high schools, even though each was a new and different environment requiring new ways of being and learning. The only negative in attending elementary school was that a student could be caned for the least infraction.

Half Way Tree Elementary school was located in the busy and well populated capital of St Andrew Parish known as Half Way Tree. You know you have arrived in Half Way Tree by sighting the famous Clock Tower in the middle of an extremely busy intersection. According to *The History of Kingston and St Andrew* published by the National Library of Jamaica, the clock tower was erected as a memorial to King Edward VII, son of Queen Victoria, who ruled England and her colonies, including Jamaica, from 1837 to 1901.

Until age twelve I was a student at Half Way Tree Elementary School, where all students wore uniforms: navy blue skirts and white blouses. The school was a huge two-story wooden structure with two open-air classrooms of equal length extending from the back of the building into an open area. The second floor was a large open space with four classes; two each of the same class, facing each other and separated only by movable blackboards. Downstairs had the same configuration as upstairs, with the two extensions at each side of the building containing the first- and sixth-class students respectively. Although each extension had a roof, all sides were open.

When there was rainfall, there was a real scramble to get away from the seats nearer to the open sides, so as not to get wet. Those were also fun times, with much pushing and squealing as we tried to move to dry seats. A separate stand-alone three-sided building facing the back of the school building housed the very young children in one large classroom, and a large asphalt playground.

Inside the main building, near the front entrance, was a small stage used for assemblies and performances, especially elocution, a favourite activity at our school. Many students honed their talents as future elocutionists and communication experts on this stage. To the left of the stage was a small open area, no walls, housing our headmaster and his desk. Teacher James was a serious gentleman of dark brown complexion and average height, always impeccably dressed, as I recall, in a white suit. He would wander around the classrooms, cane in hand, causing everyone to be a little nervous. His cane was a long, thin, bamboo instrument, about two and a half feet long. Teacher James's presence struck fear in every student who saw him approaching, cane in hand, ready for action. He would often strike students for no apparent reason except for a deeply held conviction that he needed to do so. It was reputed that a brain implant made him act irrationally at times. Whether this was true or not, we never knew.

However, one day, during a lesson, I felt a sudden sharp pain on my shoulder. I cried out and turned around. There was Teacher James, cane in hand, and I was the target. Even my teacher was surprised, because I never caused any conflict in the classroom. This strange behaviour resulted in a visit from my mother to talk with my teacher and Mr. James. (Jamaicans call this behaviour someone "taking a set on you".) At some point in the discussion, and seeing that he was not being responsive to their comments about me, Ms. Daly quietly reminded him that my father, Egbert Spence, was a graduate. Now, Ms. Daly was one of the oldest teachers in my school and had taught my father as a student. When she called my father's name, Teacher James was immediately alert and described Daddy as having been a brilliant student, one of the few students accepted into Kingston Technical School, a desirable high school placement for bright young boys. From that day forward, Mr. James never raised his cane to me again, but instead, would always greet me with a smile while inquiring about my father.

The school attracted students from all walks of life, and from all parts of the city, so there was a healthy mix of children from different economic and social backgrounds. The school also attracted fruit and other vendors who sat outside its gate to promote their delicacies. There was "mack-a-fat," a small fruit with a hard outer shell and a powdery meat covering a small brown nut inside; only the powdery meat would be eaten; asham, a stove-roasted corn and sugar mixture, dry but delicious and served in a cone-shaped wrapper. I used to save whichever fruit or dessert-like food as the last item to eat; but one day when I decided to save my one ripe and juicy mack-a-fat for the end of lunch and was looking forward to savouring this delicious fruit, a school friend approached me and reminded me that I either owed her, or had promised to give her, a mack-a-fat, and to my great chagrin, I had to give up my prized possession.

The only teacher I feared in the Half Way Tree elementary school was Mrs. S. Students called her "Mother Wasp" behind her back, because she was so stern. Students in second and third classes came together weekly for maths exercises to encourage maths problem solving in our heads, rather than on paper. Known as "mental arithmetic," this approach created much anxiety for me. If your answer was incorrect, you would invariably feel a whack over your shoulder with the cane. I soon discovered that if you looked as though you were seriously thinking about solving the maths problem, Mrs. S. would not call on you. She just wanted to ensure that you were actively engaged in trying to problem solve. Using "mental arithmetic" was a useful skill that stayed with me for years in both my personal and professional lives.

On other mornings my classroom teacher, Miss Russell, whom I adored, and Miss Berry, the other teacher on my grade level, led the combined classes in general knowledge and English. Those were easy sessions for me; I was always prepared for my classes and was an active class participant. Ms. Russell was young, attractive, and kind, and did not use the cane to threaten children. I recall being teased that I was her "favourite." Children know these things. Anyway, I was so happy when, at the end of the school year, I was skipped to fourth class and so did not have to be in Mrs. S's third grade class. I used to wonder whether Ms. Russell skipped me because she did not want me placed in the severe Mrs. S's class. The rationale was that I was ready to handle fourth-class work, and for me, a much better reason; moreover, I was placed with the gentle and much older Ms. Daly, who was a master teacher. I was so happy and very relieved that Miss Russell understood who I was and the kind of learning environment that suited me best, a supportive and nonpunitive one.

In sixth class, we were between eleven and twelve years old, in our last year in elementary school, and most of us were preparing for high school. We all hoped to get accepted with a scholarship, since high school entry was very competitive, required an entrance exam, and was also costly. There was, however, another real barrier to obtaining a high school education. If a student was not accepted into a high school by age twelve, that was the end of his/her dream of graduating from a reputable high school. Jamaica's education system prior to its independence was still based on the more traditional English system, where only a small number of students were eligible for secondary education. In addition there were only about twenty-three secondary schools across the island during 1944; this number was increased to forty-one in 1960 to enable more students to receive an education.[2]

If students wanted to teach, they could sit for the required entrance exams during elementary school and hope that they would be accepted into one of the teacher training colleges. Alternatives were enrollment in a commercial school to study stenography and become a secretary, or in a correspondence course, usually from England or Canada, quite popular in those days, but to which I was not attracted. Moreover, unless medicine or law were one's professional goal, the next career goal and probably the most popular at that time was to become a government civil servant, perhaps somewhat typical of individuals living in countries under colonial rule.

While I was focused on doing well in school, I was also quite aware of the boys in our class. I used to have long discussions with Ramon S., a quiet, very intelligent, and nice individual who became a good friend. We lost contact because we went to different high schools and lived in different parts of the city, but I have often wondered which career Ramon pursued. He was such a bright student. Years later, while I was a student at NYU, I met another classmate, Errol Rhoden, who was then studying at Cooper Union to become an architect, a goal he accomplished, and he now has his own company in the US.

Our elementary school class had many bright and ambitious students. One student stood out as the smartest, and the nicest, girl in our class. She was Yvonne Patterson. Yvonne came from a family of educators and excelled in all the subjects, so we knew that she would gain entry into St Andrews High School, then the elite private high school in Kingston, which she did. (St Andrews would be comparable to the Spence or Brearley independent schools in New York City). Yvonne was also the only daughter of her parents. She lived in a huge house with her six or more much older brothers, who took excellent care of her while their parents taught in rural Jamaican schools and came home on some weekends and during vacations.

After taking the exams for high school placement, my classmates and I all waited anxiously for the results. What a great relief for me to receive a letter stating that I was accepted into Excelsior High School with a half scholarship. Receiving a scholarship during those years was similar to wearing a badge of honour in Jamaica. That meant that you were bright; it had little to do with family income. With a half scholarship, my tuition was about three pounds, £3, each term (then a little over $12 USD), which in the fifties was still a substantial amount of money in Jamaica. I looked forward to attending high school, because, most excitingly, there was no caning of students by teachers. In addition, XLCR was a coeducational high school, not the norm among the prominent secondary schools during the fifties. High school sounded wonderful.

Intertwined with all my experiences and events was music, which was everywhere in Jamaica, especially calypso. Music was often played on sound systems throughout Kingston and the countryside; its pulsating beat was heard and felt by grownups and children alike, whether you were in a small town or the big city. Although calypso had its origin in Trinidad, this genre was very popular in Jamaica, especially Trinidad's most famous Lord Kitchener, whose music was colourful, bold, and filled with sexual innuendos. However, Jamaica also had its own local calypsonians, like Lord Power, Lord Flea, and Lord Creator (they were all "Lords"). As a young child, I enjoyed listening and translating the real meaning of the texts, which were often sung in metaphors. Lord Flea sang about "The Naughty Little Flea," while Everard Williams's "Healing in the Balmyard" and "Rough Rider" were hugely popular. Also popular on their release were "Mommy, Out the Light," and "Big Bwoy and Teacher." "Big Bwoy" was a fictitious comic character who challenged teachers with his combined humour and insolence. You could also learn about the biblical Samson "and his great fall, (which) should be a lesson to one and all," from the popular calypso "Samson and Delilah," sung by A. Bedasse, with music by Chin's Calypso Sextet. This is among my favourite calypsos, because

Delilah learned what she want to know
And poor foolish Samson got the blow.
He lost his strength; he lost his sight.
Guess what she take and win the fight?

Many parents, especially the more conservative and strict parents, and there were many of them in Jamaica, tried to prevent their children from listening to the latest calypsos. A few of them were successful. I knew the words to almost all of the latest calypsos and was never prevented from listening to or singing them.

Those local calypsonians were also "journalists" for Jamaica. Through their songs, they described significant events so comprehensively that everyone could understand the totality of that event. For example, after each hurricane, a calypso would be released almost the next day describing the hurricane, its impact and devastation on the people and the island. Calypsonians also addressed political and social issues, giving voice to the concerns of the general populace. Significant events like the murder of a famous person or the activities of a local hero were "documented" in calypsos. Social satire was also regularly seen in the newspaper through the drawings of the famous artist Leandro.

Mento was an early form of Jamaican music, influential in the development and growth of ska and reggae music. Mento, much like calypso, told stories about everyday living and blended music and dance. In an interview with Monty Alexander, Jamaica's famous musician, he was quoted as saying that "mento has to do with a whole world of social circumstances. . . . [It] came from the pain and struggles of the grassroots people. . . . It is people reaching out beyond their [poor] circumstances."[3] I recall how as children we would act out one particular mento selection, "De river bin come down, and a how you come over." It was a call-and-response with singing and creative movements, and was so much fun to act out. Another popular song, which aptly described the daily struggles of poor Jamaicans, especially market women, was

Carry me ackee go a Linstead Market,
Not a quattie wut sell (repeat)
Everybody come feel up, feel up
Not a quattie wut sell. [a quattie is one penny and a half]

Those words convey the ongoing, daily struggles that women—and they were mostly women—who sold their produce in the busy markets endured. Jamaican customers loved to haggle for the lowest price, with little thought about the difficult life of market women. I used to feel sorry for them, because I could often see the despair in their faces. However, these women did not keep their grievances to themselves, and customers who annoyed them in any way would often get a "tracing off," beginning with a "cut eye" or "Missis, is who u tink you a deal wid?" and then the customer would be soundly criticised about her physical appearance, from head to toe.

My generation was also heavily influenced by R&B music, such as Lloyd Price's "Just Because," the Chantels' "Maybe," Mickey & Sylvia's "Love Is Strange," the Platters' "The Great Pretender," and Dean Martin's "Memories Are Made of This." These are among my favourites, as are of course our very own Byron Lee and the Dragonaires, who played every kind of music.

Ska, uniquely Jamaican, followed in the late sixties, by which time I had left Jamaica for the USA. Reggae music by Peter Tosh, Bob Marley, and other reggae artists appeared on the music scene much later. I was completely unaware of reggae or Bob Marley's fame until an American colleague's husband talked with me about reggae, assuming that I knew everything about it and Bob Marley. Following that discussion, when I felt quite embarrassed that I did not know what was happening in my own country, I began to take an interest in this genre, and when Bob Marley performed in New York City in 1980, my friend Wynsome and I were in the audience. I was thrilled by Bob Marley's performance and soon became familiar with the rhythm and tempo of his music; he was also an engaging performer with the ability to draw his audience in with his music. I loved his "No Woman, No Cry."

Vivid memories and nostalgic feelings about the music from the forties and fifties are never far away. I recall with delight dancing to "The Great Pretender" by the Platters, and other slow and melodic R&B music at house parties. In dancing with a favourite partner, young people would "rent a tile," a metaphor for close, slow dancing. Music and certain aromas like "Lily of the Valley," "Khus Khus," or "Evening in Paris" were very popular in the forties and fifties, and usually evoke wonderful memories and pleasant feelings about my youth in Jamaica.

Another effective documentation of Jamaican life on all levels came from the poems of Louise Bennett, "Miss Lou," as she was affectionately called. An Excelsior High School alumna, she used the local vernacular, Jamaican patois, in all her poems. Students became experts at reciting her poems, which required acting out the expressions and gestures intimated in the poems. As Jamaicans, we all loved her poetic versions because they portrayed the real Jamaica, the social and cultural climate, its norms and values; it's people, their strengths, culpabilities and idiosyncrasies, and all her words were in patois, also always commanding "belly laughs," spontaneous laughter that had individuals holding their stomachs for control.

Prior to Miss Lou's works, educated Jamaicans could recite, by heart, all the famous English (British), Irish, and Scottish poems. We studied Byron, Shelley, and Keats in high school and read from *The Story of English Literature*. I studied poems like "The Prisoner of Chillon" and "The Deserted Village," as well as Chaucer's *The Canterbury Tales*, which we had to memorise while simultaneously translating from Old English. I was moved by English lyrics like "Drink to me only with thine eyes," the Irish "Believe me, if all those endearing young charms," and Scottish "Loch Lomond"; they were all taught in our high school.

Despite my knowledge and appreciation of English literature and songs, I remain captivated by the beat of Jamaican music, and learning about Jamaica's cultural and intellectual impact in the USA and abroad. I am drawn to the hypnotic sound of Peter Tosh, who died too early, and the unique, hoarse-sounding voice of Shaggy, the innuendos in calypsos, the local stories within mentos, Miss Lou's poems and the colourful sounds of the island's patois. Many Jamaican writers today frequently use patois to convey that authentic Jamaican voice.

In my reflections on Jamaican culture, the images that immediately appear to me are those associated with the grassroots or rural people, the folk songs, ghost and Anancy stories, and the annual December Junkanoo, or John Canoe Festival, when dancers and musicians celebrate on the streets. I think of the country women riding on donkeys to take their ground provisions to the market, local artists selling their wooden carved images and the bartering that often accompanies a sale. There is also "pardner," a popular system of saving among a group of individuals who contribute a standard weekly amount called a "hand" to the "banker"; each week one individual gets the "draw," the sum total of his or her contribution. Many individuals use this form of savings for significant purchases like the down payment on a house.

Then, there is the natural beauty to enjoy in Jamaica's awesome mountains, rivers, and streams, blue Caribbean sea, natural caves, mineral springs, and variety of birds and fruits. Having produced a significant number of scholars, athletes, musicians, artists, poets, writers, educators, beauty queens, and others, and with less than a three million population, Jamaica is a source of pride for the majority of its people regardless of where we end up living.

•   •   •

It was at Half Way Tree School that I was reunited with my sister, Audrey. I was about to exit the school gate after classes one afternoon when I noticed a small group of children playing "Mother and Children," a popular children's game where the coveted role is the mother. Anyway, after observing the game for a few minutes, I approached the leader and asked if I could join them. She told "her children" to remain where they were while she talked with me. On introducing ourselves, we recognized that we had the same Spence surname.

Then I remembered that Audrey and I had met as young children when visiting our father but hadn't seen each other in years. We were thrilled to reconnect, so after hugging each other, Audrey invited me to accompany her home.[4] I will never forget that reunion. Audrey's mother, Sybil, her Aunt Linda, and Audrey all lived with her grandmother, known as Aunt Jo; they were so happy to see me and had numerous questions for me about school, my mother, and where I was living.

When we repeated the story of our meeting, there was a lot of laughter and jokes. We had such a good time together. My mother and Sybil had known and liked each other. Sybil had also met me when I was about four or five, which is probably when Audrey and I first met, and we remembered each other. I was one year older than Audrey. Sybil and my mother should have been rivals for my father's affection and attention before his eventual marriage to my stepmother when I was around nine years old. However, they weren't.

But then, my mother got along with everyone, and I rarely heard her say anything negative about anyone. Not even when she heard of Daddy's marriage to my stepmother. I was sure that she was disappointed, but she kept those feelings to herself. Although I felt sympathy for my mother's loss of her relationship with my father and was surprised at the news, I was not upset, since he hadn't lived with us. I didn't feel his marriage was a loss for me at all. I was also aware, even then, that this was a common experience for many Jamaican women. Having visited many homes throughout Kingston and other cities, I had observed that so many mothers were unmarried but lived with acceptance, and safely, within their extended families. Personally, there was no change in my feelings for my father, even though I instinctively knew that my mother was very disappointed, and maybe even heartbroken.

My main reaction when I heard the news was wondering why he hadn't told us before his wedding. Regardless of how she really felt, my mother never uttered one word against him and insisted that I still visit my father during holidays. Aunt Dor felt differently and openly voiced her displeasure at his behaviour, which then had me defending my father. Daddy was so outgoing, charming, and intelligent that he was well received wherever he went, and I enjoyed meeting all his friends and colleagues, as they were pleasant, caring, and welcoming. And I adored my father. But many of his colleagues from work knew my mother and, from their comments, were as surprised that he didn't marry her.

On introducing Audrey to friends over the years, they would all say that she was beautiful, and I was so happy to hear that; I called her my beautiful sister. Audrey and I remained in close contact until I left Jamaica. We lived less than two miles apart and visited each other regularly. I have fond memories of each of us walking the other one home following those visits.

"Walking one's friend home" was a common activity in Kingston, but all young children and youth knew that you shouldn't say goodbye at a street corner. That was rumoured to be bad luck. Because Audrey and I were always engaged in conversations, we would realise too late that we were at a street corner. Then we would turn around to walk the other one "part way." That meant we had to keep walking until we could say goodbye in the middle of a block. The result was that Audrey and I would often spend time walking each other back and forth, which was always food for much laughter and teasing.

During those preteen years, I was also quietly looking for answers about me; who was I within the larger scheme of living, and what kind of person would I be as I grew older? Who did I resemble? My mother, who everyone said was so beautiful and gracious, with long black hair and beloved by all who knew her? Or my father, who to me and others was tall, dark, and handsome, intelligent, and very sociable? It was reputed then that if girls looked like their fathers, they were supposed to be lucky, so I was happy with individuals who said that I resembled my father. I read all the available descriptions of individuals born in a particular month or day of the week and then compared how closely I resembled those descriptions. I recall a poem declaring that the child who was born on a bright Sunday would be happy, merry, bright, and gay (cheerful). Those words partly fit into my vision for my personality and my life's purpose.

Finally, my search for the right word that appealed to me and was close to how I wanted to be was answered many years later when, as a college student in a pre-social-work course, my professor Mary Keeley was talking about values, the desire to do good and entering the helping professions. Somewhere in her presentation, she concluded that our goal in life was to be "a good person." I couldn't believe my ears. It seemed so simple, and yet here was this learned individual actually saying what I wanted to hear.

That was it. In my heart and head, all I wished for, besides being happy, was to be of use and to be a good person. And that meant being helpful to everyone who needed help, and to never deliberately hurt anyone. That was my purpose in life. I also wanted to be wise like some of the many Jamaican adults I knew. They seemed, to me, to have the right answers for every problem; of course, my thinking was based on my youth then. I thought that I was already pretty wise for my age.

Between the ages of eight and nine, I rode the tramcar to school, a fun adventure all by itself. Electrically powered, the tramcars ran on rails in the middle of the road and were open on both sides, so they could be boarded from either side of the road. Sometimes, the cars would be so overcrowded that people would be hanging from the steps, and the conductor couldn't get to everyone to collect fares. There were lots of free rides then. The tramcars were replaced by buses in the late forties and were missed. Few of my current Jamaican friends recall the tramcars, but then, several of them grew up in the country while trams were in Kingston. They really missed a treat and that part of Jamaican history.

There were numerous individuals who influenced me in one way or another during my school years and, later, my professional years. Besides my teachers, I recall the three lovely adult sisters who lived across the street when we lived on New Lincoln Road. They were all attractive, light complexioned, very pleasant, and good neighbours. Even as a young child, I often wondered why they never married. But that was a fact of life for many Jamaican women who then lived within extended family structures. There just didn't seem to be sufficient eligible men. Or maybe the sisters never found anyone that they wanted to marry. Abrahams noted, "The 1943 Census showed 638,796 women to 598,267 men and indications are that this disparity has in no way decreased in the intervening years."5

Those men who were eligible were already married, although that did not deter many of them from having girlfriends on the outside. Moreover, since so many women were unemployed and there was no national unemployment safety net, many of them were supported by funds from male companions, married or single. During those years it was rare to see an unmarried woman or man living on her or his own; some houses were large and there seemed always to be room for an additional relative or boarder. If you were lucky, you could be treated as family. Some of those boarding experiences were not happy ones, especially for children and youth whose parents or parent had emigrated. I have heard many sad stories from friends and other individuals as they recounted some unhappy days as young boarders.

When the eldest sister learned that I attended Half Way Tree School, she invited me to eat my lunch in the bar where she worked as a barmaid/

manager. The bar was a short walk from my school. Now, working in a bar was not a respected occupation for women, especially middle-class women, in Jamaica; however, jobs for women during those years were very scarce, and most women took the jobs that were available. Anyway, this job worked for my neighbour, who had a respectable, no-nonsense, and businesslike air about her; her customers were well behaved, and policemen were never far away. So I ate many lunches at a small round table in the bar, and she would often offer me a soda. I felt very safe and well cared for.

During the spring Lenten season, my teachers would get students prepared to walk, "a little ways down the road," about three or four blocks (blocks were not used to describe distance in Jamaica), from the school to the St Andrew's Anglican Parish Church to a religious service acknowledging the crucifixion of Christ. To some children, this was free time from school. I looked forward to going to the church, since we sang hymns that were melodic and spiritual. I also enjoyed reading Bible stories, each one of which taught a lesson about being kind and helpful towards others. The first book I ever owned, a gift that I cherished, was from my father. It was a book filled with alphabetically arranged Bible stories, with each letter assigned to a biblical figure or episode. The full stories then followed. I read that book over and over until I could recite every story by heart.

Jamaicans took religion and its religious holidays quite seriously. The forty days of Lent, a very holy period on the island, beginning with Ash Wednesday and ending with Easter Monday, included Good Friday, the only day when the Carib Theatre "Back Gate" was locked. No, or very few, Jamaican households cooked on Good Friday, the most holy of days; all government and other offices were closed and everyone ate Jamaican spice buns and cheese and fried fish throughout the day. It was also a day for visiting relatives and friends after attending church services, one of which lasted three long hours; the refreshments consisted of, yes, more buns and cheese and fried fish.

The Lenten season culminated in a rousing celebration on Easter Sunday with the singing of joyful Easter hymns. Sonorous voices could be heard from the churches to the streets proclaiming "He is risen!" Adults and children were dressed in their new clothes and hats, and everyone in church seemed very happy. Easter Monday was a national holiday when there were plenty of house parties for dancing throughout Kingston, beginning around noon and lasting through the evening. In those days, people danced on their verandahs (all houses had verandahs), and doors and windows were left open because

people felt safe in their homes. Stories about gun violence and random kill-
ings were extremely rare. When a violent death did occur, it was talked about
for months. In fact, there might well be a calypso documenting the event.

I remember the many foreign religious groups, mostly from the US
Midwest, who frequently visited Jamaica to "spread the word." Some held
revival meetings in tents, attracting hundreds of local Jamaicans to sing and
pray. I have never attended any of the American evangelical revival events,
which did not resonate with my far less conservative beliefs. However, on one
of my frequent visits to see my father, when I was about nine years old, he
took me to a much smaller local revival experience in the country. Held in a
medium-sized shed, and hosted by a young, very handsome Jamaican pastor,
the meeting was packed with local Jamaicans from the nearby communities.

Being the stationmaster, my father knew almost everyone in the community, including this young pastor who was visiting Albany, and had invited
him to the meeting. I was amazed and awed by the singing, swaying, and
clapping, which on reaching crescendo resulted in women and men swoon-
ing and being caught and supported by fellow worshippers before they fell
to the floor. The helpers, all women, wore white dresses and were already
poised to support worshippers who were about to fall.

During that time the pastor continued to preach in a soothing and rhyth-
mic voice about forgiveness, love, and other everyday topics. Soon people
began making their way up the aisle towards him to ask for his healing
and blessing. This experience was such a strong contrast to my own more
restrained Anglican church experience in Kingston that on our way home, I
peppered my father with questions about why the people fainted, why they
sang and jumped up, and were they really healed by the pastor. I have often
thought about that pastor and how comforting, pleasant, and emotionally
available he was to the people who needed his help. However, I knew that I
was more comfortable with my church, perhaps because my early introduction was to the Anglican way of worship and, moreover, it was familiar to me.

RELEVANCE OF COLOUR AND CLASS

Even at a young age I used to wonder why all the ballet dancers were, in
the Jamaican language, fair-skinned (white) children or adults, not only
on the movie screen but also in Jamaica. Perhaps they were the only ones

who danced in that way, on their toes? There was a famous ballet school in Kingston at that time, but I rarely, if ever, saw a dark or brown-skinned child going to or coming from that school. Maybe there were one or two, but they were not visible. I concluded then that was how it was. Only white or fair-skinned children were ballet dancers. But why? Noticing the differences between classes of people and colour of skin, and how they were differently involved in society, began early for me. The differences were even more evident in the notable high schools, where only a small percentage of eligible twelve- and thirteen-year-olds were enrolled.

In addition to the top-rated high schools for girls in Kingston—St Andrews, Wolmer's and St Hugh's, with the latter two seeming to enrol more black and brown students than St Andrews—there were three popular Catholic high schools: Immaculate Conception, Alpha Academy, and Holy Childhood. It seemed to me that Jamaicans of Syrian/Lebanese and Chinese backgrounds tended to gravitate to those schools, but my impression was also that Alpha Academy had larger numbers of black and brown students at that time than Immaculate and Holy Childhood. Those observations are no longer as valid, since the government now funds the high schools, and they are more accessible to the larger black population.

The famous boys' schools then were the Priory School, with many fair-skinned children, some of diplomats, and financially well-off Jamaicans; Jamaica College, or JC; Kingston College, or KC; Calabar and St George's Colleges; and Cornwall College in Montego Bay. In writing their names now, I am struck by the fact that the boys' high schools were all "colleges," while the girls' schools were not similarly named. JC then seemed quite populated with white or light-complexioned boys, while KC had more black, brown, and mixed-heritage students, more representative of Jamaica's diversity. KC and Calabar boys were quite popular among girls in our high schools. There was a quiet rivalry between KC and Calabar boys at that time, and not only around sports. Other well-known and reputable high schools were Merl Grove, started by Jamaican Ms. Speid, Ardenne, Queens High School, and others.

Every Saturday morning a live show called *The Quiz Kids* featured a panel of five to seven bright boys and girls from the selective high schools, who would respond to questions from the host. There was John Poxon Jr., whose father was Reverend Poxon of my high school; David DaCosta; and one or two girls and other boys whose names I have forgotten. The same students were on the radio every week. I often went to the live shows to be in the audience. I noticed that only David D. had an olive complexion and wavy hair; all the other panelists were very light complexioned or white Jamaicans; I used to wonder why dark or brown-skinned Jamaican youth from other than the two or three "elite" high schools were not included; we had some really brilliant students in those other high schools.

My observations of colour differences are relevant in my story because skin colour and class were the realities of Jamaican life during my youth. One major difference between the USA and Jamaica during those years was that there was no legal racial or colour barrier in Jamaica, whereas segregation was the norm in America. Jamaica was a predominantly black country with a mix of ethnic groups, including Chinese and Indians, Jews, and Lebanese, often called Syrians. These groups came to the island at different points in Jamaica's history and brought unique and different skills that were well utilised as the economy and culture developed; and as they interacted, the island began to identify another group of "halves": half Chinese, half Indian, half Jewish, half Syrian/Lebanese.

The other "half" was presumably black. Moreover, one's complexion often played a role in how one was perceived. Jamaicans generally felt that the lighter-complexioned people were more successful and had more opportunities, especially for women and girls, than those with darker complexions, a carry-over from colonial rule. And of course, when they looked at sales clerks, banking staff, and private companies, the images they saw in those early days confirmed their beliefs. This situation was changing during my youth as more black- and brown-skinned Jamaicans graduated from high schools, gained advanced degrees from England, Canada, and the United States, and assumed a variety of leadership positions throughout the island. I observed then that while skin colour once dominated social and professional mobility in Jamaica, for black and brown Jamaicans, a high school or college education, in addition to having important social connections, was quickly becoming as important to moving up the career ladder.

I do not recall Jamaicans ever using the word "Negro" during the forties and fifties; all descriptions were related to complexion or skin color. Even the word "white" was rarely used; English people were white, but white Jamaicans were usually called "fair-skinned" or "Jamaican white." The current use of "black" was also not typically used to describe a race of people but to describe skin colour, a complexion. However, even in those times, the lighter skin colour was preferred. (On a visit to Jamaica in 2019, I learned, to my chagrin, that bleaching one's skin to achieve a lighter complexion has become popular among some young women.) When the local people were arguing with or cursing each other, they used whatever skin colour their opponent had, from fair to black, as well as their other physical attributes, to curse them, or in the Jamaican lingo, "to trace them off."

In her 1963 edition about personality and conflict in Jamaica, anthropologist Madeline Kerr offered her perspective that "the Jamaican today is a man who has been exposed to many diverse cultures. He cannot return to African ways because it is never possible to go back psychologically and because during this time he has developed ways of living alien to the country of his origin. Very few people, too, are of pure African descent."[6] She later amplifies her observation "that because Jamaica was the 'product' of so many different cultures and traditions (English, Scottish, French, African, Spanish)[,] eventually, the country would have to create from that diversity something that is new and vital and essentially Jamaican."[7] I believe that the development of that "essentially Jamaican" quality gained momentum following its 1962 independence, catapulted through the revolutionary lyrics of Bob Marley, Jimmy Cliff, Peter Tosh, and other local reggae musicians, as well in the local literature, patois, art, political and social life, and media.

In writing about my early life experiences in Jamaica, I often pondered why I had not learned more about slavery and its resulting impact on the local population. Maybe I wasn't paying attention in class. Or maybe, if the subject was in the curriculum, which I doubt, not only was it too distant, as indicated by Abrahams, but also I do not recall any intentional connections being made between Jamaicans and Africans, and discussions around slavery did not appear prominent in the existing cultural discourse to which I was exposed.

CHAPTER 4

HIGH SCHOOL: MY EXCELSIOR YEARS

I entered Excelsior High School, known as XLCR, in 1951 and graduated in 1955, after the required four years. My high school was located on Mountain View Avenue, a very long main road connecting Old Hope Road, a well-established residential area in the parish of St Andrew, about two miles to Windward Road, a more heavily populated area, and the main thoroughfare leading to the former Palisadoes airport. Today, the airport is called the Norman Manley International Airport, after Jamaica's very erudite former premier. Jamaicans used to say that Mr. Manley, a barrister by profession, was one of the "seven most educated men in the Western world," and we Jamaicans were so proud of him, whether or not that was indeed true. Jamaicans take such pride in their intellectuals, athletes, musicians, and all others who have been successful in creating, innovating, or leading.

Excelsior School was founded by A. Wesley Powell, an influential and amazingly progressive educator whose ideas about education were years ahead of the prevailing British/colonial-oriented model. As a young student, I was totally unaware of his progressive philosophy until I read, in the nineties, his autobiography, *The Excelsior-EXED Story*, published in 1989. However, I had always sensed that Mr. Powell had done something remarkable in creating this unique high school. He used to tell and retell his story at almost every student assembly, and, though as students we would sigh, "Not again," we listened; over these many years, I have been so grateful that he never ceased repeating that amazing story. Stories like Mr. Powell's that reflect perseverance, courage, and selflessness are so important for children and youth to hear. Later, as a professional, I have often recalled and retold with fondness the story of the founding of Excelsior High School, to our sons, my friends, and colleagues.

Prior to starting his school, Mr. Powell wrote that he taught himself short-hand and became extremely proficient and fast in using this skill. As a result, he was hired in 1929 by Marcus Garvey to take notes at his convention to form the Universal Negro Improvement Association (UNIA) in Jamaica. Mr. Powell wrote that he was mesmerised by Marcus Garvey's presence and ability to hold the attention of his listeners, especially given his physical attributes. According to him, "growing up in the Jamaican middle-class, one automatically ingested the prejudices ingrained by an intentionally divisive colonial policy. Even people who were themselves black (as in complex-ion) had racial prejudices. . . . I marvelled at the man Garvey—short, squat, thick-lipped, quintessentially negroid—that he should have such power over the minds of people. Whenever he spoke it was with a powerful delivery, a sonorous voice, and an articulation which rolled and rang the words towards his listeners. His was a most dignified personality."[1] Mr. Powell saw in Garvey "a man of extraordinary vision and courage" and credits knowing Jamaica's first national hero as "one of the richest experiences of my life."[2]

The birth of Excelsior was seen as part of an educational revolution during the thirties. Many educated Jamaicans, men and women, especially those who had travelled abroad, recognized that huge numbers of young Jamaican youth had no access to quality high schools, so a few of them had started independent secondary schools across the island. The existing traditional secondary schools were excellent in academics, few in num-bers, selective, expensive, and more British-oriented in their curriculum. Hence, the newly emerging independent schools were meeting a real need in educating larger numbers of young people following their graduation from elementary school, even with the worldwide depression in the thir-ties. Excelsior was one of those new schools focused on providing access to a high-quality secondary education for a more diverse student body. However, the move to educate the populace began much earlier, when, following emancipation, there were free men and women who realised that education was important to build a stable society. And as the formerly enslaved people with the help of churches and other groups began to pur-chase land, communities were formed across the island, and the teaching of reading began with learning to read the Bible.

Mr. Powell told us that he started XLCR as a private secondary school in 1931, with five students on the verandah of his parents' home in downtown Kingston. Three of the students were his relatives; the teachers, in addition to himself, were his father and other relatives. As the number of students enrolled in XLCR increased, so did the school's reputation. By the end of the first year, enrollment had increased to thirty students. XLCR's reputation grew rapidly because of the high percentage of its students passing the overseas Cambridge School Certificate exam. Mr. Powell then decided that he needed to pursue higher education. He enrolled in Columbia University for a B.S. in geography and geology, and later, in Teachers College (TC), for his master's degree in international education. At TC he met many progressive educators (John Dewey was also there) who broadened his professional knowledge and educational perspectives, chief among them a Dr. Kandel, whose speciality was international education.

On returning to Jamaica after only three years with his two degrees, Mr. Powell knew that he could not immediately impose the progressive approaches he had embraced in America; Jamaicans still revered the British model and did not appreciate higher education in the United States. Therefore, he began with small steps: he introduced one free period each week for students to pursue their interests, offered weekly career talks by alumni, formed student councils, and developed the first loan program for teachers wishing to study abroad.

Mr. Powell's early graduates did exceptionally well academically and professionally. The school's passing rate for the Cambridge Overseas Examination was very high (100 percent), and many of his early students became quite famous. For example, Arthur Wint, an Olympic sprinter (1948), was a graduate who later became a medical doctor; Louise Bennett, Jamaica's folklorist, poet, and writer, was an early graduate. In his book *The Story of the Jamaican People*, Philip Sherlock noted that Louise Bennett's use of dialect in print and onstage "helped the Jamaican dialect to gain acceptance at all levels of society."[3]

Excelsior was about twenty years old with an excellent reputation for academics when I entered its huge campus. Located on Mountain View Avenue, then a sparsely populated area called Antrim, Excelsior's campus embraced fifteen acres of land. Spread across the sprawling campus were seven new buildings. Each building housed two classrooms separated by a wall. However, two of the seven buildings had movable walls to hold weekly assemblies. The latter consisted of prayers, the singing of a hymn, a motivational talk by Mr. Powell, and general information for the week. The classrooms were spacious, with high ceilings, a large blackboard on one wall, and huge windows on two sides of the rectangular room, facing each other. As a result, the classrooms were always full of light, which contributed to wandering gazes through the windows while listening to our teachers. In the middle of campus was the only old wooden building, the administrative office, on XLCR's relatively new and modern campus. Teachers could be seen eating their lunches on the back verandah with its open-lattice-worked wall. The building also hosted the famous Tuck Shop, where students could purchase a variety of food items.

Jamaican students in high schools across the island all wore distinctive uniforms that immediately identified the schools they attended. I wore, with pride, a beige outfit with a green and gold striped tie, a green cloth belt, and a "Jippi Jappa" (straw) hat with a wide brim. Boys wore a khaki uniform with long pants and the same green-and-gold-colored tie. Oftentimes, when our school teams played against other schools, my friends and I would attend the games to support our players. Then we would shout these verses:

Excelsior School, new yet old,
Glorious in her green and gold,
Green for honour, gold for fame,
Cheer up boys, and play the game!

Our teachers impressed on us the importance of good behaviour on the streets at all times so as not to disgrace our school in any way. Even today, as an adult, I find it really hard to eat on the street. Those Excelsior lessons were so compelling for me.

The first day of high school arrived. What excitement! Dressed early in my new beige uniform with its pleats crisply ironed in place, I could hardly wait to arrive at XLCR. With a sandwich for lunch and probably a shilling for a drink at lunchtime and a sixpence for bus fare, I left home early for the walk to Cross Roads, a main hub for all buses, to catch the bus to Papine stop. On alighting from the bus at Stanton Terrace about fifteen minutes away, I crossed the road to await the connecting Mountain View Avenue bus that stopped at XLCR, less than a ten minutes' ride, but about a twenty minutes' walk. This was also a two-fare zone, so a group of us students would frequently walk to XLCR, to save on the extra fare.

During the years at XLCR, my fellow students and I also looked forward to car rides from the Reverend Hugh Sherlock, who lived in the Mountain View area and frequently drove by as we waited for the second bus. Reverend Sherlock was a kind and gracious individual who always seemed pleased to assist us in arriving at school on time. Soon we became familiar with his schedule and would time our arrival with it so that we could ride with him. Reverend Sherlock was connected to the school by his service on the Methodist Board of Governors for XLCR. The Sherlocks came from a well-known and respected Jamaican family, with Hugh, a minister, and his brother Sir Philip, an educator, historian, and storyteller.

Many famous Jamaicans lived in the Mountain View area during that period, including the Hon. William Alexander Bustamante, affectionately known as "Busta" to all, Leader of the Opposition party, the Jamaica Labour Party and founder of the Jamaican Industrial Trade Union. With his huge crop of white hair and his outgoing personality, Busta was a Jamaican icon, recognizable and admired by almost everyone for his colourful personality. There are many "Busta" stories: many years ago, a new governor arrived in Jamaica from England, as was the custom every four years. Bustamante met Sir Hugh Foote, the new governor, at the airport and extended his greetings to "Sir Hugh Foote, Lady Foote and the little Feet," the governor's two young children. I was always thrilled to see Busta when he drove by and waved to us, even though my family belonged to the ruling party, the People's National Party whose leader was Norman Washington Manley, the brilliant lawyer. Although most middle-class residents did not usually vote for him, Bustamante was especially well liked by working-class Jamaicans. It was reputed that both party leaders were actually cousins; they worked harmoniously together, and they were both of racially mixed heritage.

MY CLASSMATES AND ME

On the XLCR campus, as new students, we were welcomed by prefects, seniors who directed us to our new form rooms. All the scholarship students were placed in form 4A2. Form 4A1 had the paying and perhaps special admission students. Moreover, I believe it was one year later, or it could have been much earlier, a new form was added for students who were now fourteen years old and whose prospects for enrolling in a good high school had previously been very dim. Mr. Powell had made another major policy decision to provide access to these older youth, many of whom were quite smart, gifted, and developmentally more mature.

Many of the graduates of that class have had successful careers. Paul Harris, good-looking with the easy smile, later became a supreme court judge in Jamaica; Karl Rodney founded *Carib News*, a weekly newspaper in New York City; Leslie Clarke, father of Congresswoman Yvette Clarke, became an architect and is the spouse of the famous councilwoman Una Clarke, also a Jamaican of Maroon ancestry; and my friend Rose Browne, whom I have dubbed a trendsetter, because she was the first in our group to wear an Afro hairstyle and to purchase a home in the Hamptons. Rose retired from NYC's Housing and Preservation Department and then became a senior vice president at the Community Development Corporation. Rose and I were also undergraduate students at NYU and have been neighbours and close friends on Manhattan's Upper West Side for over fifty years. Her only daughter, Michele, married Michael Culver; they now have a daughter in college and a teenage son, both of whom are skiers, and very much a part of our family.

After settling in our individual desks and chairs (as opposed to six students sitting together at a long desk in elementary school), our form master, Mr. Probyn Aiken, arrived to introduce himself, gave a welcoming talk, and provided us with our schedule for the term: Latin, maths, English, religious knowledge, English literature, geography, home economics, seven subjects each day with two breaks in between. We learned some information about Mr. Aiken; he had studied abroad, earned his degree in Latin, and had taught for several years. He looked forward to getting to know us and hoped we would be happy at XLCR. Mr. Aiken had a very amiable personality and a pleasant voice. I liked him immediately.

As a group, my fellow students and I were so excited and proud to be in high school. Besides being in a new environment, I now had to become accustomed to being called Fern instead of June, because while both were correct (Fern June), Fern was the first name on my birth certificate, which the school had used to enrol me. From then and throughout my educational and professional lives, I was Fern, while my family and friends from earlier times still call me June. Once I became used to being called Fern, I responded equally to either name.

While we waited for our form master to arrive, we greeted each other, speculated on what we thought would happen in high school and looked forward to learning new subjects like Latin. Laurice Russell, of mixed Indian background—a lovely personality and very likeable—and I connected that first day and remained friends until her father, with whom she lived, removed her from XLCR after the first year. I doubt that her mother was actively involved in her upbringing, since I rarely heard any information from Laurice about her. Anyway, Laurice was such a very pleasant and unassuming person that I was sad to lose her friendship and always wondered what became of her.

Mr. Aiken was our form master for two consecutive years, in forms 4a and 4b. In my third and part of my fourth year, forms 5a and 5b, Mr. Muñoz Bennett, a tall, relatively slim and trim individual, who walked with a deliberate and slow stride and tried to sound serious but actually had a good sense of humour, became our form master. We were already aware that many Jamaicans had left the island to work in Cuba or in Panama; some had returned, with or without families, while others had remained in Cuba and in Panama. Hence, with Munoz as his first name, Mr. Bennett could have been born in Cuba or Panama of Caribbean parents.

After Mr. Bennett left the school in 1954, Mrs. Knight joined our class for a brief period, and then Mr. Wong arrived, striding across the campus towards our classroom as we watched in eager anticipation. My fellow classmates used to tease me because I admired Mr. Wong. He was tall and handsome, and had a quiet confidence without seeming pompous. He looked and was half Chinese, like so many Jamaicans, meaning that he was a mixture of a Chinese parent, usually the father, and a mother of African descent. The Chinese were brought to Jamaica as indentured labourers in the mid-1800s, and, according to Abrahams, "Jamaica had absorbed them to such an extent that at least one-third of the entire Chinese community [12,394 according to the 1943 census, which made a breakdown on race and colour lines] were Chinese-coloureds."[4] The Chinese have contributed much to the commercial and industrial growth in Jamaica as well as to its music industry, for example, Byron Lee and the Dragonaires, and Miss Pat Chin, who now lives in New York and recently published her memoir, *My Reggae Music Journey*.

The words "of African descent," would not have been used during that period, since Jamaicans described everyone by skin colour and almost never by race as is known in the United States. I believe that Mr. Wong taught us English, a compulsory subject, and I am sure that I performed well in his class. Miss Morgan, who was another of my favourite teachers, taught us English literature. Miss Morgan had an interesting voice that undulated as she described the plot of a story or read a poem. She was an excellent teacher who also had a college degree. My fellow students and I were impressed by her credentials. Behind her back, students called her "Putus," a term of endearment. Almost every teacher had a nickname.

My four years at XLCR were rewarding ones with so much learning taking place. I enjoyed high school, was learning a lot, especially Latin, and if I missed a day of school, which I doubt, I must have been really sick. In addition to academics, school also provided a safe space away from adult problems where I could imagine possibilities.

My classmates and I got along well, and I made many friends among both boys and girls. Boys and girls became more comfortable with each other so there was less of a mystique about boys among us girls. There were about twenty-five students in my form, of which about ten were boys.

In 2014 I looked at a photograph of my class and could name all but three students. Still, I remembered them all. We knew that the very modest and unpretentious yet pleasant Dede Simmons was the brightest student among the girls and that the deliberate-speaking, slow-moving, and thoughtful Carlyle Welsh was the most studious and intellectual among the boys. Years later I learned that the two had married each other. Although I was friends with many of my classmates, my closest friend was Pauline Knight. We usually ate lunch together and talked about our observations of our classmates, teachers, schoolwork, and families. Pauline was authentic, direct in her quiet way, generous, empathetic, and just a very lovely person. We corresponded regularly after I left Jamaica and kept in contact over many years. When the older and more mature Claude Knight was placed in our class, he was attracted to Pauline, and that relationship flourished following graduation; despite numerous challenges, they eventually married and had four children. We kept in touch over many years: through her divorce from Claude, whom I had really liked for Pauline; through her second marriage and move to Roanoke, Virginia; until her untimely death there in December 2016.

My other classmates included Shirley Kong Quee, who invited me to study in the USA, Marjorie O'Sullivan, and Erna Brodber, who became a sociology professor, a writer, and later, an organic farmer in the country. In 2018 Erna was one of eight writers to receive the prestigious $165,000 Windham-Campbell award from Yale University. I had the pleasure of meeting her again at Barnard College's Caribbean Conversations in 2019—a reading and discussion by Erna and Jamaican author Nicole Dennis-Benn. Another more mature and unassuming classmate, the lovely Louise Shaw, met an untimely death while we were all still in high school, a shocking experience for adolescents, who typically expect our peers to live and have a future.

I performed well in all subject areas except maths—I should have asked for help but didn't think I should—and was especially fond of literature and religious knowledge. Geography and Latin were next in line, along with Spanish and home economics. Music was included in our high school curriculum and was taught by Mrs. Hyacinth Lloyd, an attractive, more mature woman, who walked with a slight tilt to one side. I really liked Mrs. Lloyd, who was an excellent teacher, was also very pleasant, and always talked with me directly. She taught us the difference between classical and romantic music, as well as many English, Irish, and Scottish songs that I still hum and often sing quietly today. I was happy to be learning so much about music and was always prepared for, and involved in, the lessons. It was Mrs. Lloyd who, in my senior year, took me aside and said, "Fern, begin to think about a profession, now that you will soon graduate." Seeing that she was very serious, I queried, "Why, Mrs. Lloyd? I will get a job after I graduate from high school." She responded quietly but firmly, "When you have a profession, no one can take it away from you." I never forgot her advice.

Anyway, one day, to my surprise and joy, Mrs. Lloyd told me that she was giving me a music scholarship to study the piano and that she would be my teacher. Each Saturday morning, I would make my way, walking some distance to her home in a different community in Kingston, to play the piano. I did not have a piano at home, and so practising during the week was a challenge. Although I visited Mrs. Frankson, our neighbour across the street, almost daily after school to practise on her family's piano, Mrs. Frankson and I would instead sit and talk for hours. She was such a wonderful woman, and I loved visiting and talking with her. Mrs. Frankson's husband owned a heavy haulage business, so they always had several pieces of trucking equipment in the large open area to the left side of their enormous house. A spacious verandah surrounded almost one half of the house, facing the active yard area. We would sit on the verandah, and she would tell me about her life, her six children—two of whom were also my friends—while I combed her hair. As a result, I did not advance in the skills required to play the piano, but I learned much about the complexity of adult life.

Of course, since "practice becomes perfect," and I lacked much practice, I felt that I had disappointed Mrs. Lloyd, but she was a trooper and kept me as her student for almost two years. I practised enough, however, for her to feature me in a small concert in the music room at Excelsior. I played my one piece okay but was so extremely nervous that I was determined to never repeat that agony. Nevertheless, I have always enjoyed and appreciated music, especially the human voice, the most versatile of instruments, so whether the songs are English or Irish airs, ghazals, leiders, Gullah, or Jamaican mento songs or calypsos, listening to them is always pleasurable, evoking many wonderful memories from my youth and adult years.

HIGH EXPECTATIONS OF US

XLCR held weekly assemblies for the entire student body. By then, XLCR had over five hundred students enrolled, the largest number among the well-known high schools. We crammed into one long building on campus and stood the entire length of the meeting. In addition to their semireligious tone, the assemblies were designed to get students in the mood for serious study and to focus on our education. We were told that our main purpose during those adolescent years was to focus on school, our main responsibility until graduation, when we would go to work. I know those words served as a guide for me and probably for many of us, since we all graduated as a class.

While studying sociology at NYU many years later, and learning about the various challenges for adolescents in the US, I was puzzled because our roles and responsibilities in the Jamaican culture were so clear: do well in school, then get a job or prepare for university entry. No one talked about the challenging teenage years that I can recall. Adolescent sturm und drang was certainly a new concept for me. Our roles as children and youth were well defined.

In addition to the assemblies, Mr. Powell also invited alumni, now professionals, to talk with us monthly. These alumni talked about their professions and the path each had taken to achieve his or her career goal. This activity was to expose students to the range of career possibilities that could be within our reach upon graduation. Each speaker also emphasised the importance of being focused and diligent to achieve our goals. Our headmaster was always extremely proud of his graduates, many of whom had excelled in their chosen fields, and he took every opportunity to expose us, his current students, to these models for success. He expected the best from all of us;

his message was clear, as reflected in the school's name, Excelsior, signifying "Yet higher," and its motto, *Age animo* (Do it with thy might). He instilled a feeling of pride, confidence, and a heightened sense of responsibility and ambition within us as we prepared to enter the world of work. I remember Mr. Powell visiting our class prior to graduation to give us a pep talk, but he also demonstrated how to fold our job inquiry letter into three even folds before placing the letter in the envelope. His high expectations for us were so ingrained in our psyche that achieving them had to be our goal, and that goal was never directly related to making money but rather to follow the path to acquiring good values and to live meaningful lives.

THE OVERSEAS SENIOR CAMBRIDGE CERTIFICATE

During our third year, we began to think and talk about the pending exam we had to take in order to graduate. The Overseas Senior Cambridge Certificate examination was prepared in Cambridge, England, by British educators, and sent to the then British West Indies, including Jamaica. The fifth-form classes, of which there were three or four levels, had a year to prepare for this exam; all the books on which we would be tested were assigned by British educators and were known as "set books." If, by the end of the year and prior to sitting for the exam, teachers deemed a student not ready to take the exam, she or he would not be recommended.

Miss Morgan worked with us in a supportive way to understand and interpret *Macbeth*, on which we would be tested and about which I became thoroughly versed. I spent many hours thinking about Macbeth's meeting with the three witches and whether their predictions were genuine or whether Macbeth felt compelled to make them come true. For the final exam, I selected eight subjects on which I would be tested. The only compulsory subject for everyone was English, which every student had to pass. My eight subjects were English, English literature, geography, religious knowledge, Latin, Spanish, history, and home economics.

I studied really hard during my fourth year, and finally it was time for the examinations, which lasted about two whole weeks. Those were the most tense weeks I have ever experienced. Sheer agony. I felt that I could not have lasted beyond the two weeks; so much of my future rested on passing that exam. The exam papers were sent to England to be read, graded, and the results returned to Jamaica. The waiting period for results took a few months but seemed to be forever; these were first published in the *Daily Gleaner*, Jamaica's major and respected newspaper.

For me, failure was always unthinkable. The self-imposed feeling of shame if I were to fail was too much to consider. Besides my father, I would be the first in my immediate family to graduate from high school, and I wanted my father and mother to be proud of me. A failure after four years of high school would be such a huge disappointment. The three passing categories were: distinction, credit, and pass, and most of us hoped for a credit rank. Imagine my joy and delight when my name appeared, along with numerous other students', under the credit category, in the *Daily Gleaner* of March 1956. That meant that I had passed all eight subjects, several of which, including English, were with credit, a respectable result. I believe that all my classmates but one passed the Cambridge School Certificate. My parents and family friends were very proud and happy, and my anxiety disappeared as relief and sheer joy took its place. At my high school graduation on campus, all the girls wore white dresses. Prizes were awarded and I received an award, a book of Shakespeare's plays, for some aspect of my character that is now a vague memory.

CHAPTER 5

REFLECTIONS ON JAMAICAN LIFE

During the fifties Jamaica held its famous Ten Types—One People beauty contest. I was fascinated and excited by this unique concept. For me, regardless of the controversy surrounding this creative idea, the contest democratised the concept of who was beautiful in a place like Jamaica; a woman from every complexion or ethnic group represented her group as the beauty queen. Jamaica was initially called Xaymaca, "Land of Wood and Water" by the Arawaks, the original inhabitants. I believe that the pageant organisers decided that since there were about ten types of people of colour in Jamaica, the contestants would represent ten colours of the country's wood and flowering plants.

The ethnic/complexioned groups were black, brown, light brown, Chinese, Indian, Middle Eastern/Lebanese, half Chinese, half Indian, half white, and white, and they ranged from Miss Ebony, the darkest wood and complexion, to Miss Mahogany, medium brown complexion, Miss Satinwood, Miss Allspice, Miss Sandalwood, Miss Golden Apple, Miss Pomegranate, Miss Jasmine, Miss Lotus, and Miss Apple-Blossom, very light-skinned Jamaican or white Jamaican. The result was that there were ten winners instead of just one. Their photographs were on buses and in the newspapers. I was excited by the competition sponsors' recognition that there was beauty across all colours and complexions. The ten beauty types are featured in the book *Jamaica, an Island Mosaic*, by Peter Abrahams.

Although skin colour in Jamaica had often played a significant role in one's career advancement, being well educated and having the right connections, that is, knowing individuals in high positions, could make a huge difference in obtaining one's desired employment. While in high school, I was fascinated to learn that a black female had been hired as a clerk by, I believe, the Bank of Nova Scotia, a first in the history of Jamaican banking. She was a graduate of my high school, so I was motivated to see her in person. I recruited my friend Pauline to accompany me to the bank to see if this news was indeed true. I was pleased to see her sitting poised and confident at her desk. She was contributing to a needed social change in Jamaica. Of course, the concept of social change was not in my vocabulary then; it was simply recognizing and welcoming a longed-for attitude change: that individuals with dark skin deserved the same opportunity accorded to fair-skinned ones. It was about treating everyone fairly and equally. Besides, the adults and children in any one Jamaican family were often a mix of all hues and complexions, from black to brown, light, and fair complexions, and they were all related to each other.

I read later that she was actually a test case to have banks hire dark-skinned Jamaicans.[1] The media had brought to light that no dark-complexioned individual had been hired in any of the banks, and so a group of XLCR alumni decided to address the problem. As a student, this individual was brilliant and had planned on a medical career when the alumni approached her to become the test case. Her academic record was outstanding, and she scored the highest on the bank's entry exam, so the bank had to hire her. My middle son, Javaid, an educator, has challenged my analysis of skin colour. He feels race was the key factor, and he may be right, but my perspective comes from a vivid recollection of my experiences growing up in Jamaica, where race was not front and centre for me, and was not even a prominent topic in my immediate environment as it is in the USA; our population was a numerical majority of black and brown people, unlike in the US, where African Americans were a numerical minority among the majority white population.

As indicated earlier, I was always aware of the relevance of skin colour, not race, because mentioning his/her complexion was the way Jamaicans described individuals about whom they were talking. I heard phrases like "You know her, she is that dark-skin [or brown or light skin], good-looking girl," but I knew that class was also an important factor in how individuals were perceived and then treated. The word "race" I do not recall hearing among the groups within which I interacted. We were Jamaicans of different hues and classes, and that was a given. We were not subjected to the relentless obstacles and disenfranchisement experienced by African Americans. During the 1980s an African American colleague visited Jamaica for the first time. On his return he could hardly wait to tell me how excited he was to be in Jamaica. He explained how validated he felt entering a place where he was no longer a minority. According to him, "The pilot [then Air Jamaica] was black, the customs officials were black, the taxi drivers were black . . . I was part of the majority group for the first time ever!" He said that he finally understood Jamaicans' unique experience.

The author Peter Abrahams's observation as an outsider captured the prevailing spirit about race and colour during that period. He wrote that "Garvey failed in Jamaica . . . because Jamaicans did not think of themselves as Negroes . . . let alone 'Universal Negroes.' Their world was Jamaica. . . . Africa was so long ago and so far away as to be unreal. . . . Race was an entirely alien factor."[2] That was close to my experience during my early developmental years in Jamaica; it was about being Jamaican, regardless of economic or social class. Of course, today's Jamaica is far more acutely aware of, and more outspoken about, racial issues locally and globally. However, it was only during my research on Jamaica years later that I became aware of the simmering dissatisfaction and impatience of the island's intellectuals with British rule and the prevailing educational system designed to perpetuate and educate the middle and upper classes. The much-needed educational reform in the late fifties provided greater access for poor and working-class children to secondary education, and in 1962, after years of preparation and anticipation, Jamaica received its independence peacefully from Britain under the leadership of its two most prominent politicians, Norman Washington Manley and Alexander Bustamante. Britain was ready to do so, anyway, as its colonies were becoming a burden.

Nevertheless, even with Jamaica's independent status, some Jamaicans still held warm feelings toward Britain and the royal family. Prior to independence, a governor was sent from England to oversee the country. He lived in King's House, where all the important social activities occurred. This situation has changed since independence. The prime minister now recommends to the king a local Jamaican to be appointed as governor general of Jamaica.

Again, while I was aware of colour and ethnic differences among Jamaicans, my awareness was more related to the natural curiosity and general observation skills typical of young children. As I indicated earlier, race was not a theme in my conversations, while skin colour was; descriptions of individuals usually included complexions. However, the reality for many families, given the island's mixed racial heritage, was that the existence of siblings of different complexions and facial features was common among them.[3] But beneath the surface, there was often among some people a preference for individuals of lighter complexion, to the chagrin and, often, hurt of the dark-complected family member.

I was aware that there was another small group of people with whom most of us typical Jamaicans had little in common and with whom we rarely interacted. They were the British nationals and well-off Jamaican whites who seemed to be a class by themselves. This group represented the capitalist ruling class, British-descended white Jamaicans and white expatriates of the banks, those in the British colonial service and the upper ranks of the Jamaican Civil Service. As a child my life did not seem touched by them, since black and brown people were the island's majority, many of whom were already in prominent positions in government or politics; some were highly esteemed educators and were well known across the island; others were civil servants, worked in banking, commerce, or other capacities. In other words, as students we had a plethora of role models looking like us from which to choose.

Given the intersection of colour, class, and education, there would be more options available were you perceived as being middle class or educated; if you were both, skin colour was rarely a factor. Being well educated was a top priority, along with how one spoke. For me, the impact of the "Ten Types" concept was a recognition that individuals of all complexions were valued in the society, and this, from my perspective, was a major step towards a form of equity for its citizens.

Many Jamaicans were quite aware of, and alert to, the barriers that kept dark-skinned people out of certain places. For example, while I was still living in Jamaica, there was an uproar when the owners of a hotel in one parish tried to prevent the local people from using the nearby beach. The newspapers carried the story, there was a protest, and the hotel had to reverse its position. So the Jamaican people usually kept a steady watch on, and actively resisted, any overt discrimination against them, whether from their own or from external groups. However, decisions by politicians could sway the balance between decisions beneficial to the island and its people or to the business world, where profit is often the main motive.

My early years in Jamaica were those in which the English were mostly admired; our history books were also written by English/British historians. However, it was much later, while engaged in conversations with thoughtful and well-informed friends and colleagues, beginning at NYU, that I began to embrace a different perspective on the real impact of colonial rule, especially the class construct, with its resulting consequences in Jamaica.

Reflecting on my earliest knowledge of Jamaica's history, two significant dates remain etched in my mind: 1494, when Columbus landed in Jamaica with his three ships, the *Pinta, Nina,* and *Santa Maria;* and 1655, when the English arrived as colonisers and soon drove out the Spanish, who had brought the first slaves to the island. Many of the enslaved individuals, along with those slaves previously freed by the Spanish, fled into the mountains where they were safe. Called Cimarrones by the Spanish, this group soon became known as Maroons. I believe that they were the first free black people on the island. Until a treaty was signed in 1739 giving specific rights to the Maroons while requiring them to cooperate in reporting on escaped enslaved individuals to the British, they were thorns in the white overseers and Englishmen's sides, conducting many raids on the plantations and often taking female slaves with them. During my youth, I heard many Jamaicans boast with pride that they had Maroon blood in their veins.

The Spanish inhabited the island for 160 years before the English arrived, so many of Jamaica's rivers, such as the Rio Grande and Rio Cobre, some cities like St Jago, and mountains like Mount Diablo have Spanish names. Once the English settled in Jamaica, two distinct groups of people inhabited the island: white Jamaicans and enslaved people. Peter Abrahams notes that with the growth of the sugar industry, the demand for labour grew; sugar mills increased in numbers across the island; and by 1700, there were over four hundred mills producing sugar for export to Britain. To meet the labour demand, Jamaica imported 610,000 Africans, including women, as slaves.[4] England and Scotland grew wealthy from the Jamaican sugar industry.

Meanwhile, the majority of estate owners returned to England, leaving the management of their estates to their lawyers, overseers, and bookkeepers. The overseers meted out harsh punishments to the beleaguered slaves, who were seen not as human beings but as property. Many escaped to join the Maroons in the mountains. Female slaves were exploited for their productive and reproductive capacities; however, even within that inhuman system, they were able to exercise agency by becoming higglers who sold provisions and goods on the streets and in marketplaces. These higglers played an important role in developing an economic foundation carried forward through emancipation and into today's marketplace. Some enslaved women were kept as mistresses by those estate caretakers, who were often unmarried. Abrahams noted that "in time this concubinage of the black or brown female slave to the white planter or his agents became a set pattern in Jamaica society under slavery."[5]

In the meantime, rebellions were many and were led by the enslaved people. Although abolitionists played an important role in ending slavery, two significant rebellions stand out as having been the main triggers in Britain's move towards emancipation: Tacky's Revolt in 1760, and the Baptist War led by Sam Sharpe in 1831. Freedom and justice for all were central to Sam Sharpe's very soul. As leader of the largest and most significant uprising, he rejected slavery "by claiming freedom as a human right and by making the issue one of morality: The whites had no more right to enslave the blacks than the blacks to enslave the whites."[6] While the leaders were caught and punished severely, the numerous uprisings and continual unrest finally led to the abolishment of slavery in 1834.

Prior to emancipation, however, between 1770 and 1808 there emerged a new class of racially mixed individuals known as free coloureds, or mulattos. Their children were free coloureds; children of freed blacks became the free blacks; meanwhile, both groups were still considered inferior by the white plantocracy. Those individuals who were favoured either worked in the house, were freed, or were given a piece of land to cultivate. Since the Englishmen were the ruling class, the classes below them, a middle class, tried to emulate their ruler's behaviour, and by the 1800s, the differences between colour and classes were well established. The favoured enslaved individuals looked down on the field slaves, a pattern that continued over the decades, and as the coloured population increased with their lighter skin colour, a middle class emerged that intentionally excluded black-skinned Jamaicans in their social interactions.

In her research on class and colour in Jamaica, Madeline Kerr describes the lengths to which the middle-class individuals would go to maintain their status, such as never carrying parcels on the street or just not daring to "lose prestige by doing anything that can be done by a servant, or that the upper classes might have done by a servant."[7] In other words, their behaviour was modelled on that of the white Jamaicans or the Englishmen's behaviour. Those class-conscious behaviours were in vogue during my developmental years in Jamaica; sometimes they were subtle, and at other times, less so.

However, over time a cultural and attitudinal shift occurred in Jamaica due to increased knowledge about their history, now taught in schools, and hearing the many stories of resistance by formerly enslaved people like Tacky, Sam Sharpe, Cudjoe, Paul Bogle, and Nanny. Paul Bogle, Nanny, and Sam Sharpe are now among Jamaica's seven National Heroes. In addition, the continuing resolute voices of Jamaica's intellectuals, still frustrated with the vestiges of colonialism, continued to advocate for, and in the sixties received, independence from England and freedom from colonialism. Sherlock and Bennett attributed the cultural change to a recognition, finally, of Marcus Garvey's intellectual genius, and the importance of his urgings that Jamaicans become more aware of the impact of slavery and colonisation on their racial identity, and of their connection to Africa.

With its cultural and historical consciousness now heightened, Jamaica's intellectual awakening grew stronger and resonated positively with the populace. The island's current affirmation of its racial identity "is radically changing the Jamaican self-image to one of assertiveness and racial equality. It has projected Jamaica onto the world stage politically and has moved increasing numbers of black people into leadership roles in their country."[8] Marcus Garvey is now celebrated as the first of Jamaica's seven national heroes, a fitting tribute for someone whose advocacy was ignored for decades.

The slow unravelling of that admiration for the British may also have occurred with the latter's recently published hostile attitude towards those Jamaican immigrants of the "Windrush generation." The *Windrush* was the ship bringing five hundred Jamaicans and other Caribbean nationals to England in 1948 to increase the country's labour force following World War II. According to news reports, this group, coming from a commonwealth country, thought they were already citizens and so never applied for citizenship. Among the Caribbean immigrants who landed in England was the famous calypsonian Lord Kitchener, who immediately expressed the high expectations of the immigrants through his melodious calypso "London Is the Place for Me." Hope was in the air for the immigrants.

However, in 2018 they became the brunt of attacks by conservatives who denied them human services, deported some individuals, and threatened deportation for others. Britain's prime minister finally apologised after prominent voices were raised on the immigrants' behalf. The significant contributions the Jamaicans and other immigrant groups had made by filling the labour shortage gap in England after 1941 seemed to have been deliberately erased from the English politicians' memory.

Discrimination towards Jamaicans and other nonwhite groups had existed in England once they began to arrive in large numbers during the forties and fifties. Jamaicans who returned from England during those years told stories of being asked, especially by children, if they lived in trees like monkeys. To my young mind, such questions were astounding, given that we had studied their history and literature; they should have known more about our history and culture. I did not appreciate that lack of knowledge about our island and its culture.

Historically, almost all of Jamaica's twelve parishes had a Great House, typically located on a hill overlooking one or several villages. The custos of that parish, whose role was to represent the governor-general and to greet all dignitaries visiting the parish, lived in the Great House. The custos was an honorary title with many benefits. Until independence, the custos had always been an Englishman whose traditional charge from the governor was to represent the governor in the parish, be the chief magistrate, make recommendations for the appointments of justices of the peace, and perform other social function activities.

The role of custos changed following independence. I was delighted when visiting Jamaica with a group of educators from Bank Street College in 2002, we met with the then-custos of Trelawny, the Hon. Royland Barrett, who was a local dark-complexioned Jamaican, a barrister, and a graduate of XLCR, my former high school. He was also a scholar who held our attention as he talked with us about the influence of the churches, Methodists, Moravians, Baptists, and others in helping formerly enslaved individuals to own property in Jamaica following abolition. My group also visited a former Great House, the Good Hope Great House, now available for guests but where we learned some information on its history and its current use as a place for weddings and other social events.

Philip Sherlock, in his book *Keeping Company with Jamaica*, describes the Good Hope Great House as "an excellent example . . . [of] something satisfying in a harmony of man's buildings with nature's work."[9] As I stood on the verandah and looked over the estate and the breathtaking view below, I thought of the English poet William Cowper's words

I am monarch of all I survey,
My right there is none to dispute,

as so apt for all the former colonial custoses who basked in seeing, living on, and sometimes owning acres upon acres of Jamaica's amazingly lush vegetation and panoramic views of that beautiful land, filled with fruit trees and covered in exquisite flora and fauna, on a daily basis.

In a 2006 interview for a curriculum on immigrants in New York City, I told my interviewer, Dr. Richard Lieberman of LaGuardia Community College, that I have always been an observer of what was happening around me. That's how I made sense of my world. Growing up in Jamaica, I interacted early on with many different types of people, especially older people, perhaps because I was the oldest child and, I was told, my grandfather's favourite grandchild, in my immediate family. I enjoyed talking with adults who responded positively to my questions and felt comfortable in sharing their stories with me.

When I lived in Kingston, relatives from the country would appear to visit my family, often unannounced, since we did not have a telephone; friends and neighbours stopped by to talk; vendors selling mangoes, star apples, and other fruits, or ackee, the national fruit, spent time at the gate convincing us why we should buy their goods; and neighbours would spend time talking over adjoining fences.

LOCAL DIALECT, METAPHORS, AND FOOD

As a curious child interested in everything around me, I listened to my family describe some individuals as "sweet mouths," indicating that they will flatter you, so be careful about trusting their words. The metaphors used to describe personalities were precise, pithy, and easily interpreted by the local listeners. Philip Sherlock, the famous Jamaican scholar and historian, described the Jamaican language as that "of people with a strong sense of the ridiculous, a gift for vivid imagery, for ridicule and irony, for nicknames and epithets, for earthy humour and bawdy cuss-words."[10] Some people were "flighty flighty," or unable to focus; some were "fenky fenky," or very picky; a female with thin legs would be "mauga legs"; a male with a large head might be "big head Joe." A village in the mountains resembling the Alps in every way except being snow covered is called the "Jamaican Alps," and the Luminous Lagoon in the parish of Trelawny is called "Glistening Waters." Egret birds who sit on cows during the day and return to the trees at dusk are called "cowbirds." Anyone who talks too much would be "chat chat" or "mouthamassy," and gossip is described as "carry go, bring come." Jamaicans called the person or thing the way they saw either one.

Almost everyone had a story to tell, some real and moving, while others were hilarious. I also met and listened to individuals who had been farm workers in the United States recount some of their experiences while picking oranges in Florida or fruits in Maine or New Hampshire, or harvesting tobacco in Enfield or Somers, Connecticut. Some farm workers returned with a "twang," an imitation of the American accent, which was often cause for much amusement. I was in the mix of all of these experiences and was always attuned to how different individuals behaved and how other people responded to them. With a bent towards being organised, fair but critical, I had decided early on which behaviours I admired and which I neither condoned nor would emulate. Often my reactions were based on my teachings from home, Bible stories, and the vivid parables through my membership at St Luke's Anglican church. I admired people who were kind and generous of spirit, possessed integrity, were easy to relate to, and showed respect for everyone regardless of class, education, or work.

Moreover, as soon as I was old enough to travel alone, about eight years old, I also visited my close friends and relatives in their homes. My family called me "walk about" because I was always going somewhere. These visits offered another opportunity for me to see how other people lived and treated each other. The households represented the mix in family composition: some had parents who were married and lived together with their children, and often with an older parent or another relative; others had one parent with the other parent either living elsewhere, in America, England, or Canada; many had a single or divorced mother living with her mother or with relatives in an extended-family situation. Some parents were very strict with their children, especially their daughters, and did not allow them much interaction outside their homes, perhaps concerned that they may associate with individuals of whom these parents may not approve or, for girls, the fear of unplanned pregnancy.

My family was definitely more relaxed, but I also knew that my mother's trust in me was unwavering, so I would not behave in any way to change her belief in me. I saw how quickly my mother came to my defence in the very few situations that arose. While still in elementary school, I believe that I ignored a male classmate for some reason that I have forgotten. Anyway, he punched me on my shoulder, and I cried in pain. On hearing my story, my mother was at my school the next day talking with my teacher about the incident. The teacher included the offender in our meeting, and after listening to both sides of the story, he was punished and warned not to hurt me again. My mother's coming to the school again was unusual, because in Jamaica the teacher was held in such high regard that most such issues were left up to him or her to resolve. Parents trusted the teacher's ability to handle the problem. I realised that my very quiet and easy-going mother was fierce when it came to protecting me, and I was not only happy at this revelation but awed by this other side of her. In my adult years, I realised that my mother also really knew me better than anyone else, a fact that mattered much to me.

There were times when I felt that Jamaicans seemed to be more alike than different in so many ways, even across the ethnic groups and glaring class divides. A common trend among Jamaicans was food preparation according to the weekdays. In many households, one could almost predict the dinners prepared according to the days of the week: on Fridays, there was usually Escovitch fish perhaps served with bami (a cassava flatbread) and vegetables; Saturdays delivered up beef or chicken soup along with side dishes, while stewed chicken, rice and peas, or curried goat and rice were usually served on Sundays. The menu during the rest of the week varied from oxtail, ackee, and codfish, stewed peas and rice, "turn cornmeal," boiled dumplings or green bananas, yam or other ground provisions along with fried plantains, and other local provisions, all depending on available funds. Of course, not every family followed this pattern, especially if they lived near the sea, but many did. Like mangoes, breadfruit was a versatile staple in households: breadfruit could be boiled, roasted, baked, fried, or cooked in soups.

My favourite meals were rice with stewed chicken or beef, stew peas and rice, roast breadfruit, banana, fried or boiled dumpling, some yams and all kinds of porridge, such as green banana or cornmeal porridge, and I loved cow's foot jelly. Dinner was eaten early in most households, so it was always ready when I arrived home from school around 4:00 or 4:30 p.m. I was very happy when there was rice and either chicken or meat for dinner, and very unhappy if rice was not visible on my plate. My mother would try to console me by reasoning with me. In my heart I knew there was a good reason for the lack of rice; there was often a ration on white rice, imported from abroad, which increased its cost; I also enjoyed spreading the imported New Zealand 'best butter' on my bread when we could afford to purchase that expensive item.

I enjoyed stews like oxtail, cow's foot, as well as roasted sweet potatoes or corn, "tie-a-leaf," a cornmeal mixture with raisins wrapped and tied in a banana leaf and then boiled, and a rich variety of other vegetables and fruits, including the ever delicious mangoes, sweetsop, star apple, and jackfruit. During mango season almost every home bought or picked mangoes from their existing trees and ate so much that often they could not eat dinner. Julie, Bombay, and East Indian were the most precious and sought-after mangoes; however, the small black mangoes were also delicious and popular, and I often saw individuals seated on low stools in their yards happily devouring a bucket of black mangoes.

After this feast of mangoes, star apples, guineps, and the island's rich variety of other fruits during the summer months, children had to face the consequence: "a washout," the dreaded annual dose of that awful-tasting castor oil on one day, and senna and salts on the following day. Adults shared a common belief that children developed worms from the feast of fruits, and so the "washout" was necessary for their healthy return to school in September.

On my annual visits to Jamaica between 2016 and 2019, I was intrigued by the number of individuals who spoke patois during their normal interactions; in my youth, middle-class individuals spoke "good English" even if they knew and were fond of patois.

Use of Aphorisms as Cultural Norms

Most Jamaican children were brought up and socialised through "sayings" or aphorisms. Parents and relatives were consistent in their use of aphorisms to explain life. For example, if an individual tended to not learn from others' experiences, the explanation would be simply "You can take a horse to water, but you can't make him drink" or "Children who can't hear will feel" for disobedient children. A spanking is coming. Another popular saying was "Stop coming and come" for individuals who always delayed other people with the phrase "Soon come." "She little but she tallawah" was applied to a small or fragile-looking female who was actually quite tough, and "patient man ride donkey" describes the experience one would have in riding the slow-moving donkey: one cannot be in a hurry.

To reassure a child or an adult who might be fearful, one may hear a Jamaican proclaim "Duppy [a ghost] know who to frighten," meaning that if you seem vulnerable, bullies can sense this and will pick on you. Every adult I knew used some of these and other phrases in their daily interactions with family, friends, and other people. The phrases could be used as a warning, to reassure, to teach values, or to explain. They were usually crisp, direct, and rich in the use of metaphors. Some were in standard English, but the most poetic and colourful ones were in the local Jamaican patois. Some others were:

*Chicken merry, hawk deh near!
Danger can lurk in the most unexpected places. (This is a warning.)
*Dawg no howl ef im hab bone.
People do not become upset if they are comfortable.
*Cockroach no business inna fowl fight.
Let well alone!

Using these sayings saved Jamaicans from providing long explanations in social interactions. Community members knew and understood them, and as children developed, they began to learn and use them. Sayings are not unique to Jamaica but are universal among different cultures. Similar sayings are also found among the Gullah/Geechee people in South Carolina and Georgia Sea Islands as well as in the midwestern states. I have, however, often wondered whether adhering to some of these sayings was missing an opportunity to do something about a particular situation, to think about what may be behind a behaviour, and then develop a plan to address or correct the behaviour or feeling, rather than simply accepting the saying. While colourful and useful for the deliverer of the words, there seemed to be something passive about some of them, especially as used in Jamaica and within the English-speaking Caribbean islands as well.

DEVELOPING MY SENSE OF SELF

In addition to learning about Jamaican values and life from everyday experiences, my close friends and I attended Sunday School at St Luke's Anglican Church, where we read and absorbed Bible stories that taught the values of kindness, modesty, generosity, humility, treating others as you want to be treated, and so on. I learned to dissect parables. which we were told were heavenly stories with an earthly meaning, and I enrolled in confirmation lessons at the end of which I was able to receive Holy Communion on Sunday mornings. I was also busy being involved in some church activities for children during the week, such as Brownie meetings.

My favourite reasons for going to church were the calm feelings evoked by being present, and by singing the hymns, most of which I knew, and still know, by heart. The words were like poetry to me, and each hymn seemed to be teaching a life lesson about love, sacrifice, humility, forgiveness, or engaging in rituals. I did not enjoy sermons unless there was a special story that was inspiring or imparted wisdom.

And so over my developing years, all the positive, meaningful, challenging, and humorous experiences coming from home, school, church, friends, and influential adults converged and crystallised in my developing a strong sense of who I was, embracing my values and my identity, trusting my instincts and becoming the person that I hoped to become. Although I had friends in my age group, I spent many hours with adults. While I enjoyed listening to their stories and conversations, they too seemed to enjoy having me with them. These relationships were largely based on a sense of kinship among us, even though we may not have been related by blood.

I spent many weekends with the Nairns, a very large family of about eight siblings, five of whom were in America. Together they pooled their resources and built a large house with a modern kitchen and bathroom, formal living and dining rooms, and several bedrooms where they could stay when visiting Jamaica. The house was occupied by two of the sisters, one of whom was the cashier for Crooks Haberdashery, a large and popular retail store on Slipe Road, a main street in Kingston. The other sister was Aunt Anna, who was fond of me and so always invited me to visit her family. In Jamaica children were taught to call unrelated adult family friends "Aunt" or "Uncle," out of respect. To my family's chagrin, I used those titles only if I felt those adults deserved them.

So, I liked Aunt Anna who had those qualities that I admired; I didn't mind walking almost two miles to visit on weekends. I would go everywhere with Aunt Anna, including the Copacabana Beach Club, visiting their friends, and Sunday Mass, since the family was of the Roman Catholic faith. Soon I could recite the rosary and sing the hymns while remaining Protestant. One sister who had done financially well in the States, married the owner of a liquor store, and owned a brownstone in Brooklyn met me on one of her visits to the family house. Apparently she was quite impressed with me and so talked to Aunt Anna about adopting me because she had no children. They then suggested that I talk with my mother about returning with her to America. Walking back home, I became terrified at the thought of leaving my mother, even with the promise of material advantages and a richer life. I really feared that the love and safety that I felt from being with my mother and aunts might be absent in a new situation. Besides, the personal freedom that I enjoyed might not be available to me elsewhere, and that was important to me even then.

Then I became even more worried about my mother's response. What if Mama agreed that I should go? What would I do? I really did not want to live with another family. Even though I was bold in talking with adults, I was still a child, and this was a life-changing decision. On arriving home I told Mama of the offer. Without hesitation and with a hint of indignation, she declared, "Of course not! Why would I do that? I will not send you to America with anyone, regardless of promises!" And that was the end of that conversation. But for me, there was only great joy, a huge relief, and much appreciation for my mother's good sense.

Somewhere along my middle years, I embraced words that I had heard from my family, "You come from somewhere!" I saw those words as affirming, that I was rooted somewhere, and that I had a remarkable family history. During my undergraduate years in the States, when there was a particular challenge, I would be comforted by the feeling that I could always return to Jamaica. Of course, I knew that I would not give in to such a move, but it was comforting to know that I could return home if necessary. Moreover, I was always optimistic and held to the maxim that everything happens for a reason. It was left to me to figure out the "why," and since I loved figuring things out or, perhaps, justifying what had happened, there was little room for too much disappointment. I was often told, for some reason, that I was lucky, and I believed it, perhaps because of all those many positive experiences I had as a young person. Besides, my determination to succeed, though quiet, was an ever-present and motivating factor.

I also found poems to be useful in explaining feelings and providing encouragement when needed. I reread the inspiring words in my autograph book many times over the years. I could always find the right words to brighten my spirits or to embolden me in making a wise decision. Among my favourite poems were

Mind is the power that moulds and makes and man is mind:
And evermore he takes to the tool of life, and shaping what he wills
Brings forth a thousand joys, a thousand ills.
He thinks in secret and it comes to pass, environment is but his looking glass.
(G. Anglin, January 1955)

The second poem was written by one of my teachers, Ms. Dorothy Scott, in 1955.

Be master of your petty annoyances
And conserve your energies for the big worthwhile things,
It isn't the mountain ahead that wears you out
It is the grain of sand in your shoe.

I took those words seriously. It was up to me to make or create the life I desired, including being happy. During the months following graduation from high school, I spent time visiting my friends, wrote letters to my pen pals living in South Africa, read at least one book daily—all love stories—and fully enjoyed them. I also saw many movies, especially those with my favourite actors, Jane Russell, Esther Williams, Errol Flynn, and Victor Mature. Reading books and poems about love and living a fulfilling and purposeful life resonated with me.

But reality soon appeared, and the vacation period ended. I was ready to work. To begin my job search, I received a letter of recommendation from my minister, the Reverend Canon Maxwell in May 1956, which stated that I was "a keen and faithful young member of our congregation . . . and I consider her to be conscientious, industrious, well-mannered and of high moral principles."

CHAPTER 6

Becoming a Civil Servant

Beginning my job search at age sixteen, I sent out several letters applying for jobs, but nothing materialised until my mother contacted a family friend who was a prominent civil servant. He immediately offered me a clerical position in the Jamaican Civil Service. I began working the following day. My sisters, Phillippa and Hope, respectively seven and five years younger than me, told me that following their high school graduation, they also got their positions after our mother made a call for each one of them. My mother knew so many people, and she was always there to help her family as well as other people needing help. While I was in college, my mother became the manager for the New Bell Cleaners in Kingston and was much loved by all her customers. She treated everyone with so much kindness, caring, and graciousness that her leaving to join me in the US in the late sixties created a real vacuum for that business.

I worked in the Collector General's Office (CG) located in the heart of downtown Kingston, from 1956 to 1957 for a salary of five pounds weekly, about US $20. I was excited and happy to finally become a civil servant. My building was one of about four or more impressive, cream-coloured (they may have been white at an earlier time) historical government buildings on both sides of King Street, facing each other. King Street was the main thoroughfare in Kingston, with most buses ending and beginning their routes in front of these buildings.

North of the buildings and bus terminals and with their entrances sharing a common covered corridor were all the popular stores: Nathan's, Issa and

Co., Henriques Jewellery, and others. In Kingston the large businesses were generally owned by ethnic groups: Jamaicans of Lebanese descent (often called Syrians) owned the huge haberdashery stores; wealthy Indians owned the expensive jewellery stores; Chinese owned the grocery stores and food emporiums, while the majority of black and brown Jamaicans tended to be in the civil service and in education.

There were some exceptions, of course. There was the Keizs Furniture Store, owned by the father of former York College president Dr. Marcia Keizs and her sister Jean, who was my classmate at XLCR. Mr. Keizs was a dark-complexioned Jamaican, while a brown-complexioned Jamaican owned Crooks Haberdashery, where one of my "aunts" worked. I also knew black and brown Jamaicans living in the country areas in other parishes who owned smaller shops, haberdashery or grocery shops.

RIDING THE ESCALATOR

The Times Store on lower King Street was the first store in Kingston to install an escalator, and I remember going there just to see and experience this innovation. This was a short escalator to the second floor. I stood for a while just watching others step onto this moving staircase and was transfixed. That was amazing. I wanted to step on the escalator but was scared that I wouldn't be fast enough and might fall off. As I watched, no one fell off; but there were other people like me who just stood and watched as the escalator made its way slowly to its destination. So on my first visit, I was happy just watching others get carried up to the second floor. Subsequently, I returned to the store, gathered my courage, and rode the escalator safely to the second floor.

KING STREET AND PARADE: THE HEART OF KINGSTON

The middle section of King Street had beautifully designed government buildings with manicured spaces between the buildings, all of which had balconies stretching along the entire front of the building. At lunch or tea break, staff, including me, from various units of government would appear on the many balconies, to survey King Street, talk to each other, or just to relax while surveying the environment.

Jamaican civil servants worked a half day on Saturdays. So, every Saturday after work without fail, young women would wear their prettiest dresses to walk up and down King Street pretending to shop but hoping to be noticed by anyone, especially the young men who usually stood at the same corner spot to talk and to watch young ladies as we passed by them. That was the Saturday ritual in Kingston for both young men and women. Those were such fun days. South of the buildings were the Bank of Nova Scotia, Barclays Bank, Times Store, and other stores, offices, and restaurants.

Then there was South Parade, a circular area at the northern end of King Street. Parade bustled with taxis, trucks bringing or selling fruits and other goods, brightly decorated carts, shoppers, market people, and many stores surrounding one side of the circle. At one end of the Parade was a huge, stately tree usually surrounded by higglers selling their produce. Parade was a busy and congested area, but it was also the ending or beginning of many major streets flowing into and from its centre, like spokes in a wheel. I have heard that Parade is no longer in existence.

A few yards away from the Parade was Jamaica's famous Coronation Market, where one could purchase ground provisions, fresh fruits, fish, beef, crafts and more. Jamaican markets are an experience unto themselves. Determined to sell their produce, the market women could be either aggressive in their approach or sweetmouth to induce the shopper to buy their varied items. If they were displeased with your attitude or nonpurchase, you might catch their "cut eyes" at you or hear an insulting remark. Saturdays were market days for my family. As a little girl, I loved to visit the sprawling open-air market in our community, Crossroads Market, with Mama and Aunt Dor, and observe how they would haggle over prices with the vendors. On the corner of a street, one block over from the market, was a small haberdashery store with this unforgettable sign: "If absence makes the heart grow fonder, this store has many friends!"

I had many friends at the CG office, and although the clerical work was monotonous, my colleagues made coming to work a joyous activity. At lunchtime my former classmate and friend Pauline and I looked forward to our usual fare of a beef patty, that delicious Jamaican staple seasoned with a combination of mouth-watering spices that after eating one, although quite filling, I always yearned for another. Patties were generally sold at patty shops and restaurants throughout Kingston, with Bruce's Patties being the Cadillac of patties. Paired with a Horlicks malted milk at The Milk Bottle, a small restaurant behind our building, that was the most luscious lunch ever. As we ate, Pauline and I talked about our experiences on the job, the boys we admired, relationships in our offices and information about any upcoming dance parties. After all, we were young adults, and those were the topics of interest to us then.

Pauline worked one floor below me in the customs office. All the government offices had a similar layout pattern, large open spaces with long rectangular wooden desks on which clerks performed their daily tasks. On my floor I sat at one end of a wooden desk about six to seven feet long with three or four other clerks. There were similar furniture and staff configurations throughout the huge room, which on one side opened onto a balcony facing King Street. A medium-sized, glass-enclosed office for our supervisor was situated in the far right-hand corner facing east. We were on the third floor. My task was to wade through a pile of motor vehicle receipts and check each one off with a long tick (check) mark. Working with my office colleagues was fun, but the work left nothing to stimulate thinking or creativity. I often thought the work was redundant, since these were receipts indicating that the five shillings (5/-) motor vehicle taxes had already been paid. I was never sure what happened to the bulk of receipts after I had ticked them off. However, their existence provided work for us civil servants, and I was thrilled to be working in the government office, the dream job of my youth.

With a significant number of young people working in the building's various government offices, there were many social interactions and friendly conversations happening while we worked. We were all government clerks who felt comfortable in moving around the huge, open offices and socialising with colleagues even as we were supervised by mostly older and experienced managers. I also met my first boyfriend at the CG office. Ernle worked on the floor below mine, but he and his friends would come to visit on their breaks, and soon we were talking on a regular basis. As an athlete Ernle was a high jumper and had participated in the 1955 Olympics in Australia, along with Mel and Mal Spence, Keith Gardner, George Kerr, and other athletes. They were soon all recruited to enrol in universities in the USA, where they encountered, for the first time in their lives, racial and climate challenges. One athlete told me that he was so shaken when he saw the pile of snow outside his dorm that he returned to sleep instead of going to class. He, like me and some other Jamaicans, had never seen snow until we arrived in the US. Then his friend said that he did not know he was black until he came to the United States.

We had heard stories about racial prejudice in the US but didn't quite understand the nature and depth of that racial reality. Nevertheless, I understood the athletes' feelings of confusion and frustration; they were well known and were a source of pride in Jamaica; neither their colour nor race had been a factor. Some of them returned to Jamaica before completing their degrees, while others dealt with the challenges and completed their degrees.

MY BIRTHDAY PARTY

In addition to the friends from my office, I had close friends who lived in my neighbourhood and who had attended other private high schools. I used to visit these friends frequently because they lived within walking distance from my home, whereas I recall visiting only three of my classmates: Shirley Kong Quee, who lived near XLCR, and we usually walked by her home after school; Una Savage, who lived within a thirty-minutes walking distance; and Noelle Scott, whose father worked at the university and whose family lived on campus. My other classmates lived in communities where I would have had to take at least two buses to reach their homes.

Among my friends were the two Lazarus sisters, who self-identified as part Syrians and lived with their mother, a nurse; and the very pleasant and even-tempered Sonia Brown, who lived with her aunt in what was then a very upscale Jamaican neighbourhood. Sonia's mother had left Jamaica for America years before, thereby achieving the goal of so many Jamaicans. Sonia attended Immaculate Conception High School along with friends Pearl Mitchell, Joy Lazarus, and my sister Audrey. Pearl and Sonia, who now live in the USA, and I have remained lifelong friends. Sonia also attended NYU and now lives closer to her two grown children in California, after retiring from a very satisfying position at Yale University. Audrey, who had married in the US and had two daughters, my nieces Linda and Lisa, had also graduated from NYU and worked in medical social work for many years. Sadly, she passed away in 2015. I have missed our sharing of childhood memories.

When I was thinking of celebrating my sixteenth birthday, Sonia's aunt graciously offered to host my party in her home. I had saved some money for a celebration and so was quite excited by the idea. I then ordered a fancy cake from a bakery whose name I have forgotten. I had agreed to end the party by midnight, so we enjoyed the time dancing to popular music and waited to cut this beautifully decorated cake by 11:30 p.m. With eager anticipation, everyone gathered around the table for the cake cutting. The young people looked longingly at the cake. They just knew the cake would be delicious because it was so beautifully decorated. We were a happy lot, anxious to sink our teeth into that fabulous-looking cake.

And then, there was a gasp and my total embarrassment. As my knife entered the cake, the batter oozed out and the slice fell apart. It had not been fully baked and was totally inedible. When I told the owner of the bakery about the situation, he merely said that he had not done the baking; it was baked by one of his workers. Needless to say, not only was I very upset by his attitude and no apology but also had to deal with my guests leaving without the taste of a birthday cake but with a juicy story to tell others. I was so embarrassed. Later, I thought about how much money I had spent on that party and wondered whether it was really worth it. But I soon got over that disappointing event, probably buoyed up by one of our sayings: "It was too good to be true!" Besides, there were lots of letters to write to my pen pals, and several dance parties to look forward to attending, so I soon left that unpleasant experience behind me.

THE SOCIOLOGY OF TRAIN TRAVEL

Travelling on Jamaican trains has always been a source of great satisfaction and delight for me. I well remember my many train rides on the Jamaica Government Railway as wonderful adventures where I was free to observe the behaviour and customs of local Jamaicans and tourists, or to simply daydream about how I envisioned my future. I would have a good job and save my money to travel, while also helping my family to purchase a home in Kingston or St Andrews; these were themes among my daydreams.

Often travelling in the first class coach, a small compartment furnished with individual wooden cushioned chairs, because of my father's position in the railway, I was always fascinated by the rich surrounding vegetation as the train sped through the countryside. I noticed that first class typically attracted more English people or tourists than local Jamaicans, while travelling in second class was like being part of the audience in a theatre. Second class was a mix of everybody, including market women who shared hilarious experiences with each other about their relatives or the customers who tried to outsmart them. I had such an enjoyable time listening to their comments and the humorous stories they told. Each train had two or three freight cars that transported goods and materials to different parts of the island. The trains were such a vital mode of transportation for the island, moving people and goods from Kingston to Montego Bay, or Port Antonio, the two major routes, or to Ewarton, a shorter route focused on transporting materials like fruits or bauxite. The route to Portland was constructed to facilitate the export of bananas produced by the United Fruit Company (UFC), and the small banana growers. The story of the short-lived success of the peasant banana growers in Portland has been well documented in Sherlock and Bennett's all-inclusive history of the Jamaican people.[1] According to them, the "early manifestations of a national will indicate the same quality of spirit that the Portland and St. Thomas banana cultivators displayed in the 1870's. . . . and so during the 1870's, large numbers of [peasants] bought small parcels of land of 10 acres or less from planters in financial need."[2] These banana growers did well until they were forced out of their profits by the UFC.

During summer vacations from school, I travelled from Kingston to the country to visit my father. During the three-hour train ride to Kendal, where my father was the stationmaster of the Kendal Railway, I would play a quiet game of reciting the order in which each station would appear before the train arrived at that station: Kingston, Gregory Park, Grange Lane, Spanish Town . . . etc., with the final destination being Montego Bay. A village in the parish of Manchester, Kendal became famous when in September 1957, there was a disastrous train crash on the near-midnight return journey from Montego Bay to Kingston. According to reports, over two hundred people were killed, and about seven hundred were seriously injured. Since the accident occurred near the railway station, my father was awakened by the loud noise and the train whistle. He got dressed and walked on the railway tracks to the disaster site, about half a mile from the station.

I was in Kendal at the time of the Kendal crash. I was about to leave for the US on my student visa and had visited to say goodbye. I vaguely remember when he left the house, since I was still asleep. He later described an unforgettable scene, with mangled bodies everywhere, people crying or screaming for help, and most of the train resting in a ravine. This was the worst train disaster in the history of the Jamaican Railway, leaving an indelible imprint in the memory of all Jamaicans old enough to remember the disaster.

In 2007 *Reapers of Souls* by Beverley East was published, rekindling the memory of that fateful first day of September. The train was packed with individuals who had gone on an all-day excursion, a favourite Jamaican holiday, to Montego Bay. As the train approached the Kendal railway station, probably going too fast, the driver is said to have lost control, and the train derailed. Ms. East lost fourteen relatives in that Kendal train crash. Typical in understanding unusual events in Jamaica, numerous stories circulated about the reason for the crash, some linked to religion (some nuns were on the train), others to fate, others to superstition.

For me, travelling by train allowed me to see parts of the geography and social conditions of the towns and villages through which the train passed. While the backdrop from one side of the train was the mountain range running from east to west across the island, the other side often showed a combination of gullies and dilapidated huts erected parallel to the train tracks. In some places, the soil was red, indicating the presence of bauxite. Local fruit and vegetable stands were frequent along the train route, and children, often barefooted, could always be seen playing in the yards and waving as the train sped by.

The people who lived along the tracks were quite poor with few resources and little hope that their lives would change. Very few of the adults had a salaried job, and their livelihood depended on the fruits and vegetables displayed along either the train routes or near the parallel high-ways where cars or truck drivers might stop to purchase their products. I used to think then that if only I had a magic wand, I would eliminate poverty by providing better economic, training, and educational oppor-tunities to improve their lives.

Where huts could no longer be seen, the vegetation appeared, thick and lush and always breathtaking. Jamaica was so full of contrasts, amazing island beauty versus abject poverty, especially in the cities; people full of life, lively music, and good humour versus the reality of a hard life due to lack of jobs and, for so many, an inadequate education. Nonetheless, each railway station provided an opportunity to boost the economy of the town or vil-lage in which the train stopped to discharge or welcome passengers. Trains passed through the designated stations twice daily, whether they were bound for the Kingston/Montego Bay or Kingston/Port Antonio routes. Aware of the predictable schedules, the vendors hastened to each coach window to sell their products. Various musical voices competed with each other, some smooth, some aggressive, but all urging us passengers to "buy yu orange," "buy yu star-apple," "Miss, yu wan roast cashew?" As the train whistle blew to signal departure, those who were brave enough to come on board would negotiate a reduced price for his or her item to ensure a sale. These vendors were such amazing salespeople.

Jamaican trains always departed Kingston at 9:00 a.m., on time. Should you arrive one second after the scheduled hour, the gate to the platform would be locked. I am certain that was due to the earlier British influence. Anyway, as the train pulled out of the Kingston station, I would settle back in my seat and listen to the wheels of the train as it gathered speed, first slowly, then gradually increasing its speed, and within minutes, the wheels went faster and faster until the rhythm familiar to my ears appeared, and I would quietly hum the Jamaican train song to the rhythm of the wheels:

Mi bat a come, mi bat a go
Mi bat a come, mi bat a go
Tell me bout the tunnel but no tell me bout the viaduct
Tell me bout the tunnel but no tell me bout the viaduct.

I still have no idea about the origin of those words, but I had learned them from somewhere or from someone who had listened closely, and in wonder, to those melodious sounds singing from the wheels on the steel rails. The tunnel referred to the few tunnels through which the train passed on its journey, one of which was really long, though perhaps less than a mile. Darkness loomed in the car during this time, and with my eyes closed, I would try to anticipate when the train emerged into daylight. I guess the viaduct seemed dangerous, as it was a bridge over a huge expanse of water.

Visits to My Father

I was very close to and proud of my father. He was strikingly tall, slim, jovial, and handsome in his black pants and white shirt, the uniform of all the stationmasters in Jamaica at that time, and we were always very happy to see each other. I remember hoping that as I alighted from the train, the passengers would be watching and thinking, as we greeted each other with hugs, how lucky I was to have such a good-looking and affectionate father.

My father graduated from the Kingston Technical School at a time when one had to be academically gifted to be accepted into that special high school. His name was also listed in the October 24, 1930, *Gleaner* as among "Successful Students in Pupil Teachers' Tests," which also meant, I assume, that he could teach. I doubt that he ever taught, but he became a civil servant with the Jamaican Government Railway at a young age and remained there until his retirement in the early seventies. Among my favourite memories of my father were the fact that he always, with great satisfaction, completed the crossword puzzle in the *Daily Gleaner*; that he had these huge ledger books filled with the words of every song that appeared each day in another newspaper; and he collected *Mutt and Jeff* and *The Phantom* comic strips from the daily newspapers, possibly the *Star*. He had collected these songs and comic strips while he was still single and had been posted at other stations across the island. I learned the words of most of the songs and read and reread all the comic strips as I sat in his office. I also loved to listen to him sing, his favourite song being "Jesu, Joy of Man's Desiring," tell stories, and just talk about his work. My father loved and enjoyed his job, and I was moved and inspired by this devotion to his work. I knew then that work would be important to me; I wanted to be like my father.

The technology used by stationmasters to communicate the movement of trains or to share special news was the telegraph, on which my father was an expert. Because of this, a group of his railway friends dubbed him "Sir Egbert Telegrif." As his greatest fan, I used to watch his performance in his office as he prepared to announce the train's departure from his station to the next station. Seated at his spotless and full-width, brightly polished, and shining wooden table, he focused intently on the instrument with the small brass base securely fastened on the table's upper right corner. Secured on this base were two brass arms about two to three inches long, with each arm bearing a black key at its tip. With his right arm on the table, my father would open the black keys with one movement, close his eyes in deep meditative concentration, and begin "the call-and-response" pattern of communication using the Morse Code. He returned to earth only when the messages were delivered and the responses came back as received. His was a performance worth seeing.

My father had a relatively large office in Kendal Railway's one-level building, with doors that opened on both sides of the room for easy access from the entrance to the office and then to the platform, and a third door leading to the huge storeroom, where I loved to explore among the stored items. His office was always immaculately clean, with a gleamingly polished wooden floor, a quiet ceiling fan that kept the office cool, all official papers neatly stacked on one of the two large tables in the room. A narrow side table under the window faced the platform. Each table had a chair eagerly awaiting the start of another day's work. "Sir Egbert" took great pride in having an impeccable office space. A woman came each day to dust the furniture and sweep or polish the floor.

There was also a small window between his office and the passenger waiting room through which customers bought tickets for travel to various destinations. Each day while visiting, I looked forward to being in the office with my father; he allowed me to sell travellers their tickets, all neatly arranged according to the designated stations, and then to reconcile the sales at the end of the day. If the figures did not match, and I was adamant that my calculations were correct, Daddy's mantra was always, "Figures don't lie, but liars figure." Then I would have to review and repeat the sales reconciling process until the figures were correct. He was always right in his calculations.

Every stationmaster was provided with a relatively large house near the station, since they were on call. Daddy went home for lunch, usually the main meal for the day, but he enjoyed having his cup of tea in the early afternoons, around 4:00. Separating my father's house from the railway station was a long, very wide driveway and parking lot extending several yards to the main street in the village. A huge rectangular white gate at the end of this driveway and parallel to the street suggested that the property belonged to the railway. The open area near the office provided much excitement for me and others when Banana Nights happened. That's when farmers brought their green bananas to be weighed, counted, inspected, and bought by the fruit company, then to be shipped abroad for consumption. The transactions between the "tallyman" and the farmers could last way after midnight, and I observed all those transactions until my eyes began to droop, and I would leave for home, which was just a few steps away from the office.

During my visits to the country, I would first spend some time talking with my stepmother, Ma Lin, short for Linda and my name for her, who had graduated from Merl Grove High School and had been a community worker prior to marrying my father. Ma Lin and Daddy had a good marriage, and they complemented each other well. Ma Lin was very pleasant, outgoing, and accomplished, and we had a very good relationship. We used to sit together on the verandah and talk about her prior endeavors as a community worker helping families in rural Jamaica. That was fascinating to me, since I had not met any such individuals in Kingston. Ma Lin loved to bake and always baked cakes at Christmas, and Easter buns for the Lenten and Easter seasons.

Though small in size, theirs was also the very first library I had ever seen in any of the many homes that I visited in Jamaica. A circular wooden bookshelf with partitions, it was filled with books and dubbed the EGLIN Library, their combined names. I spent time looking through almost all their books but do not recall whether I read any of them. Daddy and Ma Lin had five children together, two sons and three daughters; we were all raised as siblings and have always related positively to each other. I am "Sis" to my brothers Louis and Emile, who retired as bankers in Jamaica; married, they each have two adult children who are both professionals. Residing in the Bronx, sisters Lois, retired, and Dahn, who works in the public schools, keep in touch through emails, phone conversations, and special family events. Dahn, family historian, acknowledges all our birthdays and is the historian for the Spence family. The very lively, bold, and outgoing Joan, a true force, passed away after a brief illness in 2010. After her children had grown, Ma Lin became the librarian and unofficial counsellor in Old Harbour, where Daddy had built a house, and was much loved by the community.

Following our conversations where Ma Lin updated me on events and people, I made my rounds visiting neighbours, including the two postmistresses who lived on site, typical throughout the island; Lloyd French and his family, who had known me since I was a little girl and who always asked about my mother; and the two nearby groceries near the railway station. The owner of one store usually allowed me to stay behind the counter to take orders. I enjoyed serving customers and had learned to weigh and securely wrap loose sugar and flour by the pound or half pound in precut brown paper so that neither product would fall out of the wrapped item.

Directly across the street was Dan's Chinese grocery, where his nephew Lascelles Chin also spent summers and assisted in the shop. A Chinese shop could be found in every village, town, and city in Jamaica. Lascelles and I were about the same age, and whenever we met in Kendal, we would talk about school. He attended Wolmer's High School in Kingston. Today, Lascelles is CEO of perhaps the largest holding company in Jamaica, LASCO Affiliated Companies, and funds education, health, and other important local services.

I was really happy to read of Lascelles's generosity and commitment to supporting the various community services in his country.

Kendal was somewhat typical of rural communities throughout Jamaica.
The class divisions were apparent based on levels of social and economic
status, and although residents lived close to and knew each other and got
along well, they showed deference in relating to anyone they deemed being
of a different social status. The Great House, still in existence and positioned
on a hill not far from the railway, was occupied by the Clark family of English
or Scottish background; their unmarried adult daughter, "Miss Helen," taught
Sunday school for children in the community.

CHAPTER 7

The Letter of Invitation

In 1957, almost a year after I began working at the Collector General's office, I received a letter from a former classmate that changed the trajectory of my life, forever. The day was a regular 8:30 to 4:30 routine, pleasant enough, and I had, as usual, looked forward to having lunch with Pauline, my school friend and coworker. We were now both seventeen years old, having graduated from high school the previous year. Pauline usually visited me on her breaks at least twice daily, when we had a cup of tea or lemonade in the nearby staff room. So I did not expect any surprise upon leaving the office for home.

However, on arriving home my mother greeted me with a warm, mysterious smile. "Hi, June, you got a letter from the States today." As indicated earlier, "the States" was how most Jamaicans referred to the United States during my youth. I saw the airmail envelope in her hands as she walked towards me. With heightened curiosity I searched the envelope for the sender's name. Who could be sending me a letter from the States? My aunt who lived in New York City usually wrote to my mother, so I knew the letter was not from her. I turned the envelope over, and there on the back were a name and address. My letter was from Shirley Kong Quee, my former classmate and friend.

In her letter Shirley explained that she was enrolled as a foreign student at Chicago's Roosevelt University, on an F1 student visa, and lived with her brother, his wife, and their two-year-old son. She was inviting me to join her, also as a foreign student, at the university. To earn her keep, she worked in a Chinese restaurant, and if I came, she had a job waiting there for me, and I could live with her and her relatives.

I read and reread the letter with a mix of interest and curiosity. Of all our classmates, why did Shirley choose me to invite? Perhaps she was lonely and needed company in that new environment? While in high school, we had a good relationship. I often visited her home, where she lived with her married sister, a well-known and highly respected high school teacher. When we walked to her home, we talked about school, our classes, teachers, and life in general. Her sister's house was then a relatively new and highly desirable design for Jamaican houses. On my first visit, I was immediately attracted to its flat roof. I thought of all the dance parties that could be held there. Even the floors now covered with ceramic tiles were attractive and unlike the wooden floors common in Jamaica's older houses. But then, Shirley had never indicated that she had held any parties on that flat roof. After all, this was her sister's house, not hers.

However, I could not recall indicating to Shirley any interest in travelling to the United States. All these thoughts were moving like lightning through my head. While many Jamaicans yearned for an opportunity to travel to the United States, Canada, or England, largely to improve their economic conditions, I was not yet one of them. It was easier to go to England or Canada, because they were, like Jamaica, commonwealth countries; however, obtaining a visa to immigrate to America was very difficult, especially following the introduction of the McCarran Act of 1950. This act limited the numbers of people allowed into the US from the islands and other countries with black and other nonwhite populations. I knew about the McCarran Act as a young child because my mother and aunts always talked about how that policy hindered their chances to leave Jamaica for the States.

The story swirling within the Jamaican society was how financially well one could do in America, and so Jamaicans continued to be optimistic about obtaining that treasured visa. Many women designed what are known today as "vision boards," rectangular or square cardboards with pictures of their dreams pasted on them; every board contained a plane, a ship, and other dreams for fulfilment, like a house or marriage. As a child I had listened to the laments of adults who could not obtain a visa to emigrate, as well as to the stories from seasonal farm workers who had returned from picking apples in various American states or harvesting tobacco in Connecticut's tobacco fields.

Mr. T visited my family on his familiar bicycle each year on returning from America. He shared some of his experiences as a seasonal worker picking or harvesting apples and curing tobacco in the Connecticut valley. He did not talk about any hardships he had endured, such as poor and inadequate housing facilities or harsh working conditions, but shared that he was able to earn more money in America than he could earn in Jamaica. He had now saved enough money to build a house in Jamaica and was always happy to be home with his family again. Many other farm workers told a similar story. Their motivation to work and earn was so strong that they could tolerate any unpleasant conditions for the financial gains they could not earn in Jamaica. They saved enough money to now live comfortably until the next harvest season when they would return to America. According to Abrahams, "Going abroad as migrant workers had, over the years, become a pattern of Jamaican life. It had begun seriously in the 1870s when de Lesseps started the digging of the Panama Canal. Later, the growth of sugar plantations in Cuba, the banana boom and the opening of large plantations on the Central American coast stepped up the process. [However] . . . the greatest rush of all, to the United States, began in the 1890s and kept up as a steady flow until the United States Government introduced quota regulations."[1] Moreover, many of the women who now lived in the US but vacationed in Jamaica spoke of their work in hospitals or with American families and how well they were treated.

I used to reflect on those stories and wasn't at all certain that I wanted to leave Jamaica, a safe and predictable place for me. There were sporadic rumours about racial tensions in the US, but these were not headlines for the Jamaicans I knew who believed in and were proud of our motto, "Out of many, one people." Yet I had also heard that America actually cared very much about its children, and that was appealing to me, since I had often felt that many Jamaicans were too strict with their children and often punished them too harshly. I did not pause to wonder which group of children were cared about in America.

So, even with my very modest salary, Jamaica was home to me. Besides, I felt very supported and loved by my family, had many relatives and friends nearby, and had, since graduating from high school, actually once enrolled in an extension course at the University of the West Indies.

Shirley also indicated that with the job, I could work and pay my way through college. Now, that was interesting and was a motivating factor in the equation: resign from my job and go, or stay and keep my secure civil service position. I had also heard that when civil servants retired, the retirees were rewarded with a gold watch, as an acknowledgement of their service. I did not know whether this was indeed true. Then two factors clinched my decision. I soon figured out that Chicago was not that far from the University of Illinois, Champaign, where my then-boyfriend was a student. Moreover, my best friend, Wynsome, was already in New York; I would be able to see her again. After talking with my mother and Aunt Dor, I responded to Shirley's letter, indicating my interest in joining her in Chicago.

In preparation to leave Jamaica, I began to save more of my salary, since I had only a few months before the fall semester began. Saving was not a problem, and a reduction of spending for a few nonessential items was quite easy. My first savings account had been opened at around age nine with one shilling at the Half Way Tree Post Office, near my elementary school. Because Jamaica was still under British rule, our currency consisted of the sterling pound, shilling, and pence. The postmistress produced a small beige passbook, entered the amount, and handed it to me with these encouraging words, "Now, keep your savings book in a safe place, and bring it with you when you have more money to deposit."

My savings habit continued over the years. Now employed and earning a salary, I recalculated my £5 weekly salary, and after my weekly house contribution, transportation, and lunch expenses, I could save an additional £1 to purchase my plane ticket and pay at least some of my tuition. Although I was previously unaware of Roosevelt University, the faculty from my UWI Extension course knew an anthropology professor there and gave me his name. I applied to the university and soon after, received my letter of acceptance. I obtained my passport and scheduled an appointment for my very first physical examination by a doctor. Throughout the island, except for annual visits by a doctor to elementary schools, most illnesses, especially minor ones, were treated with local herbal medicines. The doctor asked me a few questions about my health, then gave me a routine physical examination, the required inoculation, and the official "Approved" stamp on my health form.

A Visit to the American Consulate

With the necessary papers in order, I prepared to visit the American embassy for my visa. Since my appointment was in the late morning, I first went to work for two hours, then walked a short distance to the embassy. The night before my appointment, I was concerned about an appropriate outfit to wear for this important meeting. I was aware that many Jamaican women wore stockings to such meetings, and even to work, but I was certain that our hot climate mocked that habit. Then I wondered about wearing my crinoline, a petticoat and a favoured look among my peers. Worn under a flared skirt, the crinoline gives the skirt a balloonlike look. But this was a serious interview. I wanted to look my best, so my mother's good judgement prevailed. She always had good judgement about clothes. I decided to wear a beige, boatneck linen dress with a belt, no crinoline, and a simple white bolero. I left home feeling quite confident.

Although I have no memory of being anxious, I am sure that I experienced some anxiety when my name was called to meet the examining officer. Since an applicant's fate hung on the examining officer's approval or rejection, entering his office was an anxiety-producing event. Furthermore, this was my first visit to an American establishment on the island, and I had no idea what to expect. The officer, a white American, was seated behind an attractive yet modest wooden desk. He was properly and professionally dressed for his position, wearing an immaculately clean and well-ironed white shirt, tie, and dark trousers. The room was relatively spacious and uncluttered, with an American flag in one corner, a bookcase against one wall, and a ceiling fan. He greeted me politely and pleasantly and invited me to sit. Whatever anxiety I had lessened tremendously, and I relaxed and prepared myself to answer all his questions.

Glancing around the room, I thought about the many stories this room held quietly to itself over many years; stories of joy and relief, where so many lives were transformed, and the years of hoping and waiting to be "called" were at last fulfilled; some individuals had "gotten through" that unpredictable process and now they could begin a new chapter in their lives. The same room had also seen tears of disappointment and real sadness when the officer had rejected or turned down an applicant. The room probably wished that it could offer some comfort but couldn't. If only the room could talk, it would have comforted that applicant. On leaving the American consulate, the applicant would have to tell everyone, "I didn't get through." But he or she would persist and so would apply for that visa again and again.

After looking at my application and having a brief conversation, the officer asked about my intentions on completing my college degree. I replied confidently, "I will return to Jamaica to work." He looked at me and seriously stated, "Miss Spence, you will not return to Jamaica."

Imagine my surprise at his statement. Of course, I protested and stressed that I knew I would return to Jamaica. He listened attentively but knowingly, said no more, approved my application, handed me my visa, and wished me well. I was on my way to study in the United States.

Many years later, and long after receiving my US citizenship, I was reminiscing about my journey to America and recalled that officer's statement. Admitting to myself that he was so right in his prediction, I still wondered how he could have known that I would not return to Jamaica, and what was there about me and my responses that made him so sure. I will never know, but I will always wonder.

THE SEND-OFF

In September 1957, two weeks before my eighteenth birthday, I left Jamaica to become a student at Roosevelt University in Chicago. Seeing someone off at the airport in Jamaica was a big deal; it was a community event. Family and friends were usually very excited to see that a relative or friend was flying to another country: in today's Jamaican vocabulary, "to foreign." Furthermore, travelling by an aeroplane then was an occasion for being well dressed, and I was no exception. I felt appropriately dressed for the occasion in a newly made pink and navy blue outfit, new shoes, and stockings, with twenty-five dollars in my purse, but I was not worried, since I had a job waiting for me. My flight on the British Overseas Airways Corporation (BOAC) had a stopover in Miami, and I recall having to catch my breath on seeing, from the air at night, an amazing expanse of bright, dazzling lights, glittering like a wonderland over Miami. Although the lights of Kingston were awesome looking down from houses on the surrounding hills, the Miami lights were more breathtaking and seemed endless. I was on an adventure, a new and thrilling experience. I was enthralled, breathless, and full of excitement for what the future held for me.

Simultaneously, there was a bit of nostalgia for the Jamaica I had left behind, the comfort and security of home and my extended family, my job, and my many good friends, the predictability of daily living and the good times, the ever-pulsating sounds of our music, opportunities for dancing, which I always enjoyed, and the musical sounds of "peeny wallies," also known as "lightning bugs," during the late nights. A bit of uncertainty crept in; did I make the right decision in leaving behind all that was familiar, including my connections, experiences, and memories for a new country? As I reflected on the latter, my confidence returned and instead of being sad, I felt confident, excited, and ready to take on this new challenge.

Now, whenever I travel by plane, and in particular at nightfall, and see cities blanketed by multicoloured lights, I still recall and recapture that mixture of glee and wonder at my first view of those Miami lights.

CHAPTER 8

COMING TO AMERICA: CHICAGO TO NEW YORK CITY

On arriving in Chicago, September 1957, I was met at the airport by Shirley and her brother. After the introductions, we drove to their apartment at 47th and Drexel Boulevard, next door to the famous Sutherland Hotel. I later learned that this hotel featured celebrity performers, the majority of whom were African Americans, known as Negroes during that period. Coming home from college or work in the late evenings, I often saw groups of the most glamorous Black women I have ever seen, all dressed up in fur coats, usually with a male escort, heading for the numerous performances offered in the Sutherland Lounge. Using my Jamaican lenses, I figured that they were part of a special well-to-do class in the society because of their appearance. Their appearances confirmed my then-naive thinking that most people were doing well economically and socially in America.

I began working at the Chinese restaurant on the day following my arrival in Chicago. Shirley accompanied me to meet Linda and her husband, the Chinese couple who owned the restaurant, and Charlie, the cook. Donning the pink waitress uniform was not initially comfortable for me, but I did it and found that I really enjoyed serving my customers. I became a very good waitress. Then the first of several challenges of living in Chicago appeared. The weather was cold and windy, and I had no winter clothing. This was September; the weather should not have been so cold. I had few available funds to purchase warm clothing. Room and board accounted for almost two-thirds of my fifty cents an hour salary; tips ranged from 10 cents to 50 cents on average, and there was tuition to pay. Fortunately for me, a group of Jamaicans living there, on hearing of my plight, provided me with a coat and some warm clothing. The Jamaican community in Chicago was doing well educationally and economically. Given the extremely windy and cold weather, I now desperately wanted to return to Jamaica.

However, achieving balance in life and being realistic have always been central in my decision-making process. Recalling the potential opportunities in dealing sensibly with the challenges rather than taking the easy road of a return to Jamaica, the logical side of me won. I have this tendency to find a positive in every challenging situation with which I am confronted. And I had realised early on that identifying and resolving most presenting problems usually lessens any ensuing stress, such a deterrent to the happiness in which I fervently believed. The facts were that I enjoyed attending college as well as working in the restaurant and actually would not think of returning to Jamaica without a degree; "shame" was the operative word in Jamaica, not "guilt." With my modest salary and tips, I was able to pay for my college tuition and room and board, and have a small amount left for transportation and sundries. Besides, when I translated fifty cents an hour into Jamaican currency, it appeared that I was making a lot of money.

However, another of many challenges was yet to come: managing Chicago's elevated trains. My first experience taking the "El" to Chicago's Loop, where Roosevelt University was located, clearly showed the difference between Jamaican and American cultures where haste was concerned. I soon learned, after having the doors close practically in my face several times, that I had to move fast to get on and off those trains, or else I would have to find another mode for travel. None existed for me. One of my first classes at Roosevelt University was held in a huge lecture hall holding over a hundred students. Given my challenges with the trains, I was usually late during the first two weeks. Then, to get to my seat, I had to pass the professor, who stood behind a podium, looking up at students while he lectured. There were several mornings when I paused before entering the room because I had to pass by the professor, feeling all the students' attention on me, the latecomer. I was so embarrassed. I often felt like not entering the room, but I did, persevered, and completed the semester.

In the meantime, I lived with my friend, her brother, his wife, and their young son on Drexel Boulevard. Although I met many wonderful and kind

Jamaicans, I was not happy in Chicago. I cried quietly over many nights and wished to return to Jamaica, where life was far less stressful. But I persevered and remained at the university for two semesters. While still enrolled there, I had the pleasure of meeting Dr. St. Clair Drake, a well-known anthropologist and an African American, recommended by my Jamaican professor.

From Roosevelt University to New York University

I did not return to Chicago following a visit to New York and with my favorite aunt, Aunt Juliet, during the summer of 1958. Instead, on leafing through the telephone directory for a university to continue my studies, I discovered, visited, and enrolled in New York University, still maintaining my foreign student visa status. I actually fell in love with New York City. There, I met my lovely Aunt Bea and her American family for the first time. Aunt Bea was just like Mama in temperament: calm, gentle, and very good natured. She had left Jamaica long before I was born. My two aunts were terrific. They taught me to navigate the subways and to travel between Queens and Manhattan. I was thrilled to see chewing gum machines in the subway. The cost was one cent each. Amazing. And, again, there was so much more to learn. New cultural customs, new kinds of food, new sandwiches like baloney and cheese, and even getting used to the American way of spelling, for example, "neighbor" instead of "neighbour." My relatives here provided hugs and kisses each time we met, so I also became used to hugs and kisses.

When I wrote Shirley requesting that she mail the few clothes that I had left behind, she responded that upon learning I would not return to Chicago, her brother threw away all my clothing. Not completely surprised by his reaction, I was relieved that I had brought to New York the few items that had special meaning for me.

Working in New York City

During my first two years in New York City, I earned those much-needed dollars for tuition by babysitting for the Pinskys' two young boys, Robert and Jeffrey, on Kings Highway in Brooklyn. During the summers of 1959 and 1960, I visited the NYC Department of Employment, which referred me to two positions during those respective years. I encountered such kindness and willingness to help from everyone I met in the city. First, I worked decorating gloves in a small glove company off Fifth Ave., and in 1960 I wrapped expensive gifts for customers in the former Black, Starr and Gorham store, well known for its exquisite and expensive silver items, and located on Fifth Avenue and 48th Street.

It was there that I first met a diverse group of Americans and West Indians who were welcoming, and with whom I had many thoughtful and fun conversations while we wrapped gifts or packages on a long table in the store basement. My cousin Lurlene, who lived in the Bronx, worked nearby in the accounting department of W & J Sloane's, a then-fashionable furniture store on Fifth Avenue and 38th Street. We met frequently either for lunch or after work, enjoyed many social activities together, and held numerous conversations about our families and friends. Lurlene lived with her mother and stepfather in a beautifully furnished Bronx apartment that sparkled clean; I spent many weekends visiting them and talking with her mom and stepdad about being a college student. It seems strange today, but Lurlene's parents were so proud that I was in college, and so were the other Jamaican families that I met during that period. They had not met many young Jamaicans who were here to study as full-time college students. Those Jamaicans of my age were already working in banks or in other industries, and had arrived in New York City from Jamaica as permanent residents, not as foreign students. Examples included my best friend, Wynsome, who lived with her mom and two brothers and worked with BOAC. While there, she met Joy Penso, also Jamaican, and soon we three became close friends. Both friends lived with their respective families in middle-class communities in Queens where their families owned their houses. I was impressed that both friends had the then very desirable Princess phones in their bedrooms.

Wynsome, light-complexioned with long brown hair, was striking and walked with the confidence of having once been a model. However, as we talked about my courses, college life, and my professors, she began to take an interest in college. Some time later, Wynsome, who enjoyed learning and the ballet, enrolled as a part-time student while she continued to work and some years later graduated from Hunter College; she then shifted her interest to social work. We always got along very well, so I was very happy when, one summer in the early sixties, we had an opportunity to work together as social workers in a Lower East Side Housing Project. We loved to help the tenants who were our clients.

Work has always been important for me; even at an early age, I saw the personal satisfaction and economic advantage provided through work. Work could provide freedom and financial independence, which many adults, especially women in Jamaica, often had to forgo because good jobs were so hard to find. The lack of good jobs was one main reason that so many Jamaican women, and men, left for England and Canada, and when they could obtain a visa, America. One unfortunate result of these actions, however, was that some parents, more often mothers, had to leave their children behind with relatives or guardians for many years. Some mothers or parents were able to reunite with their children early; but for those whose reunion took years, the missing developmental years sometimes created a sense of loss or neglect on the children's part, resulting in uneasy interrelationships or uncomfortable communication between them. Of course, the opportunity to rebuild/ strengthen the parent/child relationship depended on the understanding and patience of both the parent and the particular child.

Most parents felt that their leaving for economic betterment would be beneficial for the children, and financially that was usually the case. The dollars sent home paid for school tuition, clothing, and general upkeep. But emotionally many children suffered, especially when left in an unsupportive environment. I have had friends who expressed their unhappiness at being left behind with families who were totally unresponsive to their emotional needs. They really missed their mothers, often the main parent.

But, continuing my story, I also have to enjoy the work in which I am involved, regardless of the type of work. Moreover, getting along well with my coworkers makes all the difference in the work environment. I was also aware that developing good relationships matters. The three elevator operators for Black, Starr and Gorham were all Jamaicans. My observations about the impact of race and the division between white people and black and brown people in the USA began then, because while these men were seen as only elevator operators, I knew from the way they comported themselves that they would have had a middle-class status in Jamaica and would have been treated differently there. Puzzling to me then was why their white bosses did not seem to look beyond their service positions to see them in the same way that I saw them, as being very respectable, intelligent, ambitious, individuals who also had personal and family goals. I doubted that their bosses saw the whole person in each of these individuals, which certainly had implications for any advancement on the job, such as becoming supervisors. However, coming from Jamaica where their cultural identity was already shaped, these Jamaicans knew that they had made a conscious choice to immigrate. They came to America because of the positive financial earnings that enabled them to live a much better life. One of them, Mr. Richards, invited me to meet his family in Queens, where they owned a beautiful home and were such gracious hosts. I was still using my Jamaican lenses in interacting with Americans, white or black.

THE GULLAH/GEECHEE CULTURE

Hearing an accent among the wrappers, I asked, "George, which Caribbean island are you from?" I was sure that he had a Jamaican background. His response was, "Caribbean island? No. I am from Georgia." I wasn't sure that I believed him then. Many years later when I visited St. Helena's Island off the coast of South Carolina, I learned about the Gullah/Geechee people and then understood why I thought he was West Indian. The Gullah language is very similar to Jamaican patois with almost the identical cadence. Prior to the sixties, Gullah culture flourished intact due to its isolation from the mainland. There were no bridges connecting the sea islands to the mainland. Thanks to Congressman Jim Clyburn, there is now a Gullah/Geechee Cultural Heritage Corridor stretching from North Carolina along the coastline through South Carolina and Georgia to Florida in recognition of the cultural contributions of the Gullah/Geechee people. In addition, bridges provide access to cities, and increased research on this culture is illuminating its richness. One positive outcome is that Gullah people are today more open to discussing and celebrating their identity and rich cultural heritage. At that time George did not tell me that he was Geechee.

I also became more aware of how closely related we Jamaicans are to the Gullah people, because the slave ships on leaving Africa dropped off some family members in Jamaica, Barbados, and other islands, and others to South Carolina, Georgia, and other states. While I had read briefly about the Middle Passage in high school, that history had seemed so far removed from us and so inhuman that I couldn't believe it as the truth. As a young student, I was aware of the wars in Europe, but that seemed so far away, and besides, my history book was Europe focused; the brief description and one photo of individuals chained and bound together on a slave ship was too cruel for me to absorb as true. Today, Caribbean history is the curriculum in Jamaica, unlike the focus on English history during my youth. I think that independence from Britain on August 6, 1962, created a cultural, historical, and psychological shift among Jamaicans, permitting the acquisition of formerly suppressed knowledge about their real connection to slavery and enslaved people.

The one Bajan in the store's group kept us in stitches as we worked, and then there was Richard Hutchinson, the only other young individual besides me who was in college. He was African American, studying to be a minister at a Baptist college in Alabama. We had many philosophical conversations over lunch, and it was obvious then that he was a brilliant student with a strong bent toward social justice. It was through our discussions that I became more consciously aware of the historical injustices against African Americans. The impact of these injustices has kept the majority of African Americans from advancing economically. Years later I reconnected with Richard, who was by then coordinator of veterans affairs at the Borough of Manhattan Community College, and famous for his intellect as well as his use of complex words. At his funeral in Harlem a few years later, all his colleagues spoke of his erudition and his penchant for eloquence during conversations. With his confident presence and leadership abilities, Richard could have made an even greater difference, but, sadly, he died too young.

BALANCING STUDY, WORK, AND A SOCIAL LIFE

Among the most surprising new experiences in learning about American urban life was listening to American college students talk freely about, sometimes openly critically of, their parents. I had never heard my Jamaican friends talk against or blame their parents openly. They kept whatever feelings they may have had about their parents to themselves. This unwillingness to criticize one's parents is probably no longer true in Jamaica, but then, I have not surveyed a significant sample of Jamaicans. In addition, the word "neurotic" peppered many conversations during my first year at NYU. I never quite understood this new word and its meaning until much later, through my classes. I was sure that a precise and colorful descriptive word for a "neurotic" personality exists in Jamaican patois, but I have yet to discover that word. Also, *The Prophet* by Kahlil Gibran was among the most popular books being read and discussed by college students during the late fifties to early sixties, but I was too absorbed with work and my studies to do much external reading. I did, however, later read and use, quite frequently, lines and verses from *The Prophet*.

By my junior year, in 1960/61, after a short sojourn in Brooklyn, I moved into NYU's only dorm, the Judson, on Washington Square South. My room-mate was a truly wonderful and spirited young Iranian woman named Afsar Esfandiary, aka Affie. We related well and easily; Affie was such an affection-ate and caring young woman with a huge heart, who was already engaged to marry Faramaz, following graduation. I was also tired of commuting to Brooklyn for work during the academic year and was fortunate to obtain a position at NYU's Institute of Fine Arts, the IFA, housed in the impressive James B. Duke mansion at Fifth Avenue and 78th Street. I remained at the IFA through my graduation in 1962. My college days were glorious, with simple and inexpensive pleasures. I was very busy balancing study, work, and enjoy-ing my life but still within an academic environment. On my limited budget, I feasted on orange drink and cream cheese on raisin bread from Chock Full O'Nuts located across the street from NYU's main building. The cost was very reasonable; the food was delicious and filling. Besides, whenever I visited my two aunts in Queens, I always brought back delicious sandwiches for lunch or dinner. In the dorm students had access to the kitchen and a refrigerator. However, if you wished to see your refrigerated food again, you had better ensure that your name was clearly visible. When I used the kitchen, I cooked simple, low-cost meals like omelets, rice, and some vegetables, mainly corn, which I loved to eat, especially creamed corn, that I did not recall eating in Jamaica. Our corn was always fresh: we ate it boiled or roasted. I learned to cook some basic dishes while at NYU.

Moreover, living in the dorm brought me closer to learning about events that were occurring daily in the city and the larger society, since students would talk about them in the kitchen/dining room or in the student lounge. Soon my friends and I were heartened by news in the media about the emerg-ing civil rights movement and the Freedom Rides in the sixties. It was the era of President Johnson's "Great Society," and a significant expansion of social programs, including Head Start, was happening across the nation. I could hear Malcolm X's booming voice on television as I passed through the dorm's living room and, at times, even paused to listen for a few minutes. Stokely Carmichael, Trinidadian, was creating excitement and controversy by his call that "Black is Beautiful," and individuals wearing dashikis were quite visible in NYC. I was surrounded by all these societal changes and challenges but was not a participant in any movement. As a foreign student, I lived a very protected life in academia, feeling that I was in, but not of, all that was occurring. But I was quietly aware of it.

SUMMER STUDY FOR TEACHERS FROM THE SOUTH

Although students who lived in the dorm usually returned home during the summer vacation, I remained a resident. I could not afford to travel home to Jamaica. It was over two summers that I first noticed, and then met, a significant number of African American graduate students, mostly women—I know there were also men, but the Judson was for female students only—who came from the South to study for their graduate degrees at NYU. At the time I had no idea why they were at NYU and did not think much about it. I became friends with two of the women, one of whom, Mattie Gilliam, invited me in 1963 to visit her home in Courtland, Virginia, about an hour's ride from Richmond.

I sat in the front seat on the Greyhound bus without any problems and enjoyed a smooth and pleasant ride to Richmond, where I was met by my friend. I spent a delightful week with Mattie and her husband, in their beautiful house built by her husband, in the then-segregated South, my first real exposure to this system. Mattie drove me around her community, introduced me to her colleagues, most of whom were teachers and middle class, and introduced me to life in the South. We visited a small movie house where African Americans had to sit upstairs, while whites sat downstairs; I told Mattie that I preferred upstairs anyway, because then no one could throw anything down on me. We both shared a laugh, knowing that the real issue was, among other values, freedom and free choice and not just safety, although safety was indeed an important issue for African Americans living in the South. I was learning firsthand about segregation and how African Americans were systematically relegated to second-class-citizen status by Jim Crow laws. These laws affected every area of their daily living, including the key institutions like church and schools; they were all segregated. I visited Mattie's school, where her students were all Black, so polite, curious about me and my accent, and responsive to me as a visitor.

Mattie and her husband were gracious hosts; I was treated well and enjoyed every moment of my week with them. In reflecting on that trip, I thought about the stress of living under such a restrictive system for African Americans: the inability to freely try on clothing in stores, to choose the best school for their children, and the courage it took to accept that way of life. But, as in the past, meetings were organized to develop the strategies necessary to gain their deserved human rights and to combat segregation. After several restaurant sit-ins, bus boycotts and marches organized by students, civil rights organizations, and other activists, the Civil Rights Act was passed and signed into law by President Lyndon Johnson in 1964. This Act outlawed discrimination based on race, color, religion, gender, or national origin and guaranteed equal protection for all citizens, outlawed segregation in schools and on public transportation, and protected voting rights. However, over these years, I have realized that even when a right or goal is achieved, being vigilant is necessary to preserve the gains made, because threats to weaken these rights are ever present.

Years later, in the late seventies, I revisited Mattie with my husband, Ismail, and our then-young sons: desegregation was in effect. The smell of peanuts from a factory permeated the air, and the county was bustling with activity that was not present on my first visit. I asked her about the impact of desegregation in her school and community. Mattie answered, "The Black students lost; we could no longer prepare them for the outside world as we did previously, since white students did not need the same information."

A Study of Black Schools in the South

In 2012 I read Dr. Vanessa Siddle Walker's book *Their Highest Potential*, her extensive research on the important role of Black schools in educating and providing the critical social/emotional support for Black children in the South during segregation. I had met Dr. Walker, professor of education, through our third son, Nafees, then a PhD candidate in education studies at Emory University. Among her interests in this area was to counter the usual negative perception of how poorly southern Black children were educated. Her findings illuminated the high value placed on education and on teachers within the Black community, and how parental support and advocacy helped the generally and deliberately under-resourced and underfinanced

Black schools to achieve their educational goals for children. In their interviews with Dr. Walker, Black adults recalled their school experiences in the
Black schools with fondness despite the lack of resources. They described
the high expectations set by their teachers, the focus on both their personal
development and academic success, and the extracurricular activities to
which they were exposed.

In reality, principals and teachers worked diligently and intentionally to
create school environments that promoted and supported the development
of the whole child. Teachers saw their role as critical in preparing students to
become successful adults, and because significant numbers of Black teachers
held graduate degrees from universities in the North and Midwest, unlike
many white teachers in those schools, they brought back new and more
progressive and child-centered approaches to their classrooms. According
to Dr. Walker, "the larger American society sent deprecating messages about
the Negro's value and status, but the teachers and principals within the school
constructed a countermessage"; they communicated to students that "you
can be anything you want to be."[1]

Dr. Walker also described and documented the strong network that existed
among Black teachers and principals and how they shared their learnings
from the nationwide conferences that they regularly attended, within the
network. Moreover, she described how in order to prevent Black educators
from attending the local segregated colleges and universities, several southern states and local school boards paid their tuition to enroll in northern
universities like NYU, Teachers College, University of Michigan, Michigan
State, and even colleges abroad.

As I read Dr. Walker's book, I had an aha moment. I suddenly realized
with a thrill the connection that existed between my sixties experience with
the teachers from the South in my NYU dorm and the era of segregation.
They were at NYU because, being barred from enrolling in the segregated
southern colleges, they were compelled to leave the South to obtain graduate
degrees. I had not known that fact even when I visited the South. For the
first time, I felt that I had been a silent participant in an important historical
event. I was excited at making the connection but appalled and disturbed by
the extent to which the southern white power structure would go to maintain the status quo. Indeed, their commitment was to keep segregation as a
fixed system; it took the civil rights movement, and then legislation in the
mid-sixties, to challenge segregation and to improve civil rights and other

societal conditions for African Americans. Meanwhile, the African American educators attending universities in the North were exposed to progressive educational philosophy and interactions with diverse groups of professionals; these were opportunities for increased knowledge, and professional and personal growth. They were well-prepared educators.

The unreasonable, hostile, social, educational, and economically unsound barriers placed in the path of Black educators and the Black population overall were, to me, a new arrival to America, a shocking travesty and glaring injustice. Segregation was a punitive system designed to deprive the Black community of their rights and privileges and assign them to lower-class status. Its existence also led to stress, the loss of human talent, and loss of one's humanity under those unbearable experiences. Developing an understanding of racism's reality and the disenfranchisement of Black people in America was definitely a major new experience for me. I recalled the statement of many Jamaican men whose refrain was "I never knew I was black till I came to America!"

Dr. Walker's book aroused my quiet sense around injustice and released much empathy and a new understanding for African American communities and the horrific experiences they have endured over time. Her book should be read by every educator, social worker, and policy maker to understand not only the full impact of bad, segregationist policy but also to gain an appreciation for the struggles and successes of those Black educators under oppressive circumstances. Gaining an understanding of the importance of those schools for Black children and how they supported their students' social, emotional, and academic development during segregation is enlightening.

Given my enhanced perspective, I considered that Dr. Walker's research could be of value to educators and policy makers in changing the current educational and career trajectory for Black and brown students, since inequities still remain today. Some NYU researchers have pointed out to me that not all Black schools in the South were equal in providing an enriched academic experience for their students, and that is important to bear in mind. However, there were numerous schools, for example, in North Carolina with well-trained teachers who were making a huge difference in preparing their students for academic and personal success, and that, like all positive actions, also needs to be acknowledged. Besides, I believe that balance is essential in life, and the positive, transformative stories have not received their deserved attention.

Dr. Walker's research contributed to my increasing knowledge and understanding about a deliberate and rigid racial structure that relegated Black and brown people to an inferior status, intending to limit their advancement; however, I was heartened in seeing the benefits when a community could come together to support, educate, and strengthen its members and its future leaders despite the obstacles they consistently faced. Those transformative stories need to be told and retold in schools today, and the books holding these stories should be made intentionally available for children of all colors and races to read, digest, and reflect on. I felt proud for having attended NYU, which openly welcomed this critical mass of African American educators each year to advance their studies. I also applaud Teachers College, University of Michigan, Michigan State, and all the other higher education institutions that opened their doors to welcome and expose these pioneer and heroic educators to new knowledge and progressive practices.

On my 2019 visit to Jamaica, I met an elderly African American gentleman from North Carolina. He and his family were staying in the same hotel as my sisters and me. Recalling that Dr. Walker's study had been of schools in that state, I asked him about his early school experiences, while mentioning Dr. Walker's study. Without showing any interest in the book and as though I had reawakened a very difficult memory, he responded with a depth of seriousness that I did not expect, "We lived it! And are still living it!" Then he proceeded to tell me, "I went to Black schools and a Black college. I never had a white teacher, nor did I know any white person. I coached a Black football team, and we played with other Black teams."

As I listened it was evident that I had opened up a wound that had never quite healed. He continued that his teachers had tried to prepare them for a "change" that was coming. They would say "change is coming, change is coming," but no one knew the kind of change for which they needed to be prepared. And, he added, "Change did come, but only one side had to do the adjustment . . . the Black folk! White people didn't have to make the kind of sacrifices that we Back folks had to make, and we lost, we lost badly!" He continued, "Developers used increased taxation to wrench the lands from Black folk in Hilton Head. Used to be all Black!" And, he added, another change is happening in the country now that is no better, and maybe worse, than during his early years.

This gentleman's reaction was similar to those of adults who integrated the high school in Panola County, Mississippi, discussed in chapter 18.

The pain and suffering during the era of segregation is still alive. This gentleman was correct that desegregation hurt many in the Black communities; the change led to unexpectedly harsh results for many African American principals and teachers. Many principals were demoted or fired as the schools were integrated, and some teachers lost their jobs as students moved to the white schools. These results have been documented in Dr. Siddle Walker's writings about Black schools and desegregation in the South.

THE AFRICAN DIASPORA CONSORTIUM

In 2016 the African Diaspora Consortium (ADC) at Teachers College invited Dr. Walker to present her findings on how those Black educational leaders and teachers used their network as a professional development activity during segregation. Dr. Walker's presentation was compelling and stimulated a very rich discussion among the racially mixed audience attending that event. I was happy to be present and to learn more about the important research being conducted. I was also delighted to meet Dr. Kassie Freeman, founding president and CEO of the ADC, whose mission is "to impact positively the educational, economic, and artistic outcomes and opportunities of Black populations across the African Diaspora. . . . [The ADC] . . . is grounded in the philosophy that shared lessons across the Diaspora can lead to new paradigms, and new directions for addressing the chronic challenges confronting Black populations around the globe."[2]

I learned of this important work through our third son, Nafees, then assistant professor at South Carolina's Clemson University, who serves on the ADC's Planning and Advisory Committee, and whose research is focused on the transatlantic slave trade. The ADC in partnership with the College Board has now developed and is piloting, as of fall 2019, the first Advanced Placement (AP) African Diaspora Course in eleven schools across six states: New York, Pennsylvania, Florida, Alabama, Georgia, and Ohio. Students' and teachers' reactions to the course have been exciting, and students are becoming "producers of knowledge" as they explore areas of their interest within the course's framework.

• • •

My memories of elementary and high schools in Jamaica became even more alive as I became involved in New York City's school programs during my professional years. I recalled that both my elementary and high school environments were safe and inspiring places for me and, unless I am mistaken, also for many of my classmates.

The negative experiences of African Americans arising from racial segregation and a violent history in the US were absent in my Jamaican experience. That's why I was so disappointed to read during the sixties, in an introductory text to sociology discussing generalizations, that one could generalize that it was highly unlikely that a Black person could ever become president of the United States. Coming from Jamaica, I was troubled to read such a negative statement in a textbook that would influence thousands of young and older readers. Of course, I read that statement during a time when place and history shaped the narrow thinking even of sociologists. The Obama presidency was proof that one may never know with certainty about the future and change. Change does happen, but change can either heal or hurt.

My mother, probably in her twenties, in Jamaica.

My father, Egbert G. Spence, probably in his late twenties.

My senior year class at Excelsior High School in 1954. Form master Mr. Bennett is in the middle, front row. I am on the right, holding Mr. Bennett's eyeglasses.

On a visit to Hope Gardens, age fifteen, wearing the yellow dress from NYC.

Mr. Wong, an unknown staff member, XLCR founder Mr. Powell, and Mr. Fong Kong

Mrs. Ivy Frankson, my dear neighbor, whom I visited almost daily.

The first beauty contest in Jamaica featuring "Ten Types—One People," held in 1955 to celebrate "Jamaica 300" (1655–1955).

Trip to Hyde Park through NYU's VISTA program for foreign students. My cousin Lurlene is standing beside me.

I am talking with students in a segregated Black school in Courtland, Virginia, sixties.

Ismail and I enjoy dancing at the International Students Center's annual Spring Dance, 1960.

Volunteer Team members for the International Students Center, 1961/62.

Our graduate social work student team's weekly meeting with NYU's faculty advisor.

Ismail and I are watching a performance in the sixties.

My best friend, Wynsome, me, my sisters Hope and Phillippa leave for my wedding ceremony, 1969.

Judge Herbert Evans marries Ismail and me as Wynsome looks on.

My Aunt Juliet in America.

Dean Ann Marcus of LaGuardia Community College at her desk, 1972/73 academic year.

I welcome LaGuardia's very first graduates, 1973/74. Ann Varon, a graduate, is next to me, while President Shenker waits to congratulate graduates.

Dr. Glenn Anderson signs as he talks. JoAnne Kranis, standing, is the ASL interpreter.

President Joseph Shenker, first on left, thanks bank officials for their check.

Dr. Janet Lieberman, LaGuardia CC, is a special guest at an event for seniors.

President Gussie Kappner and I visited the Bank Street Head Start Program, 1990s.

Dr. Rex Nettleford, third from left, is the guest of honor at an XLCR alumni fundraiser. Bank Street faculty Stan Chu is in front.

Bank Street educators meet the Hon. Custos Royland Barrett (wearing a tie, next to me), in Falmouth, Jamaica, 2002. Carol B. Hillman is first left, front row.

Our young sons in our Southfield, Massachusetts, barn, 1981.

Dan Rose, HEAF's founder, and me at HEAF's 2007 gala.

Ismail and I celebrate at a Thanksgiving dinner in Brooklyn.

Our family: Javaid, Gillian, and children, Justin and Laila; Nafees; Yussuf and his two sons, Dante and Kaiden; Ismail and me, Christmas 2017.

Ismail, me, and sons, Javaid, Nafees, and Yussuf.

The sisters on our annual Jamaican vacation, 2008. Hope, Phillippa, and I gaze at the view from our balcony.

Ismail's vision for our barn is achieved in 2022.

Khan family, with sister Hope, 2019

Ismail with our young sons Javaid and Yussuf.

CHAPTER 9

LIFE AS A FOREIGN STUDENT AT NYU

In retrospect, reflections on my Jamaican school days during those under-graduate years in New York City occurred later in my life. During the 1960s my energies were consumed, as noted earlier, in balancing my coursework, part-time positions, sticking to a tight budget, learning about and navigating America's diverse cultures and values, and enjoying my extracurricular roles as a member of NYU's West Indian Students Association, the Literary Club, which met biweekly on Thursdays at the Midtown Center, the citywide International Students Council, and NYU's Catholic Center, whose focus was also on engaging foreign students.

Being attracted to cross-cultural groups was natural, given that my inter-est to learn about individuals from other countries and cultures began in high school through corresponding with pen pals from South Africa. I had always enjoyed fairy tales and now was also mesmerized by stories from Isaac Bashevis Singer, *The 1,001 Arabian Nights*, and any kind of mystical/heroic stories, like *The Lord of the Rings*. My exploration into other cultures and their stories was enlightening and educational and then became a socially and intellectually rewarding reality for me through my involvement with foreign student associations in New York City. Besides, the fact that we were all "outsiders" was a common denominator to bring us together. At that time we were "in but not of" this country.

NYU's Catholic Center was under the superb, generous, and good-natured leadership of Father Andrew J. O'Reilly, who had a special interest in sup-porting foreign students and had designed a program called the Voluntary

International Students Association, VISTA. Through VISTA, Father O'Reilly arranged for us to visit the homes of Americans and took us on trips to Washington, DC, on picnics and boat rides on the Hudson River, and to Hyde Park, New York, where we actually met Mrs. Eleanor Roosevelt. I recall asking her for her autograph, but she responded that if she signed one, then everyone would want her to sign, and she had to leave for another appointment. She also suggested that I contact her secretary, who would then send her autograph to me. I did not follow up but regretted my decision years later when I learned of the important education and social reform work in which she had been engaged over many years. I am now an admirer of her work as a social reformer.

Father O'Reilly was a wonderful, cheerful, and very special human being, and I enjoyed being around him. Although I was not Catholic, he involved me in leadership roles with foreign students, most of whom were of other religious faiths, and so were reluctant to attend the center's activities. In meetings I would assure them of the purpose of the center, to expose us to American culture, to help us understand and adjust to our new cultural experiences, and that Father O'Reilly's efforts at outreach had little to do with religion. I would also indicate that I was not Catholic, was actually an Anglican (Episcopalian), and yet was very involved with the center because I believed in its mission to expose us as foreign students to American culture.

It was also through Father O'Reilly's generosity that I obtained a half scholarship during my last two years at NYU. And I did not have to complete any application for this scholarship. When I confided in him that the tuition was being increased and how concerned I was about being able to pay the new tuition, Father O'Reilly, without hesitation, referred me to meet with Dean Kastner, then-dean of registration and financial aid, whose office was located in the law school. Following a very brief conversation with the dean, I was awarded a half scholarship for my remaining two years at NYU. This was a real blessing, since tuition had been increasing annually and was then roughly in the low forty dollars per credit, a relatively huge amount at that time. Meanwhile, the City University of New York, CUNY, was still free.

Among Father O'Reilly's many roles was fundraising to build a chapel on campus. His goal was eventually achieved; however, I was sad to learn that he had died tragically in a plane crash in the sixties returning from an assignment. Prior to Father O'Reilly's intervention, there were days when I was really worried about having enough money to pay my tuition, but

I have always believed "where there's a will, there's a way," and there was usually a way; whenever I needed an extension on my tuition due date, the bursar would cooperate and give me a new date to pay, without any interest charges. Besides, I had the option of continuing to prepare slides at the Institute of Fine Arts, to earn additional funds. Another strategy to save for tuition was frequently preparing inexpensive baloney sandwiches for dinner. As a result, since graduation, over sixty years ago, I have not tasted another baloney sandwich.

NYU's Institute of Fine Arts

In my part-time position at the Institute of Fine Arts, I worked in the IFA's slide room, binding slides as tools for art history courses. The art historians opened up a whole other world to me. The IFA was a very highly regarded graduate program, with some of the most famous professors of art history as faculty. Students felt fortunate to be enrolled there, and many were in awe of their professors. The IFA's director was Dr. Craig Hugh Smyth, a real gentleman and a scholar, and an excellent fundraiser for the IFA. My supervisor was Mary Lee Thompson, who had completed her coursework for her doctorate degree but was also the full-time director overseeing the slide room. Mary Lee was of average height and build, brisk in her stride, with a no-nonsense air about her but with the ability to have fun. She had long blonde hair, which she sometimes wore in a thick braid reaching her waist.

Mary Lee soon became an important person in my life. She knew that I was working my way through college and did everything possible to support my journey. Since my salary was partly dependent on the number of completed bound slides, she gave me extra hours each week and allowed me to work on the weekends even when the institute was closed. Then she brought in a radio for me to listen to classical music on WQXR, as I worked. I played a game of identifying the music and the corresponding composers prior to the announcers' descriptions. When my Iranian roommate Affie and I got our first apartment, Mary Lee gave me household items. In those days I frequently used my Jamaican lenses and aphorisms to explain behavior, which would have her exclaiming with tolerant amusement, "Oh, June!"

We talked a great deal about everything; her early life, her mother who had moved to Mexico, the professors and graduate students. Mary Lee was an excellent administrator who took her supervisory role seriously. She was always direct and was a perfectionist, which I liked and admired. She was also quite wise, having had many challenges as a young person, and had also worked her way through college. I visited and ate several meals at her home and eventually met her lovely younger sister Toby, who visited from Mexico. Toby later opened an independent school in Mexico. Over the years Mary Lee became chair of the Art History Department at Manhattanville College, and I became a faculty member at LaGuardia Community College. Although years may have passed between our meetings, we always began where we left off the last time we met.

In many ways I was a novelty at the IFA. Even then I was aware that I was the only Black individual in the entire building, the youngest employee, and the only undergraduate. Besides, I had a very different accent and brought different lenses to most situations. I often quietly wondered why there weren't people of my color in the graduate programs. This observation was a habit that I developed during my youth in Jamaica, always looking at who (color or race) was in the room or in a leadership position. However, before I left the institute, one Indian student, my dear friend Lakshmi Sihare, who spent hours talking with me about his studies and his frustrations with his advisor, received his PhD; and one young Trinidadian, Kynaston McShine, a Dartmouth alumnus, did graduate work at the IFA. Kynaston retired from the Museum of Modern Art/MOMA, as chief curator at large in 2008, and died in January 2018 at age eighty-two. On reading his obituary, I regretted not having reached out to him over these many years. Maybe I thought that he wouldn't remember me. However, as a fellow Caribbean, I was so proud of all that Kynaston achieved in the world of art history and museums. He was described in an *Artforum* article on January 8, 2018, as "one of the most influential curators of the 20th century." Ann Temkin is quoted in the January 12, 2018, *New York Times* obituary written by Roberta Smith, as saying, "His lasting contribution to the life of the museum, and to the lives of countless artists and colleagues, is immense." These are no small praises in the art history world. And for a Black gentleman from the West Indies.

Working at the Institute of Fine Arts, I soon knew everyone in the building and was gaining new knowledge about art history, art historians and their specialties, and white Americans in general. I was encouraged by the students to study art history, but I resisted, telling them that I intended to be in a helping profession and that I would become a social worker. I challenged many assumptions of Thomas Matthews, a white student from the South, and was close friends with the colorful Sandy Eisen, who was determined to transform me from a colorful, outgoing Jamaican into a more sophisticated individual. That didn't work, but he was a wonderful friend.

There was also Dr. Peter von Blankenhagen, affectionately called "Von B," professor of classical art. He had an aristocratic air, was a kind and generous soul, and was always such a gentleman. He had close relations with a group of graduate students who were always with him. He often spent summers in Rome working on his research, and I had the pleasure of a delightful lunch with him when I visited Rome in 1967.

I soon learned that being invited to a "party" by different groups of individuals from the IFA did not mean a dance party. Instead, it was all about conversation and drinks. I still recall being at my first such party, and since I did not drink alcohol, I waited for the music and dancing to begin and upon inquiring, I learned that there was no dancing. I soon got over my Jamaican cultural expectation of "a party." Anyway, by my second year, I was promoted from the slide room to become the IFA's receptionist. I now controlled the switchboard and thoroughly loved my new position. Every call for faculty and other staff came through the switchboard, and then I had to connect the caller with the callee. Professors relied on me to monitor their calls and to mail their letters, and I did not disappoint them. I loved my new position, and everyone came by to talk with me. Besides, Dr. Smyth, the director, said that I was the best switchboard operator who ever worked at the institute.

THE INTERNATIONAL STUDENTS CENTER

I was also a member of the International Students Center (ISC), where foreign students came together on Saturday nights to dance from 8:00 p.m. until midnight. The activity was initially held in the church's community room in the East Thirties and Third Avenue, hence the midnight curfew. On learning about this activity for foreign students, I decided to pay a visit. So, accompanied by Wynsome and two other Jamaican friends, we climbed to the second floor preparing to enter the dance floor. We paused at the entrance because the music had stopped and someone was welcoming members and guests and explaining about the center.

He was standing at the far end of the room opposite the entrance where we waited. I looked at him and thought he was so handsome, with a patch of premature white hair in front of his otherwise jet-black hair. Well dressed in a dark striped suit, he was Indian, of average height, seemed so unpretentious, somewhat shy and had a kind disposition. After his talk, we approached him to introduce ourselves since we were new to the place. He welcomed us and we learned his name was Ismail Khan and that he was the president of the ISC. There was something special about this young man, his calm and likeable personality, and I was immediately attracted to him.

The contribution to enter the ISC was twenty-five cents, and everyone was welcomed even without the twenty-five cents. I have been told that the ISC was sponsored by the Greater New York Council for Foreign Students, funded either through the Mott family or the Ford Foundation. In the fifties and sixties, foreign students were fewer in numbers, were viewed as novelties, and so were generally well received. The ISC later moved to a larger space in the community room of the First Presbyterian Church at 12 West Twelfth Street. I attended the ISC every Saturday night and became friends with many of the regular participants, including members of the executive committee. I also often stayed to help clean up, ensuring that the place was left in order.

I soon noticed that Ismail was fond of merengue and waltz. I don't recall who asked whom to dance first, but since merengue was one of my favorites, we often looked for each other when that music was played. Ismail had a quiet and unflappable personality and was always gracious, helpful, and polite. We got along well, and I think that he might have been in awe of my outgoing and cheerful Jamaican personality, my youth, the fact that I was putting myself through college without ever seeming stressed, and interacted well with everyone. Soon I was voted in as membership chair, an important role in charge of admitting new members and overseeing the total membership. That year I received more votes than he did as president; that was a first for him, which he has never forgotten. There were also several committees working to organize a variety of social and engaging activities for members, including two annual camp experiences and the annual New Year's Eve Dance. We were a busy group of volunteers.

The chairs of those committees became a close-knit group, so after the dancing ended at midnight, we would find our way to one of the nearby Village coffee shops, where we would talk and laugh for several hours. Our favorite spot, which no longer exists, was Manzini's on West Third Street, a cavernous space with sawdust on the floor. I usually had hot chocolate, since my tight budget hardly allowed for any extras. However, the very generous Ismail was already employed as an engineer while working on his doctorate degree in urban planning, and beside whom I usually sat, and would often pay for a few of us.

This was also the time of the Beat Generation, and numerous cafés were present in the Village, especially on Bleecker and Macdougal Streets, where one could hear poetry and folk singing or see artists selling their smaller drawings or paintings. Though our group visited cafés like Cafe Rienzi, the Gaslight Cafe, Cafe Wha?, or Cafe Figaro, which showed old films and played the same music repeatedly, we were not a part of that generation. Some of us, not all, were just struggling college students—again, being in but not of that generation. Some of us also frequented the Coffee Mill in Midtown Manhattan, where we discussed the books we were reading.

I was the youngest student and the only undergraduate in this diverse group, but they were comfortable with me, and our interactions were always positive. The group members, including Ismail, came from a variety of continents and countries. All were graduate students and gainfully employed.

Irene Anderson was a group member. Of Scandinavian background, she was the ISC advisor as well as the assistant director of admissions for foreign students at NYU. She was actually the individual who had interviewed me. Irene was special, so pleasant and welcoming that I knew I was right in choosing NYU. Tall, stately, and blonde, with an easy and easily recognized laugh and ready smile, Irene loved the ballet and attended all performances in the city. She was compassionate, supportive, and helpful to all foreign students. She never missed a night at the International Student Center and participated in all its activities, including the annual sleepaway camp trips, which accommodated about fifty ISC members for a reasonable fee. Irene loved to waltz and was often on the dance floor with partners who could waltz. After we graduated many of us kept in contact and, annually, met at each other's homes for picnics or get-togethers. Those friendships were very important over time, and many marriages resulted from these connections. We shared a common bond in that we had all immigrated here from other countries and had met at the ISC.

Among the lasting friendships developed while I was an undergraduate was that with Beulah Joel from Trinidad. I met Beulah in my very first class at NYU, an English course. She was ten years my senior and was already a registered nurse, having studied in England, but was pursuing her bachelor's degree in nursing. Beulah was hilarious, with her sing-song Trinidadian accent and to my surprise was quite outspoken in the class. We became friends immediately, and I was a frequent visitor to her Brooklyn home, where I would feast on delicious Trinidadian food. Beulah soon bought her house, like other West Indians, and later lived and worked in Africa for many years before returning to Brooklyn, where she still resides.

THE WEST INDIAN STUDENTS ASSOCIATION

I also joined the West Indian Students Association. Under the leadership of Keith Johnson, who years later became a distinguished career diplomat as the Jamaican ambassador to the US, the West Indian Students Association at NYU provided important social support for its foreign student members. In 1960 the largest groups of foreign students at NYU were Indians, with 143 students, 138 from the Philippines, and 132 from the British West Indies. An article on NYU's Foreign Student Center was the main focus of the 1960 *NYU Notebook* special issue, which featured a photograph of six of us foreign students on its cover page. We were also featured on page 45 of NYU's Bulletin of General Information, June 27, 1960. This critical mass of West Indian students at NYU had a positive and supportive impact on the foreign students enrolled during the late fifties and early sixties. The largest group came from Jamaica, with Trinidad a close second, and most of us had a job to support our education and, for the married students, their families. Some students lived with relatives; others shared apartments.

There was also a West Indian table in the huge, nondescript cafeteria located on the first floor of NYU's main building. The cafeteria was furnished with large round wooden tables populated by students mostly engaged in intense discussions or trying to work on their assignments. The West Indian table was situated at the far end of the cafeteria near the window. I recall how on arriving at the entrance, I would look all the way across the sea of students and tables to see whether there were students at the West Indian table and then, on seeing them, headed straight across the entire length of the room to join them.

I recalled those emotionally fulfilling and fun days after reading Beverly Tatum's book *Why Are All the Blacks Kids Sitting Together in the Cafeteria?* Why shouldn't they? I pondered. All the white students sat together, and that seemed all right; few people noticed or commented. So why was there concern or a problem when Black and brown West Indian or African American students sat together? That West Indian table generated so much fun, relaxation, and laughter for my friends and me during my years at NYU. I am sure that was the same rationale for students at other colleges and universities. Those were important socio-emotional and cultural connections. So was it the laughter? Too much fun? Maybe both, but more likely, it was just our skin color that made us stand out in the predominantly white environment. But to be truthful, I was not really bothered by the perceptions about us, since I never actually heard any negative comments, and I, for one, still saw myself essentially as an outsider, a foreign student. Besides, NYU was quite a supportive environment, and I was very happy there. In the library I usually sat with the older and more studious students to work on my various classroom assignments.

Those NYU days were packed with study, work, and social activities. My undergraduate advisor, Prof. Mary Keeley, was terrific and charted out the courses I needed to fulfil graduation requirements. She also recommended me for, and I was inducted into, the Sociological Honor Society. I enjoyed all my classes, except economics, was taught by some amazing and inspiring professors like Drs. Marvin Bressler, Ethel Alpenfels, and Robert Johnson, and even took an art course with Hale Woodruff, an African American artist, but had no idea then that he was so famous.

Ms. Keogh taught speech. She was vivacious with a flair and taught at a quick pace. Each student in the School of Education had to record a speech at the beginning of the course and then record the same speech at the end of the course. Your grade was based on the improvement noted at the end of the course. While many West Indian students who wished to teach had a real challenge to pass speech in other professors' courses, Ms. Keogh gave me an A, with just two recommended changes in pronunciation and encouraged me to never change my accent. Then again, my path was sociology, not education; however, I doubt that she was aware of my major.

The one time that I felt uncomfortable in any class was when in an anthropology class on stereotypes, Dr. Alpenfels discussed the stereotype of the "smiling Negro." Sitting in the front row, I kept silent, wondering whether the students were looking at me as an example of the stereotype. After all, we Jamaicans smiled and laughed a lot, but that was the nature of our personalities and our island culture. I did not look around.

My intellectual world expanded in sociology courses and "Introduction to Philosophy," where I encountered thinkers who had wrestled with what seemed like everyday ideas that many of us had but did not necessarily articulate. I decided then that I liked pragmatism or the democratic philosophy of William James. I was fascinated with Charles Horton Cooley's theory of the Looking Glass Self. That theory made so much sense to me. I knew how important to my development was all the positive feedback I received. At the same time, I thought, and am always thinking about, young children who grew up in households where they were always being criticized or regularly punished. How would they get rid of the negatives and not incorporate them within their self-images? Some answers were available through the many research articles and stories that I read and, later, in my work as a social worker with clients.

In the yearlong "Comparative Religions" course, I read about the various religions and their origins and visited the different places of worship. Each one had a story about its beginnings, which sprang from individual cultural and economic needs but also from the human's need to explain nature or individual experiences. The stories illuminated for me the universality of the need for religion and broadened my thinking considerably. Achieving balance through following the middle path in living and not caving in to extreme beliefs or habits aligned with my personal values and so was easily understood. Receiving an A grade in religion from Prof. Lee Belford, not an easy grader, was among the biggest surprises of my college experience.

I learned about the early beginnings of sociology as a field and the influence of thinkers like Ibn Khaldun, Auguste Comte, Émile Durkheim and others in moving the field forward. Sociology is quite eclectic, as it drew heavily from psychology, philosophy, and other disciplines. I was drawn to this cross-disciplinary approach. I also began to absorb more information on Black/white relationships in the US and the work being accomplished to build positive relationships at that time, through Dr. Robert Johnson's research on intergroup relationships. He was the son of the famous sociologist Charles S. Johnson, an African American who had been the president of Fisk University. Dr. Johnson related positively to his students and even invited us for one seminar in his apartment in the Village. I took a second course with him in the School of Social Work, where he also taught. He was an empathetic, compassionate, kind, and unpretentious individual, who frequently wore his deceased father's jackets, much too large for him, to class, and since he revealed this information to us, left many of us wondering why he felt compelled to wear them. I heard later that he left NYU, got married, and then moved to Ohio with his wife. Dr. Johnson was a good, humane, and caring man and teacher.

OTHER MEMORABLE STORIES

As a sociology major, I selected a social work minor, and was placed at Inwood House for my field experience. Under Charlotte Andress's leadership, the agency was a safe place for unmarried pregnant girls and women, where they lived and received comprehensive social work services: counseling, job training, medical attention, and other essential support services to assist them in deciding on the best action for their babies and for themselves.

Inwood House did not discriminate among its clients, so they constituted a cross section of society. However, it was interesting for me to see the numbers of white women who became clients, since the sociological readings and the studies discussed in classes rarely focused on pregnancy among unmarried white women. The studies were often focused on Black and, later, Latino communities and frequently described these communities in dysfunctional terms. I soon learned to quietly question how, and by whom, hypotheses were developed, and then became more cautious in totally accepting the research results.

Regardless of that caution, being nonjudgmental is one of the very important social work values, and my learning about social work and becoming a social worker began with this placement. Although I left Jamaica as a youth, I recall the harsh attitudes toward girls becoming pregnant before marriage, and a family's contrasting reactions in addressing this situation, often depending on the family's view of themselves, socially or religiously. I was aware of a couple of situations where even though the young girl had disappointed her parents by having a baby, the baby was accepted and soon integrated into the family. I have also heard through talk from relatives and friends that the baby was given to a family member to raise as their child, without a formal adoption process.

While I was amassing an enormous amount of new knowledge, I was also very involved in reflecting on my personal/social life, that is, whether or not to be romantically connected at that stage of my life. While I saw Ernle a few times in NYC, where he had an aunt, he was studying at the University of Illinois, and over time this relationship did not survive the distance. However, I was enjoying my freedom and did not really wish to develop any serious relationship. So joining organizations where I became a member of various groups suited me fine.

I found great personal satisfaction in being independent in NYC, while recognizing that my sense of freedom and independence was also buoyed by my strong connection to my community of Jamaican relatives and friends, while I also had many American and international friends. Regardless, I maintained a compelling sense of personal responsibility for my actions and behavior. However, one result of living on my own, for example, was that within a few years, I no longer thought of Easter in the same solemn way as I did in Jamaica and so did not partake in the traditional Easter activities. Over time those solemn days with their accompanying rituals completely disappeared. I realized then how easy it was to give up one's customs when placed in a completely different environment or placed in an environment where those traditions did not have the same meaning.

During my undergraduate years, I developed many friendships among the many Jamaican students enrolled at NYU and from all my extracurricular activities and work environments. Dance parties were prevalent among my West Indian friends, and since I enjoyed dancing, I tried to get all my assignments completed by Saturday so that I could be free to attend the parties in the evening. The majority of these parties were held in Brooklyn, where many West Indian families owned their homes, usually brownstones. Brooklyn also had many shops selling West Indian food products, so whether one needed that special Trinidadian bread, Jamaican hard dough bread, patties, Milo or Ovaltine drinks, those items were readily available.

Not one to sit still, I attended numerous free classical concerts and plays over my years at NYU. During 1961 I recorded attending at least seventeen concerts, all free, including organ recitals, which I enjoyed because they reminded me of those church services in Jamaica. I enjoyed the versatility of the human voice and so also sought out concerts featuring oratorios, most of which were held at the Church of the Ascension or First Presbyterian Church. In addition, I experienced memorable performances by Miriam Makeba at the Village Gate, Nina Simone, and Pearl Primus. Pearl Primus received her PhD in anthropology from NYU during the 1959/60 academic year. Her dissertation was a dance performance, a first at NYU, based on her research on

African dance. Following her dissertation performance, some of us students were invited to a reception in her honor, a memorable experience.

Then, while on a visit in DC with former roommate Christa from Germany, she and her Iranian husband, Dara, took me to hear Duke Ellington and His Orchestra perform in a nearby park. He was absolutely amazing. That was such a real treat and a mesmerizing experience for me. Then, while visiting me in New York City sometime later, Christa told me that my insistence that she remain overnight with me rather than continue on her journey from Maryland to Maine or Vermont saved her life. The bus on which she was to travel had a serious accident; I believe it overturned and a few people died. We had a lot to think and talk about that evening.

Among my most memorable undergraduate experiences was a visit to NYC's night court located on Centre Street, in August 1961. With social work as my minor, I selected attendance at a session of night court as my social work project to learn how cases were adjudicated. Prior to my visit, I wrote the presiding judge, indicating the purpose of my visit and the anticipated learning outcomes. I arrived early, looked around the room, and took my seat among the many visitors and offenders. Then the judge arrived, and we all stood up. As soon as the judge was seated, I heard, "Will Miss Spence please approach the bench?" I could not believe my ears. That was my name. However, I obeyed the command and with some trepidation walked to his bench. Then the judge whispered in a somewhat conspiratorial voice, "Come and sit beside me. You will have a better view of the proceedings from up here!" My fears turned to excitement. What a wonderful opportunity. And to be singled out by the judge. A marvelous experience.

CHAPTER 10

NYU Graduate School of Social Work

A Professional Path

Shortly before receiving my BSc in 1962, I thought about my next move. I was supposed to return to Jamaica but was concerned about what satisfying work would be available to me were I to return with only a BSc degree. Then my music teacher's words, "Fern, get a profession; with a profession, no one can take it away from you," returned to assist me in making my decision. I knew that I wanted to work with people and so inquired about the nearest related profession to sociology. The answer was social work. I immediately applied to NYU's Graduate School of Social Work, hoping that I would be accepted.

One of the questions on the application was, "Why do you wish to become a social worker?" I wrote that I wanted to make people happy and then elaborated on why I thought being happy was so important. After submitting my application, I wondered how the readers may have interpreted my life's mission. Although being happy was important to me, it could have sounded naive and simplistic to people who didn't know me. Regardless of how or what the readers thought, I was accepted into the School of Social Work. I was on my way to another new experience: becoming a social worker and having a profession.

Financial support was readily available in the sixties, through both government and social work/ human service agencies that sought to improve social work practice as well as services for their clients through exposing their staff to graduate programs. Again, this was the era of President Lyndon Johnson's Great Society, when much funding was available for social programs, and many policies were enacted to combat poverty. Government agencies supported their staff to obtain graduate degrees in social work and related professions. Agency leaders understood that advanced education would increase their staff's understanding of the relationship between theory and practice; hopefully, they would translate the theories into more effective strategies to address structural poverty and the "common human needs" presented by their clients, resulting in the latter's improved life circumstances.

Since I was not yet an American citizen, I was not eligible for any government scholarship. The School of Social Work then referred me to the Family Service Society, a nonprofit agency located in Hartford, to explore scholarship possibilities. A meeting with its executive director, Mr. Rothe Hilger, resulted in a two-year scholarship award, including expenses for room and board, and with a verbal agreement that upon graduating, I would work with the agency for two years. I kept that promise.

Two Contrasting Placements

The schedule for all social work students was working three days weekly in an agency, known as "the field," and two days in classes on campus. My first placement was in Bellevue Hospital,[1] where we were a team of six graduate students, with Ms. Brauman as our NYU supervisor. Reaching Bellevue three days each week during my first year was an experience in travel. Living on the West Side, I had to take two trains to reach the East Side during rush hours. One was the shuttle to Grand Central Station. Negotiating the crowd of people moving shoulder to shoulder in the passageway leading to the shuttle and then, if the shuttle had a visible space left, boarding was a feat. I exited the subway debating whether to wait for the bus or keep walking those five long blocks to First Avenue. By then I was almost exhausted. However, I was part of a wonderful social work team, and as soon as I joined them, I would quickly revive.

Our work varied depending on the needs of the patients. There was much to learn from that placement: how to prepare process recording, our role as social workers, and working together as a team. We obtained transportation for patients who were being discharged, referred parents to obtain special foot braces for babies to wear at bedtime, free to families regardless of income under the existing Greenberg Law, and planned home visits. All cases were referred to us by the hospital's social work department. We also participated in cross-discipline staff conferences around the needs of individual clients and met weekly as a group with our supervisor.

That cross-discipline learning was invaluable, and the overall learning was intense. It was fascinating to hear how each discipline evaluated and described the same patient; I sometimes wondered whether we were still talking about the same individual. Since each professional presented findings on the patient from their discipline's framework, their final diagnosis and treatment did not always align with the social worker's perspective. In one instance I was reprimanded for making arrangements to have a patient discharged to her apartment because I believed her story that she was well enough to go home. After making all the arrangements, I accompanied her in the ambulette to ensure her safety and to ensure that her home environment was adequate. When the psychiatrist learned that she had been discharged, he was quite upset: he felt that she had conned me into discharging her and said I would be responsible if anything happened to her. Of course, nothing negative happened to her, and I know that she did not return to Bellevue since I had followed up with her. She was a very smart woman who had worked as a prostitute until a medical condition confined her to a wheelchair.

As students we learned how to interview patients and how to write up nonjudgmental and objective interviews with patients, through process recording, which means writing up the conversation as it occurred between the patient and the interviewer. My coursework was designed to link theory and practice, to understand the developmental growth processes of children and adults, and to understand the history and philosophy of the social work profession, a relatively new profession. A course on using literature to understand personality development taught by Prof. Tessie Berkman was illuminating. Professor Berkman was an engaging, thoughtful, and warm individual, and talking with her was always rewarding and a pleasure. As graduate students, we were encouraged to join the National Association of Social Workers and to attend local meetings for continued professional growth.

COMMUNITY SERVICE SOCIETY

Our second-year placement was with the Community Service Society, which, prior to becoming a research and advocacy agency with David Jones at its helm, had a family counseling office in several NYC boroughs. Our team of five was in the Bronx office. Unlike the Bellevue experience, we were now beginning to do in-depth counseling with individuals, marriage counseling, and working with parent/child relationships. Three of my teammates were older and more experienced caseworkers pursuing their MSW degree, fully funded by their NYC agency. There was also Monica Davidovich from my undergraduate years, and then Barney, a jovial and much older African American with a hearty laugh, who because of his work and life experience eased our anxiety around our social work supervisor, who was not at all friendly or supportive. We had weekly meetings, individually and with the group, to discuss our progress and challenges with our cases. I looked forward to the group meetings but dreaded the individual meetings with my supervisor.

One reason was that she just wasn't pleasant. New to the field, I had never performed this kind of counseling previously and had to learn so many ways to assess and engage clients. For example, I had to ask adult heads of households, a term used to acknowledge that a woman may be the only responsible adult within a family, about their income. I did not have any friends in Jamaica who ever talked about or asked their parents any questions about their income, so I found it anxiety provoking to ask, especially the men, about their income. Fortunately, my NYU advisor, Dr. Leona Grossman, was a supportive and sensible individual who once assured me that "a little anxiety can be a good thing to experience, especially before a presentation." That helped to assuage my feelings of being totally unprepared for this challenging profession. However, I was relieved when the year, and this placement, ended.

LIVING, WORKING, AND LEARNING IN HARTFORD

Following graduation from the School of Social Work, I prepared to move to Hartford, Connecticut, to begin my first professional role as a social worker. However, before leaving, there was my Iranian roommate's wedding to attend in New Jersey. Affie and I had left the dorm together and lived, first, in a large studio apartment in a West Seventies brownstone. We later moved to a one-bedroom apartment at East Eightieth and Park Avenue, only to learn after two months that the building had been sold and we had one month to vacate the apartment. We found another one-bedroom with a small terrace on West Eighty-Fifth Street, between West End Avenue and Riverside Drive. There we met and became friends with sisters Joan and Marsha Lipschitz from upstate Buffalo.

They lived in a tiny studio on the floor below us. Soon they were part of my social group visiting the ISC on Saturdays to dance. Following Affie's wedding, Christa from Germany became my roommate. We lived together until my graduation and relocation to Hartford, and her wedding to Dara, a generous and jovial Iranian doctor. During this period Joan met and married Pakistani Latif, while Marsha, who was charming, had a lovely smile and was lots of fun, continued to enjoy meeting NYC's diverse individuals, a sharp contrast to her life in Buffalo. We reconnected by phone in 2016, when I learned that Marsha had married, was now a clinical social worker, has two adult sons, and lives in Texas. Joan has remarried, has a grown daughter, and spends half the year in Cincinnati and the other half in Israel.

A Case of Housing Discrimination?

On arriving in Hartford, I lived in the YWCA, a block from my new office. After one week, I rented a room from a young African American family with a four-year-old son. The wife, Inez, was so happy to have me there, since we often dined together, and she indicated that I was company for her; we talked a lot about our different life experiences. Both Inez and her husband had full-time jobs; however, since her husband owned his own business, this necessitated his working late almost every night. Although I liked Inez and was very comfortable in that household, after a couple of months, I decided to find an apartment. My experience in trying to rent an apartment in Hartford has been written up in LaGuardia Community College's Archives as part of an eleventh-grade curriculum focused on "a nation of immigrants."

The story began when I responded to an ad featuring a one-bedroom apartment off Albany Avenue. On visiting the apartment, I was told that it had already been rented. I thanked the super and returned to my office. Mr. Hilger, the executive director who had hired me, inquired about my visit. I told him that the apartment had been rented; for some reason unknown to me, he was quite surprised. We talked for a few minutes, and then Mr. Hilger said, "Fern, this is discrimination. I am calling my friend, the executive director of Connecticut's Division of Human Rights."

I protested and said I didn't think it was discrimination. Throughout my then-seven years in the States, I had never felt or expected to be discriminated against. That was the last idea that would have occurred to me; if a behavior had seemed offensive to me, I would explain it as either bad manners or a cultural difference. Remember, I had experienced a protected and safe environment while at NYU for six years—one friend had called my experience being in a cocoon—and was now entering the world of work. Anyway, Mr. Hilger called Commissioner Green, who came to interview me and immediately said that he would take the case. The result was that within a few days, I received a telephone call from the lawyer for the apartment building, offering me the same apartment.

The lawyer also invited me to his office, where he explained that "a nice young lady like you" should not be living in the area where the apartment was located. So, he subtly implied, by not renting me the apartment, they were actually looking out for me. As I listened to him talk, I wondered whether he thought my politeness indicated that I was that naive. In the meantime I had located a brand-new apartment in a new development in Hartford's North End where African Americans and Latinos lived and decided to take that apartment. I thanked him for his efforts but politely declined the offer. I felt that whether he was being truthful or not hardly mattered, since I was no longer interested in living there. I had that Jamaican determination not to be where I was not wanted. We have pride. Besides, my new apartment was far more attractive and spacious, and I felt safe in the complex.

Related to the ninth-graders' curriculum on immigration was *A City of Immigrants*, written for fourth-graders and focusing on diverse immigrant groups in New York City. Dr. Richard Lieberman interviewed me as an immigrant from Jamaica under the chapter heading "Jamaicans: Coming to New York for an Education," in which I responded to specific questions about myself. Age-appropriate questions then followed for the students to answer after each section to assess their understanding of the content.

Becoming a Permanent Resident

My experiences at Family Service Society of Hartford (FSS) were transformative. I was learning more about American culture and how families lived and
related to each other, and to the external world around them. I was fortunate
that Mr. Hilger agreed to sponsor me in obtaining my permanent residency
status. Immigration granted permission for graduates to gain work experience prior to returning to our respective countries, so I had permission to
work. On visiting the Hartford Immigration office, I inquired of the interviewing officer whether I needed a lawyer. His response was, "Miss Spence,
so long as you can read and write, you do not need a lawyer." True to his
words, I received my green card without legal assistance, and within a short
period of time. It is true that obtaining my green card occurred in Hartford
during the late sixties, an era of social change and many social programs;
yet I had the same positive experience when, a few years later, I applied for
US citizenship in New York City.

I was anxious in meeting with the immigration officer, worrying that I
might not provide the correct answers. He was so pleasant and easygoing. He
was impressed that I worked at a college and commented that I would know
all the answers. Then he said, "I will ask you who was the first president of the
USA, and don't say Abraham Lincoln." I relaxed immediately and smiled. He
congratulated me, explained the next steps, and that was it. Today's stories
are quite different, beginning with the long lines to enter the federal building,
and I am still saddened by the tremendous cost to receive a green card and
to apply for citizenship in NYC and the USA today.

Family Service Society

At the Family Service agency, I worked with clients across race and class
and under the supervision of the experienced and progressive Art Michel.
In addition to our weekly supervisory meetings, Art invited me to dine with
his family at their home, where our conversations were culturally enriching
and especially informative about the Hartford community. In our weekly
meetings, Art and I would review my cases and my recorded interviews, and
he would provide wise suggestions and guidance. I recall the case of the only
Jamaican client I met during my two years at the agency even though there

were hundreds of Jamaicans living in Hartford. Knowing how hard it was for Jamaicans in general to seek help, I was truly impressed by her motivation. In sharing her situation with Art, I referred to her as "an average Jamaican." He immediately countered, "Fern, no one who leaves her/his country to seek a better life is 'average'; the average citizens usually remain in their country." I have never forgotten that wise and perceptive statement.

I thought that I knew a lot and was quite wise when I arrived in the United States; after all, I was always a very sensible and responsible young adult growing up in Kingston, but I soon discovered how much more I needed to listen and learn. Even when they were opinionated, Jamaicans were pretty predictable in their responses to social or political issues; a cultural connection existed. Not so in the two cities where I lived. In addition to my efforts to develop an understanding of the racial divide, there were the divergent voices from, and even within, the many cultural, ethnic, and regional groups living in America. This recognition was a humbling and daunting experience.

My academic learning in college and graduate school was freeing and empowering. However, I learned more about social work counseling at FSS in Hartford than in my two years in graduate school. The presenting problems encountered there were far more complex than those I had previously encountered, and "home visits" were illuminating. Most revealing was that Americans in general seemed to be more proactive in seeking counseling to resolve their problems when compared to the Jamaicans of my youth. Here again, I must reiterate that my youth in Jamaica was in the forties and fifties. I understand that there are currently counselors in Jamaican schools as well as therapists, so some attitudes toward seeking help have changed among the populace.

My salary in Hartford was $5,000 annually in 1964. That seemed quite a reasonable amount. I could pay my rent and all my expenses and still have enough to save. But I remember feeling that I needed to do something worthwhile, and that meant to help someone else. So I called my aunt in NYC, and when I discovered that her daughter, age eight or so, wanted to dance, I told her that I would pay for her lessons, and I continued to do so over several years until she stopped dancing. I felt better having taken this small action, being a firm believer in always lending a helping hand and lifting as you climb, or, as Kahlil Gibran wrote in *The Prophet*,

It is well to give when asked, but it is better to give unasked,
Through understanding

My agency was housed in the Webster Memorial Building, a charming eighteenth-century neo-Georgian brick building facing Hartford's Bushnell Park. The motto written on the exposed side of the building proclaimed, "It's a sign of strength to seek help!" I constantly thought about that statement. My recollections about seeking help in Jamaica were not necessarily of it as a sign of strength. I, and the Jamaicans with whom I was acquainted, kept our problems close to home and preferred not to talk about them. So, I had to reframe my thinking, and over time I actually incorporated that maxim into my psyche, so that I could be an authentic and effective social worker.

I was assigned between fifteen to twenty cases, each of which was an interesting human story. My clients ranged from housewives, to employed adults, to parent/child relationships, to a famous musician. This agency was a model for how leaders and their staff work together. Knowing how intense counseling could be, FSS provided one week's vacation in the spring to give its social work staff time out from counseling and then one month's vacation during the summer. Mr. Hilgar also provided ongoing professional development for us by inviting specialists to talk about therapeutic approaches or current mental health challenges. In this relatively small agency, administrators and staff worked well and respectfully together. We ate lunch together in the agency's narrow staff room/kitchen, had many conversations, and were a close-knit group.

My social worker colleagues were very welcoming and reached out to include me in a range of activities. Anita Lahn, who lived in West Hartford, invited me to participate in her book club, where I met new people. Wendy, a Canadian, invited me to her home for dinner, and so did others, like Gladys, Betty, and Terry. I loved Mrs. Gertrude Ress, a fellow Virgo, who returned to Smith College at over sixty years old to obtain her master's degree in social work. Gertrude's husband was a successful lawyer in Hartford. Gertrude talked with me about her life and her two daughters, one of whom had a disability; her older daughter was working on her doctorate at Harvard University. Gertrude also invited Ismail and me to a few dinners at her home in West Hartford, where she was the most gracious hostess. I was amazed that her housekeeper always appeared in the dining room when Gertrude needed her, so I shared my observation with Gertrude. She then showed me that there was an unobtrusively placed buzzer under her dining table that she pressed to summon her housekeeper.

Gertrude was also close friends with Judge Constance Motley and suggested that I ask her to officiate at my wedding to Ismail in 1969. I contacted Judge Motley, but regrettably she couldn't marry us because of her recent appointment as a federal judge; instead she suggested a colleague, Herbert B. Evans, a housing court judge in NYC, who was happy to officiate. Many of our close friends and family members met us in Judge Evans's office, surprising the receptionist, who remarked that some couples couldn't even find one witness, while we had so many.

Hartford, in the mid-sixties, had been experiencing racial tensions, especially in housing. So a decision was made to select African American families to integrate West Hartford, the prosperous suburb. Among the first few families selected was a Jamaican minister, Rev. Carlton Young and his wife, Maisie, and their four very well-mannered children. They were aided in purchasing their house by the church and were greeted by the Welcome Wagon. They were excellent neighbors, so theirs was a success story. I met the family, liked them, and we became friends. We kept in contact even after I left Hartford.

Although I loved my job and my colleagues, Hartford was not New York City. The city emptied out after six o'clock, and besides, I missed my friends and many activities in New York City, so, once my two years were completed, I thanked my friends and colleagues for their kindness toward me, said goodbye, and prepared for my return to NYC. The agency held a lovely farewell luncheon in a restaurant for me in August 1966. I remember wearing my favorite two-piece V-neck dusty pink rose linen outfit and having a really wonderful time with my colleagues. I felt fortunate to have worked with a humane and caring leader in Mr. Hilger and such thoughtful and culturally responsive colleagues, as well as my clients, from whom I learned so much. Hartford provided me with many culturally diverse learning experiences during my two years as a social worker and resident. As so often happens with nonprofits, within a few years, FSS had to merge with another nonprofit, and so closed its doors on Trumbull Street forever.

CHAPTER 11

Returning to Work in NYC

During my two years in Hartford, I returned to New York every weekend and stayed with my friend Wynsome, who had moved from her mother's home in Queens and had rented an apartment on West Ninety-Fifth Street, between Central Park West and Columbus Avenue. We spent weekends shopping at our favorite department stores: Franklin Simon and B. Altman on Thirty-Fourth Street, and Peck and Peck on Fifth Ave in the Forties. We also shopped at Klein on the Square, a popular discount store, always crowded, on East Fourteenth Street.

One Saturday, while browsing alone in Klein's, I found a lovely outfit, arrived at the checkout counter, and handed my check to the cashier. Noticing that this was an out-of-town bank, she explained that she could not accept the check without a driver's license. Not possessing such an item, I was about to leave the line behind me to return the item to the rack when a pleasant voice behind me said, "I am happy to take your check and give you the cash." Simultaneously surprised and appreciative, I turned around and very pleasantly asked, "Are you sure?" This trusting young white woman did not hesitate and instead began to count the cash that I needed to pay the cashier. After thanking her profusely, I left the store in such a happy mood, rejoicing in the fact that although I was a total stranger, this wonderful individual was willing to trust that my check was good. She had done a really good deed that day for me, and I deeply appreciated her generosity.

Another favorite place to shop for quality household items in NYC was the Job Lot, a popular discount store on Chambers Street in Lower

Manhattan. Wynsome and I usually found reasonably priced treasures in that remarkable store. Such wonderful and enjoyable adventures. I usually returned to Hartford on the 6 a.m. train on Monday mornings, arriving in time for work.

In the meantime, the relationship between Ismail and me had blossomed; for many years, we were social friends, mostly interacting within our ISC group of friends. Sometimes I invited him to Jamaican parties, which he seemed to enjoy. We were such a lively and friendly group. But while I was in graduate school, we had long telephone conversations, often discussing theories from sociology and philosophy, which he initiated. Although our discussions were intellectually stimulating, sometimes I saw them as a barrier to protect himself from any emotional involvement.

This noncommittal relationship was fine with me while I was in graduate school; however, there was a relationship shift when I moved to Hartford. Some of his self-protection was loosening, and we began to see each other frequently during those two years. Ismail owned a car, so he often drove me back to Hartford after my weekends with Wynsome. Sometimes the three of us would go out to eat or to a party in NYC. All my friends adored Ismail; he was kind, generous, polite, and an intellectual. Ismail was never about gossip, only about ideas emerging from world history or literature. Although his background was engineering, and he had graduate degrees in engineering and economics and was now working on his PhD in urban planning at Columbia University, his first love was literature. His favorite author was Proust, and he spent hours talking to me about Proust and other writers like André Gide, Herman Hesse, and Nikolas Kazantzakis. I began reading these authors, was drawn to the sense of humanity within them, and soon had read all the authors except Proust. (I actually tried to read Proust, but gave up after the first few pages). Ismail also had a quiet sense of humor and wit, which was apparent to all of us who knew him. He enjoyed and shared stories with me about growing up in India, where Hindus and Muslims lived harmoniously together in his village before Partition in 1947. He also introduced me to the fictitious Don Camillo, the Italian village priest whose adventures were hilarious. My admiration for Ismail grew over the years as he kept challenging me to think more broadly about history, culture, and cross-cultural events. It was Ismail who also challenged me to wear my hair in the Afro style many years prior to my decision to do so.

Bringing My Family to NYC

In the meantime, I had sponsored my sister Hope to study in the US. She arrived during my last two weeks in Hartford, so we went shopping for her warm clothing at Hartford's then-famous store G. Fox & Co., which no longer exists. However, by September 1, 1966, I was back in New York City and had found a spacious one-bedroom apartment in Park West Village on the Upper West Side where some of my Jamaican friends were living. My furniture arrived from Hartford with help from Ismail and friends, and my sister and I moved into the apartment, delighted to be back in the city. In addition to being awakened by the sun streaming into my eastern-facing apartment, I was charmed by the sounds of trucks rumbling down Columbus Avenue each morning, a symphony of sounds, and music to my ears. I now lived in close proximity to my friends, so once again I resumed my active social life.

With her foreign student's visa, my sister Hope enrolled in the Rhodes School, an independent high school focused on preparing foreign students to obtain their high school diplomas. The school has since closed. With her diploma, Hope soon enrolled in CUNY's New York City Community College in Brooklyn, where she obtained her associate's degree in liberal arts. She then enrolled in Hunter College, where she obtained her BA in sociology. I was amazed and so pleased that Hope seemed to be so much like me in temperament. She was easy to live with, always in a good mood, neat, and friendly with an independent spirit. When my former switchboard position at the Institute of Fine Arts, NYU, became available, Hope was hired for the position and enjoyed many happy years there until the institute transitioned to individual telephones. She was promoted to work in the Admissions Office, where she continues to enjoy meeting and assisting graduate students and faculty to this day.

Helping my family members was so ingrained in my being that bringing them to NYC was a natural next step once I could do so. I had always felt responsible for my mother and sisters. Following Hope's arrival, I also brought my mother to the US, and when she became a permanent resident, she brought my younger sister Phillippa to live with me. Now I was getting to know both sisters more intimately, since they were quite young when I left Jamaica. I was not disappointed; they were both easy to relate to and kept me laughing at the amusing stories about their escapades and fun times during their growing-up years in Jamaica.

Phillippa's first job was working at Irving Trust Company, now Bank of New York. A friend from Barbados, Dr. Courtney Blackman, an economist, author, and now Sir Courtney Blackman, held a management position at the bank and helped Phillipa to obtain her bank position. Courtney and his Jamaican wife, Gloria, were my good friends. He later became the first governor of the Central Bank of Barbados. When Rebecca Straus, a former director of Bank Street School for Children, and her husband, were traveling to Barbados, I connected them with Courtney. On their return Betty called me to say that Courtney had invited them to an incredible lunch and how royally they were treated. He had even sent an official car to receive them. That was Courtney's, and West Indian, hospitality.

Phillippa, a gifted storyteller, often kept us engrossed as she turned a simple instance into an engrossing and engaging story. Jamaicans would say, "Boy, she could tell a story!" Among her other talents, Phillippa creates beautiful and unique pieces of jewelry, is a terrific writer, and is currently working on a novel about a Jamaican family. Phillippa has two children, Tanya Yasmin Chin, a Smith College alumna and former employee, now executive director of the Amherst Cinema, and Craig Chin, a realtor, with her first husband, Maurice Chin, a Jamaican artist and half Chinese; she has since remarried and lives in Atlanta with Hepburn Wilson, her current husband. My sisters and I enjoy each other's company and continue to share delightful Jamaican stories when we talk with or visit each other.

A new chapter in my life began with my return to New York City from Hartford. By early September 1966, I began working at the Northside Center for Child Development in Harlem. This social agency was founded in 1946 by Drs. Kenneth and Mamie Phipps Clark to address the mental health and academic needs of Black children who were having very challenging experiences in the Harlem public schools. I applied to Northside Center at the suggestion of a former School of Social Work classmate, Norman Wyloge, whom I had met on one of my numerous trips to New York City. Northside Center provided comprehensive services to children who were mostly referred by the local schools for "behavior problems." Once they were evaluated by a team of a psychologist and an educator, they were referred for group or individual counseling, tutoring, or other services as recommended by the evaluators.

The clinical staff recognized early on that the children were developmentally where they were expected to be, but their teachers, using deficit lenses, saw the "restless" behavior of Black boys as "acting out" and "disruptive," and therefore, they needed counseling. I am certain that many of those educators had little awareness that the curriculum, rather than the students, could have been the problem. The lessons probably neither engaged the students nor were related to their social-emotional needs; the result was boredom instead of stimulating their desire to learn and to achieve.

Northside Center was an interesting place with some fascinating people. It was possibly the first child guidance clinic in Harlem. Later, remedial educational services were added to meet the academic needs of the children. According to his friend and scholar, Dr. Edmund Gordon, Dr. Kenneth Clark "devoted his life to scholarly analysis and responsible social action." An applied researcher, he studied problems related to segregation and desegregation of schools. Dr. Clark, of Bajan (from Barbados) parentage, achieved many "firsts." Besides being the first Black member of the NYS Board of Regents and the first Black president of the American Psychological Association, he was also the first Black faculty to become a tenured full professor at City College. Dr. Clark had also worked with Gunnar Myrdal, Swedish economist and sociologist, on the research leading to the publication of *An American Dilemma: The Negro Problem and Modern Democracy*.

The Clarks lived in Hasting-on-Hudson and spent their vacations in Sag Harbor or Martha's Vineyard, where many middle- and upper-class African Americans spent their summers. I interviewed for the position in July with Dr. Mamie Phipps Clark and Dr. Paul King Benedict; the latter was both a psychiatrist and an anthropologist. My supervisor was Victor Carter, who loved the opera and ballet, topics we usually discussed during our supervisory sessions. A social worker by training, he had worked at Northside for many years and had a very close relationship with the Clarks. Victor was also a Bajan by background and owned a brownstone in Brooklyn.

I became aware of the Black upper-middle and upper classes in the US to which the Clarks belonged; the Jack and Jill memberships,[1] and the Alpha and Delta sororities. The Deltas sponsored Black children to attend elite boarding schools through Northside Center and often met with me at the center to discuss the children's progress in the schools.

I was fascinated and actually relieved to know that within the African American community, there were distinctive ways of belonging to special groups, which provided critical support and identity affirmation for youth. I have a vague memory of being invited to a cotillion for young African American adults who were introduced into their society. All the young women wore white dresses, and after the ceremony ended, the dancing began for everyone. I later learned more about the social meaning of this activity by reading John Oliver Killens, *The Cotillion*.

My Home as a Gathering Place

I often wondered why I had never met any of these middle-class Black families when I was a foreign student, and why their homes were not included on the visitation lists. I made a mental note then to open my home to as many individuals, foreign or not, for dinners, events, or just a place to be welcomed. Our home has since been open to friends for breakfasts, dinners, and anywhere from twenty-six to forty-three families, friends, and guests for our annual Thanksgiving dinners over the last forty-five years.

I also visited NYU's International Students receptions, where I would meet foreign students like Japanese Masako Kato. I invited her and a few other students to our Thanksgiving dinners. They had nowhere else to go. Masako and her husband, Hide, came to our Thanksgiving dinners every year for over eight years until Hide was transferred to London. By then they also had three young children, and Masako had completed her doctorate in linguistics from NYU. (Masako and her children dined with us again in 2019 on her first visit back to NYC.) I have also called the International House and invited residents referred by the staff. Our guests have included visitors from South Africa, Italy, China, Japan, Uganda, the US, and even a lawyer and his sister from Mongolia. I had achieved another of my personal goals.

The years between 1966 to 1969 were quite busy and altogether productive ones. My friends and I were still attending the International Students Center on Saturday nights for dancing. There we also met a group of young Guyanese men, all Indians, who were living together in the West Thirties and attending trade schools. Soon they, along with my other friends, became regular visitors for Sunday dinners in my apartment. I usually prepared a variety of meals with rice as a staple for them. The Guyanese men would sing and perform to Indian songs, often in a call-and-response pattern, entertaining, culturally enriching, and enjoyable. A few years later, I learned that their apartments in the West Thirties were raided by immigration officers, because they were undocumented. However, I believe the action occurred because they were from Guyana, which was not then on friendly terms with the US. So all but one, who jumped to his death from a window, were deported. A sad ending for a group of very fine young men trying to improve their living conditions.

My apartment became a gathering place and a home away from home for many foreign students/immigrants on the weekends. Soon my cousin Courtney would come by after work, my Jamaican neighbor Jasneth would join my sister and me, and we would play board games for hours. We loved Aggravation. Then, at Christmas, Ismail would help me find the largest pine tree, and I would host a tree-trimming party involving all our international, Jamaican, and American friends. Although I thought about marriage once in a while, I loved my independence. Then, having read Gertrude Stein's *Three Lives*, I was fascinated by the idea of creating a salon where friends could meet regularly in my apartment for stimulating, intellectual discussions. Moreover, I had promised myself not ever to marry until I had accomplished three goals: obtain a profession, have a permanent job, and save at least one year's rent. I now had the first two and was already close to fulfilling that third goal. These were goals to ensure that I could continue to be independent whether or not I was married; they seemed sensible to me.

SEVEN EUROPEAN COUNTRIES IN FIVE WEEKS

In 1968, while still working at Northside Center, I decided it was time to travel abroad, to know other countries and cultures firsthand. Cooper Union had a promotional tour for seven European countries over five weeks for eight hundred dollars. I signed up for this tour, led by a geographer, Dr. Johnson E. Fairchild, whose knowledge of the physical geography of the countries we visited was extensive and compelling. Still in my twenties, I was the youngest and the only Black individual among over thirty retired adults, including several couples. The group was welcoming, and I was treated very well, with many of the older women deciding to look after me because of my "youth."

The first city on this tour was London. We toured famous places including the Tate Museum, Buckingham Palace Guards, and the Tower of London on our first full day. I did not have any expectations for having a good time in London. However, I called a few individuals whose names had been given to me in New York, and the responses and welcome I experienced were the best ever. Three new friends took me to a discotheque, my first one, then on to a Wimpy's for hamburgers and chips. We ended the evening at the Playboy

Club, where we saw a terrifically funny performance. I believe that was the most fun evening I had ever experienced. My new friends were warm and funny, and seemed to have really enjoyed our meeting.

On my third day in London, our very pleasant English guide with whom I had developed a positive relationship (the commonwealth connection) was quite relieved and pleased to see me, the last person to arrive for our bus tour. We headed across London to Kensington Gardens, visited the Victoria and Albert Museum, and then in the evening after dinner went to the theater to see *The Four Musketeers*, which was hilarious and had been running forever. Visiting Portobello Road, where I saw many Indians and West Indians, reminded me of my weekend trips to New York's Delancey Street, where all varieties of clothing and food were available at bargain prices.

In Stratford-upon-Avon, Shakespeare country, I attended a poetry reading and was charmed by the politeness of the English people. I was so drawn to individuals being polite. Those habits rarely die, especially coming from a former British colony. One gentleman gave me his program because the latter were all gone when we arrived. The following day, our tour bus took us through the English countryside, where I noticed with great pleasure all the white lace curtains in the windows. They reminded me of my Jamaican days. To my surprise, London turned out to be a very positive and exciting experience for me, one that I certainly did not expect. On leaving I wrote in my trip log, "So long, London, you were great fun and a wonderful experience."

Then we were on our way to Harwich, where we boarded the SS *Amsterdam* and sailed smoothly, all night, across the Hook of Holland to Amsterdam. After touring the city, we walked on a street where young women sat in windows waiting for clients. They did not have to fear the police, because prostitution was legal; we were told that the women had to report for a checkup at specified times, a requirement that seemed so sensible to me. At least the women were not harassed. Exploring the city, I had never seen so many bicycles on streets in my young life. In antique shops, I fell in love with the blue-and-white Delft pattern and purchased a table napkin with an imprint of the pattern as a souvenir. My mother used to tell me the story of the boy who kept his finger in the dike so that the city would not be flooded; she was so moved by the story that she always wanted to visit Holland to see the dike. With her sisters she did visit London but did not reach Holland.

From Amsterdam we drove to Cologne, where we visited its magnificent cathedral, drove alongside the Rhine to Koblenz for one night, then on to Nuremberg. En route fog blanketed the valley, and I had visions of Rhinemaidens dancing and having an enjoyable time through the fog. I was struck by the beautiful countryside, farmlands, and buildings with reddish-brown rooftops.

To reach Innsbruck, Austria, we drove through the Bavarian Alps with their breathtaking views; I was absolutely transfixed. At the hotel Europa, I had my first taste of venison and loved it. When I retired to sleep, the bed was so deliciously comfortable that I slept very soundly through the night. Attending an enjoyable concert featuring Tyrolean singers and dancers the next evening, our group was happy again and had fewer complaints than we had in Germany. We left Austria for Venice and Florence, traveling over the Brenner Pass and through the awesome Dolomites, which took my breath away; the beauty and majesty were overwhelming. This mountain range had such high peaks that they seemed to touch the sky. We passed through many small villages that seemed dwarfed by the enormous mountains. Arriving in Italy, we toured Venice and Florence.

Soon we left for an all-day ride to San Gimignano, a quaint village fortress town, and then on to Siena, where we visited Il Duomo Cathedral, with its zebra-looking interior. I left our group, accompanied by its most unhappy female member, to travel to Rome, where I visited the Baths of Caracalla and saw a production of *Madama Butterfly*. Dining at The Gladiators, exploring the city, and seeing the monuments and buildings that I had once known only through photographs were moments to be treasured.

The following day I visited Vatican City and the Sistine Chapel, and then met IFA's Professor Von Blankenhagen for lunch. My traveling companion wanted to explore Rome but had joined me briefly to meet Dr. Von B. As soon as she left, Von B, who was all about elegance and comportment, quipped, in his distinct German accent, "June, where on earth did you find that uncouth woman?" Then Dr. Von B and I had the most delicious lunch of Milanese veal topped with an egg. Von B was always full of sharp observations, and with his incredible intellect and wit, we had a marvelous afternoon of good food and engaging conversation before I said goodbye to see more of Rome.

Dr. Von B passed away in New York in 1990 at age eighty, after teaching for over twenty-five years at NYU's Institute of Fine Arts. He was a striking and unforgettable figure. He was very short of stature, with a sharply angular face, deeply set and all-knowing eyes, a wide forehead, and somewhat broad shoulders on a body that revealed the effects of polio. Born and educated in Germany, Von B enriched the lives of many IFA students, art historian colleagues, and friends with his passion for ancient art and archaeology, philosophy, his ever-present wit, and his friendship. At his memorial in 1990, one of his academic friends commented that she "learned that there was very little that did not fascinate P.H. [a nickname] and very, very little about which he was not astonishingly well informed." I think about him often.

Being in Rome was exciting; I loved seeing the historical places that I had always read about, but I also enjoyed the feeling of freedom in Rome. I met Bruno, a very pleasant young man who offered to show me New Rome. He seemed genuine and trustworthy, so I agreed to travel with him. We stopped at a nice outdoor café for refreshments and then drove by the old Appian Way, passed the Catacombs, and visited the Trevi Fountain, Via Veneto, and the Spanish Steps, before heading back to my hotel. Bruno was a real gentleman and was just happy to show me around his city.

I reconnected with my group in Milan. They were so happy to see me, especially my roommate, Dora; they were all concerned with my being so young and on my own in Rome. I reassured them that I was fine and had experienced a marvelous time there. We departed Milan, drove directly to Switzerland, and on to the Hotel St. Moritz, the only luxury hotel on this trip. After visiting Lucerne, Berne, and Geneva, where I spent a few hours with my Jamaican friend Cynthia Wilson and her Swiss Italian husband, Daniel, it was on to France, passing through Dijon, Tours—a charming and bustling city that I really liked—Orleans, home of Joan of Arc, Chartres, and Versailles, with its Hall of Mirrors and those amazing gardens. They were unforgettable. By the time we arrived in Paris, I was exhausted and ready to return home. However, I did get to visit the Louvre, Sainte-Chapelle, and Montparnasse, and I walked on the Champs Elysées at night.

REFLECTING ON MY EUROPEAN TRAVEL

This amazing trip was memorable for me on several levels. This was my first real vacation following graduation, and over three years' working as a professional social worker. I was open to learning about the places and cultures on our itinerary, as well as open to eating new foods. Lunch for me in New York was generally a sandwich or a hamburger. On the trip there were times when we ate only huge, delicious, and mouth-watering peaches and bread for lunch.

To my surprise and delight, the peaches were actually quite filling. Those Swiss Italian peaches were also the largest I had ever seen. The grossest food that I tried to eat was jellied eel in London. I would not chew the eel but quickly swallowed a small piece just to feel adventurous, and to later share the story with friends on my return to New York City. I also found and bought Paule Marshall's book *Brown Girl, Brownstones*, from a street vendor in Paris. That was indeed a find, a fantastic story about a young girl growing up in Brooklyn with immigrant parents from Barbados, and her experience as a Black student in Brooklyn College.

As we traveled the group dynamics became fascinating. Within our large group, individuals formed relationships with each other based on a range of factors, a normal reaction; basically, everyone related positively, with the exception of three individuals who did not appear comfortable within the group: a married couple who seemed utterly mismatched and had an unusual way of communicating with each other, and the single, unhappy, middle-aged woman who was critical of everyone and everything so much that almost everyone avoided her, which just increased her hostility. These three are missing from the group photo we took in one of the cities we visited.

On the return flight, that unhappy individual who had also accompanied me to Rome got drunk and scared everyone by walking up and down the aisle cursing and threatening the group. Neither the stewardess nor the other staff could calm her down, and we were all scared that she would cause a very severe disturbance on the aircraft. I don't recall how she was subdued. I think she finally fell asleep; we were all relieved and could breathe much easier. That was the only real drama on what had been a rich, enjoyable, and unforgettable European adventure.

RETURNING TO NORTHSIDE CENTER

On returning to my position at Northside Center, I began to reflect on where I was headed professionally. The agency had an educational component where progressive educators, psychologists, and reading specialists worked together to help children and youth succeed. Child psychiatrist Dr. Teodora Abramovich worked exclusively with children, while the social workers counseled the parents or caregivers. The staff were all progressive and qualified professionals who were dedicated to making a difference by enriching the children's lives. Besides coleading a mothers group, I counseled adults and youth. I also liked the staff, whose life experiences deserved a book. The two most colorful and fascinating professionals there were social workers Leona Lovell and Dr. Olivia Edwards.

READY TO MOVE FORWARD

After a while, however, I grew restless. The process of individuals changing their behavior and embracing personal growth was slow. I began to think about making a bigger impact with larger numbers of people. In addition, there was limited opportunity for advancement in the agency, except becoming a supervisor, and the agency did not need two such positions. By this time Ismail and I were discussing marriage, and he was very supportive of my seeking other options. But what really prompted my visit to the NYU alumni employment center was a discussion with my supervisor.

I had been talking with a colleague who came to Northside much later than I did, and she happened to reveal her much higher salary. I was shocked, because with my much larger caseload and excellent evaluations, the salary discrepancy seemed unfair. So I went to see my supervisor and wondered about the difference in our salaries. He laughed and said that I hadn't asked for an increase, while she did. I was stunned. I felt that my boss should have recognized the salary discrepancy and recommended an increase in my salary. As a young professional confronting this new situation, I was personally hurt, and my way of handling this disappointing response was to find another opportunity and move on. I had the option then to request a salary increase, which I believe he would have approved. However, the truth is, I was ready to move on, and to explore new options. This was a turning point in my career and my way of thinking, since my expectation had been to remain in a job for many years, as adults did in Jamaica during my youth.

THE EDUCATIONAL CLINIC AT HUNTER COLLEGE

Within a week I was in NYU's Employment Center to review the job possibilities for someone with my background and experience. The employment center had one interesting position at Hunter College's Educational Clinic: a social worker as part of a team to visit, test, and evaluate three- and four-year-old Black and brown children in early childhood programs for admission to Hunter's prekindergarten program. I interviewed for the position and was hired. This was a one-year appointment on a faculty line, to continue the work of Barbara DeCastro, the previous social worker, also a Jamaican, who was on maternity leave.

The mission of the Educational Clinic was fulfilling a court order that Hunter College elementary school integrate its program by enrolling one-third Black, one-third Latino, and one third-white students in its prekindergarten classes. The school had been sued for not enrolling students of color yet it was a public school utilizing tax levy funds. To comply with the court's order, the clinic hired six psychologists to administer intelligence tests to the children in Daycare and Head Start programs, ensuring that they would be qualified for entry into Hunter College Elementary School. The clinic also hired two social workers to work with the children's parents to support and inform them about the school and the school's expectations and culture. My colleague Fred and I were the social workers. Fred was an easygoing, thoughtful professional who had been a social worker for many years and so was very experienced. We shared much of our observations from visits to childcare centers and participated in team discussions about which children should be recommended.

Fred was likable and helpful. He and I supported parents in understanding the testing and application processes and provided information on the school at Hunter College. Children who were perceived as having high potential were usually recommended by their teachers or center directors to be tested by the Hunter team. Many children performed at a high level on the tests, and each year until the clinic was closed, increasing numbers of Black and brown children were admitted to Hunter's preschool program.

Simultaneously, the clinic professionals worked with Hunter elementary school teachers to help them address their concerns and, for a few, their resistance, to the new populations, Black and brown children, with whom they now had to work. This was not an easy task, since the shift in the student population was disquieting for many teachers and challenging for others. Both groups of teachers needed help to ensure positive results for themselves and, especially, for the children. Therefore, the professional development program provided by our clinic staff focused on child development and cultural sensitivity for all the teachers. There was only one African

American early childhood teacher in Hunter's elementary school. She was delighted with the change and, along with several of her colleagues, worked enthusiastically with our team.

New York City in a Fiscal Crisis

With the work being accomplished by the Educational Clinic, the ratio set by the court was achieved by Hunter Elementary School, and training activities with teachers were happening when the city experienced a major budget deficit in 1971. The Educational Clinic was closed by the college as a money-saving strategy. Parents were now instructed to get their children tested by an independent group and had, I believe, to pay for this service. The clinic had also worked with the NYC Public Schools on a new program to improve teaching called TTT, or Training of Teachers of Teachers. In this program, the clinic was a partner with Hunter's Teacher Education Program in preparing master teachers to work effectively with new teachers. I recall how responsive many new teachers were for this additional support; the latter was really appreciated and led to the new teachers becoming more confident in their classroom practices. However, with the imminent closing of the clinic, the professional staff immediately began to explore the possibility of transferring to the college's Education Department. Some were successful; others sought positions in other places.

An important outcome from this experience was acknowledgment that there were, of course, large numbers of very bright Black and brown attending day care and Head Start early childhood programs. The challenges, which remain today, included ensuring that they received a high-quality early education that prepared them for the best elementary and high schools, which were not always available in their communities, and preparing teachers and other professionals to see, accept, and build on the strengths and potential that existed among the children. The other reality was getting information out to parents in underserved communities about access to the high-quality programs existing in the city for all children and encouraging them to explore these options. The children's potential needed to be acknowledged and nurtured so that everyone, and certainly society, could benefit from their intelligence, cultural knowledge, and experience. My belief in the design and implementation of special programs focused on access and information, and improving educational outcomes and opportunities for underserved and undereducated populations, began at the Hunter Educational Clinic.

The majority of children, youth, and adults within the underserved categories were African American and Latino. I knew from my years of experience in both social work and education that when families were intentionally exposed to opportunities, received support, a high-quality education, information, and access to resources, they and their children stood a real chance of being successful, well-adjusted, and active participants in the society. Although a system-wide change would be the ideal, the wait for such a progressive agenda was too uncertain given the existing structural barriers. So I began to believe in the design of special programs or projects as alternative paths for educational and social change. I often thought of my high school headmaster, and how he strategically introduced small changes over time, even in the hiring of teachers from abroad, until his vision for a more progressive curriculum and school was achieved. He later developed and implemented the first community college in Jamaica.

In June 1969, while I was still employed at Hunter College, Ismail and I were married in a judge's office on Center Street in Lower Manhattan. Our reception was held in my apartment, which held all our friends and relatives, who had an enjoyable evening feasting on the delicious food that my family and I had prepared earlier, and then dancing to calypso, reggae, and other popular R&B dance rhythms.

CHAPTER 12

LaGuardia Community College

Among the six psychologists working in Hunter College's Educational Clinic was Dr. Janet Lieberman, a leader and innovator who always stood out from her psychologist colleagues in the clinic. Janet was energetic, bold, a mover and shaker filled with creative ideas about achieving social change. She was more focused on demonstrating the action or activity to bring about systemic change than using a therapeutic approach, which was much slower. When the clinic closed in 1971 to address the city's financial crisis, Janet was hired as an assistant dean in the soon-to-be-opened Community College #9, later renamed LaGuardia Community College and located in a former factory in Long Island City, Queens.

Working at the new LaGuardia Community College provided Dr. Lieberman with an opportunity to implement her innovative ideas unencumbered by established rules and norms. She became known as a visionary and the architect of some of the college's most innovative programs. Janet was also able to garner major funding for all these programs that she initiated, including the famous Transfer Program. These programs have generated many articles, attracted participants at special conferences, and inspired a book, *Exploring Transfer*, and all have been nationally replicated.

LaGuardia Community College was to be opened in the fall of 1971, and hiring was happening in all areas of the college in preparation for the opening. During March, Janet called me to share news about a recent agreement between the Teachers Union/the United Federation of Teachers, or the UFT, the City University of New York, and the NYC Board of Education to launch a career ladder program for paraprofessionals, leading eventually to their certification as teachers or social workers. She wanted me to be involved and requested that I develop a three-credit course to support two groups of paraprofessionals, assistant teachers and family workers, *and* be ready to teach the course within two weeks. However, Ismail and I were expecting our first child in about three months, and I had decided to wait until I gave birth before seeking a new position.

When I conveyed my plans to Janet, she was undaunted and continued to be persuasive. Given Janet's belief that I could develop and teach the course, I finally agreed. Although we had shared many conversations at Hunter College, we really hadn't worked that closely with each other, so I was encouraged that Janet had reached out to me. But that was Janet's personality, decisive, a force of nature and a huge heart. I received train directions and, with my course description and outline in hand, left my home for the subway journey to LaGuardia Community College, located in the borough of Queens, prepared to meet my students.

As the 7 train to Queens emerged from the tunnel and slowly eased into the elevated Court House Square Station, from my seat on the second-to-last car, I saw through the train windows an array of factory buildings. I had been informed that the last train car was nearest to the stairs at my designated subway stop. To my surprise, I saw several enormous billboards that rose several feet above the roofs of buildings, advertising "Silvercup Bread," "Chiclets," "Domino Sugar," and other products seeming to compete with each other. This was an industrial area and a new environment for me. I soon learned that LaGuardia Community College, initially called Community College #9, was renamed to honor the memory of New York City's progressive three-term mayor Fiorello LaGuardia. Although the college opening was scheduled for September 1971, the first classes for the paraprofessionals were to begin earlier, during the spring; therefore, LaGuardia's very first students to enroll in this new college were paraprofessionals.

The Paraprofessional Teacher Education Program, also known as the Education Associates Program, was designed to increase the numbers of minorities and women within the teaching profession by providing them access to this free career ladder program. Alighting from the elevated train at the Rawson Street station, I had to climb down the first set of stairs from the platform to the ticket-sale level, then descend another two or three levels of stairs to reach the street. With a sigh of relief on finally arriving on the street, I paused to catch my breath. Then, as I walked the two blocks to the college, I inhaled the fresh aroma of warm bread wafting through the air. Then I noticed the Chiclets odor. Soon both aromas seemed to be jostling each other for my attention. These aromas were new, pleasant, and unforgettable. I couldn't help wondering what else was ahead for me in this new place.

On arriving at LaGuardia's main building, a former factory, I was directed to the Great Hall, where I saw this huge, cavernous space filled with people gathered at different work stations with informational signs. I finally found someone familiar with the location of classrooms, and he directed me to the third floor. On my way there and in the first classroom, I was delighted to meet Dr. Roy McLeod, a Jamaican and chair of the Mathematics Department; in the adjoining room, I greeted my group of very excited, predominantly women students.

There were about three men in the group of about twenty-six adult students. A quick survey indicated an almost equal mix of Black, brown, and white women, two Black males, and one white male. After welcoming them and sharing a brief summary of my background and the course, I invited each student to describe her/his career goal and to identify the program in which she or he worked. The majority were classroom paraprofessionals intending to become teachers, while about one-third worked with families The Black and brown women turned out to be almost equally Caribbean, African American, and Latina women.

I had prepared a course entitled "Personality and Social Adjustment," appropriate for both groups since they all needed to understand the meanings behind behavior whether that of children, youth, or adults. I also invited special guest speakers with whom they could have conversations related to classroom instruction or building relationships with families and other adults. In their evaluation statements, students said they loved the course, were excited by the experience, and marveled at how much they had learned. At the end of the twelve-week course in May, the students held a surprise baby shower for me. They invited LaGuardia's president, Dr. Joseph Shenker, associate dean of student services Jeri Minter, and our guest speakers, who all joined the festivities. With numerous baby gifts and heartfelt wishes, I headed home with indelible memories of an inspiring experience with my amazing students.

Reflecting on my initial LaGuardia experience, I discovered how much I had enjoyed working with the paraprofessionals; they were so eager to learn and so appreciative of this opportunity for personal and professional development; simultaneously they brought enormous life and work experiences to enrich the class. We bonded. On June 4, less than two weeks after the course ended, our first of three sons, Yussuf, was born. Ismail and I, family and friends were all excited to welcome our adorable baby. Three years earlier I had invited my mother, who still lived and worked in Jamaica, to join me in New York City, so she was ready to assist us in caring for Yussuf. About two weeks after giving birth, I received a call from LaGuardia inviting me to interview for the full-time position as coordinator of the Education Associates Program.

Recalling those steep stairs at the Rawson Street Station, I did not feel strong enough to reach LaGuardia. An arrangement was made for me to be interviewed by the chair of Social Sciences, Dr. Dan Erlich, whose apartment was within my Upper West Side community. I approached his apartment with some apprehension. Having worked with faculty at Hunter College, I didn't feel quite prepared for the probing theoretical and research questions that I anticipated he would ask. As we talked, however, I learned that Dan was not at all knowledgeable about the program and had no questions for me, so having taught the paraprofessionals, I was able to share with him my positive experiences with them as engaged learners.

MEETING WITH DEAN ANN MARCUS

Although Dan promised to get back to me with more information, I did not hear from him. However, shortly after our meeting, I received another call from the college, inviting me to meet with Dean Ann Marcus. During my four years working as a young professional in the US, I had met some really terrific individuals and colleagues who had all worked for many years honing their craft. My meeting with Dean Marcus was an unforgettable experience. In addition to her warmth and wonderful sense of humor, she was young, attractive, smart, and politically astute. I felt immediately comfortable talking with her, and so, when she offered me the position, beginning in August, I was candid that I had no administrative experience and was a social worker who counseled individuals and groups. Ann responded reassuringly, "Oh, you will learn; there's nothing to administration!"

I was so moved by her confidence in me that I accepted her offer and left our meeting feeling excited and looking forward to beginning my new role in August. Since I had been on a faculty line at Hunter, I was hired as an assistant professor in the Social Science Department at LaGuardia and coordinator of the Education Associate Program. I soon learned that the chair who had initially interviewed me had since been replaced. These shifts were happening across the college, partly to ensure that people were in the roles where they would be most effective. Dan later became director of Institutional Research, for which he was perfectly suited. The Social Science Department now needed new faculty and courses for the students enrolling in September. The new chair requested that I review and select résumés of applicants to be interviewed. Most of the resumes were sent to LaGuardia from the Board of Higher Education, then located at East Eightieth Street.

I developed as many social science courses as possible, even as I was preparing to welcome a new group of paraprofessionals, and to design an educational program for them. Based on my sociology/social work background and the courses that I had enjoyed as a college freshman, I prepared several course descriptions, including "Introduction to Sociology," "History of Immigration," "Comparative Religions," and others that remained in the department for several years.

The air at LaGuardia was electrifying and inspiring. New faculty were taken on a helicopter ride over Long Island City and Astoria to familiarize them with the geographical community, all arranged by Dr. Janet Lieberman. Everyone appeared excited and happy to be in this young institution. Some professionals, like Associate Dean Jeri Minter, came from the NYC Board of Education, while others, like Dorrie Williams, associate dean of Cooperative Education, and Ted Demetriou, faculty, came from the private sector.

Dr. Joseph Shenker was only twenty-nine years old when he was appointed president of LaGuardia Community College. He was then among the youngest college presidents ever appointed. He brought from East Eightieth Street the team that had worked with him on the design of Community College #9. They were Dean Ann Marcus; Sheila Gordon, associate dean of Cooperative Education; Marty Moed, dean of the college; and Mary Ryan, director of personnel. Dr. Freeman Sleeper was soon hired as dean of faculty.

From the beginning President Shenker saw LaGuardia's mission as providing access and opportunity to diverse and underserved populations. He also promoted his brilliant vision of a One College concept; that all divisions, including Continuing Education, were equal parts of the whole. Collaboration and innovation across divisions, therefore, were to be collegewide values, a very unusual strategy in higher education. But then, Dr. Shenker was an inspiring and transformative leader. He developed important community relationships that worked well for LaGuardia. As a strategic thinker, he was committed not only to strengthening the geographical community through creativity and innovation but also to increasing diversity, social justice, and equity in education.

Among the early innovations were: LaGuardia as a comprehensive Cooperative Education college; the one-college concept; creative names for departments, for example, "Language and Culture" instead of "English and Humanities," and a "Division of Natural Environment" instead of "Science and Mathematics"; the quarter system, where students could attend college year round; and "intensive" courses based on experiential learning or learning by doing, combined with weekly seminars. Among those innovative intensives was "A History of New York City," developed and taught by Prof. Richard Lieberman and his colleagues.

When I began the fall semester in 1971, some 125 students were enrolled in the Education Associates program. As a new administrator, I thought that I should handle all the coordination, student advising, counseling, and general administration by myself. The work was engaging, creative, and fun, and I was thrilled and eager to use all my social work knowledge to build relationships, to listen, to learn, and then to act. Besides, I reached out to my new colleagues to share information about the program and to interest them in teaching the courses I had designed. These relationships and bridges were being built across all divisions and departments throughout the college.

Not only did I feel the excitement that permeated this amazing college community but I felt very much included, and that I was an active participant in the process of the college coming into its own, and creating its unique identity as a Cooperative Education institution. With a steady stream of significant grant funding, innovative programming continued within LaGuardia, including the development of Middle College, International High School, and the Transfer programs, all of which were initiated by Dr. Janet Lieberman. Janet invited me to serve on the advisory committee for the Transfer Program funded by the Ford Foundation under Franklin Thomas's leadership, and other foundations that had a tremendously positive impact on its students and faculty, and, later, on all the other four-year selective institutions that participated, such as New York University.

Faculty from the partner colleges spoke about being energized and challenged by the community college students, often older and more focused than the typical freshmen. LaGuardia's faculty Gil Muller, John Chaffee, Cecilia Macheski, Joan Greenbaum, and others could attest to the LaGuardia students' newly found feelings of confidence and pride that they had successfully completed a very rigorous program, initially held at Vassar College during the first summer. Having succeeded in the summer program, many of the students transferred to a four-year college prior to completing their LaGuardia degree.

Another innovative idea, especially for this new community college, and spearheaded by Dr. Shenker and Janet Lieberman, was the creation of the LaGuardia Archives, which thrives today under the expert supervision of Dr. Richard Lieberman, historian, humanist, and amazing storyteller. Richard's astute and capable leadership was supported by an archives advisory committee whose members included Judge Milton Mullin, now deceased, former city council speaker Peter Vallone, and other city leaders. Together, these individuals had accumulated a wealth of experience and knowledge about the administrations and personalities of NYC mayors and other key government officials, most of which became available through the archives. The archives became a significant component of the college, and a rich resource for anyone needing information on NYC mayors and other politicians.

As a member of this advisory committee, I met the experts on New York City's mayors and listened to their awesome stories about each mayor's style of governing and the strategies they utilized to achieve their political and social goals. Richard facilitated the luncheon discussions and was also intrigued by the stories told but always kept the focus on ensuring that the archives was a budget item within the city council. Many of the advisory committee members had close connections to the city council and so were advocates for the archives.

Meanwhile, under Dean Marcus's leadership, the Division of Continuing Education was successful each year in garnering grant funding to provide a diversity of programs for underserved populations. Through our frequent conversations, I also gained an understanding of how higher education and academia worked. Then, sometime between 1972 and 1973, Dean Marcus invited me to bring my paraprofessional program into the Division of Continuing Education from the Social Science Department. I was delighted to join Continuing Education, since Ann had actually hired me, and I admired her straightforward, easy-to-relate-to manner and quick sense of humor.

At the time I had no idea that this move would shape my future professional role in academia, nor did I see this move as relevant for any future career advancement. Consciously, I was content with the position, which to me, offered security and a relatively good salary, and I was doing "good work," meaning that I was helping a significant group of adults to advance in their careers and in their lives. I don't recall thinking long term in those early days. Enjoying the work in which I was immediately involved, getting to know my students, and ensuring that only the most caring, thoughtful, and knowledgeable faculty were hired to teach them were my main goals. However, the move did, indeed, change the trajectory of my professional journey.

Continuing Education: The LaGuardia Model

In my new division, Ann advocated for me to have a secretary and to obtain a counselor for my students. I was able to hire Dorothy Myack, my very loyal secretary, and Rick Holmes as counselor. As a result, our students received increased guidance, while I focused on promoting and advocating for the program both internally and externally. Our students felt so welcomed and supported that at our monthly CUNY-wide meetings with directors across all its campuses, LaGuardia's program soon stood out as the most successful model. Ann and I worked well together, and with her support, guidance, and good humor, I not only became an administrator but discovered that I actually enjoyed that role.

However, I soon ran into problems with the chair of one department, who complained to Ann that I had invited his faculty to teach without asking his permission. This was true. As all employees were housed in one building, I soon became familiar with faculty across divisions and would often meet them in the hallways or lunchrooms, where I would talk with them about my students and the program. Many were intrigued; they were often working with younger students who had many personal and academic needs, and although they enjoyed the interactions with their students, the opportunity to work with another distinct adult group was appealing.

Moreover, I knew that full-time faculty were allowed to teach one course as an adjunct each semester, so I didn't think I had to request permission. Anyway, when Ann communicated his displeasure to me, I called Dr. Groman, apologized for my omission, and promised to inform him prior to inviting any of his faculty to teach. He accepted my apology, and thereafter I consulted with him prior to hiring any member of his faculty. Dr.

Groman was the only faculty to address me formally as "Mrs. Khan" during my seventeen years at LaGuardia.

Adult students, especially the paraprofessionals, were usually appreciative of the opportunity to study for a degree, that they inspired the faculty teaching them. As a result, most faculty enjoyed teaching these adults. They worked hard, were diligent and eager to learn; they also had little time to waste, since they were working full-time and had families to support. The very first students to graduate from LaGCC were the paraprofessionals. A small ceremony was held at the college, and about five students who had accumulated previous college credits received their diplomas from President Shenker.

Now working directly with Ann, I had many opportunities to observe that she handled challenges with intelligence, thoughtfulness, and confidence. She always seemed to have a sensible solution to problems. I was once privy to the professional manner in which she terminated a partnership that no longer benefited both partners equally. Our partner, a bank officer, intended to reduce his contribution to an existing joint program while requiring more work from the college. After explaining the various activities required for the program's success and seeing there was no room for negotiation, Ann was straightforward in stating why his proposed plan would not work for the college, thanked him for initially supporting the program, and concluded the discussion.

Soon thereafter I had to learn how to write grants. After the first division's grant writer returned my initial attempt with red ink all over the page and with not one helpful comment, I did not attempt to write another proposal until years later, when Judy McGaughey became assistant dean to Dean Gussie Kappner, who had succeeded Ann as dean, and Judy actually showed me how to prepare a proposal. Since that time, I have written many proposals to develop and implement or expand my numerous programs.

THE PROGRAM FOR DEAF ADULTS

In 1974, while acknowledging the success of the Education Associates Program, Ann indicated that I now needed another program. Naturally, I was surprised and wondered why, since the Education Associates program was doing so well. We were preparing over 125 paraprofessionals for career advancement in education. Ann explained that because grant-funded programs were never permanent, keeping alert to local and national funding trends was critical for future program development and growth. That was important information for someone like me so new in an administrative role. Silently, I couldn't help wondering how this young person could already know so much about public policies and program management. However, I was always appreciative of Ann's thoughtful guidance and caring that really ensured my success as an administrator.

But Ann did not stop with her explanation. Her next question was, "What do you know about deafness?"

"Nothing," I responded.

"Well, let's go find out from the experts!" she offered.

Within two weeks, Ann and I traveled to Washington, DC's, Gallaudet College, the only liberal arts college in the world for deaf people, to learn all that we could about deafness in one full day. Today, the college is known as Gallaudet University. There, we received a condensed seminar about the academic needs of deaf adults from an enthusiastic Dean Tom Mayes, who was deaf, as well as the holistic approach we would need to develop a successful program. Another important message for us in our first direct encounter with sign language interpreters was to always look at the deaf person, and not the interpreter. The interpreter was a conduit for communication.

Following our Gallaudet visit, Ann and I met with members of the NYC deaf community, formed an advisory committee, and began planning an educational program for deaf adults. Our first event was an open house held at the CUNY Graduate Center's theater to introduce LaGuardia's programs to the deaf community. The event was successful, with over one hundred deaf adults in attendance. The advisory committee then recommended that the college hire a deaf professional to coordinate program activities. With President Shenker's approval, the advisory committee became the search committee staffed by one college representative. This was a most unusual situation, but it underscored the level of the college's commitment.

Glenn Anderson was a PhD candidate at NYU when we hired him to lead the Program for Deaf Adults (PDA). Glenn had been conducting research on the deaf population for several years while working with Dr. Jerome Schein, an expert on deafness and director of NYU's Deafness Research and Training Center. Glenn's research-based approach to program development first identified all the barriers to program participation and then listed the criteria to develop a successful program. We worked well together, and along with

Glenn, I attended many social events organized by and for deaf individuals, met many leaders within the deaf community, and gained knowledge about deaf culture and sign language.

While working at LaGuardia, Glenn became the first deaf African American male in the USA to receive a PhD. Already famous in the deaf community as an excellent basketball player, Glenn effectively leveraged his popularity to promote the programs for deaf adults. Enrollment in the program soared. In 1981 a major federal grant from the US Department of Education allowed us to expand the program's capacity by significantly increasing staff and support services for deaf students across the college, thanks to program officer Dr. Joe Rosenstein.

With the ending of the federal grant in 1984, President Shenker's practical solution for the program's sustainability was the development of a strategy to bring Gov. Mario Cuomo to LaGuardia. This exciting event happened in 1985. After meeting with over a hundred deaf students, Governor Cuomo hailed the LaGuardia program as reflecting "education at its best [and the college as] . . . removing impediments and doing it marvelously well." He committed $150,000 to continue program activities. Soon after, a line item was created in the state's budget securing future funding. In addition, under the superb leadership of our human resources director, Dr. Marcia Keizs, former president at York College, LaGuardia successfully negotiated tax levy job titles for interpreters within CUNY, a major feat.

President Shenker's support for the deaf program was a key factor in its growth, visibility, and impact, because he usually mentioned the deaf program wherever he spoke. Although NYC Technical CC offered a few courses for deaf students, LaGuardia was the only college in NYC providing a comprehensive program of academic and support services for deaf students, a previously underserved population. Implementing this exemplary and extraordinary program was truly among my most inspiring program development experiences. In addition to the programs for deaf adults, an Interpreter Training Program also exists at LaGuardia.

The PDA offered me many opportunities for intimately learning about an entirely new cultural group whose language was that of signing. I enjoyed meeting, having many inspiring conversations with, and learning as much as was possible from both my new colleagues and members of the deaf community. The existence of a Black deaf community and culture was especially noteworthy. Besides reading on deafness, I had hired competent staff, most of whom were deaf. My practical knowledge about deafness came from them, and they were my best teachers. One staff member, Dorothy Pakula, a wise and marvelous woman with a great sense of humor, shared deaf jokes with me and provided insight into how deaf people perceived hearing people. She often reminded me that I had admitted her into the paraprofessional program without realizing that she was deaf.

I recalled that she had been so effusive and engaging in our interview that I thought she just spoke differently. It was also Dorothy who encouraged me to offer a noncredit course on "idioms for deaf students." She explained that hearing people would understand phrases like "It's raining cats and dogs outside"; deaf people would be puzzled at not seeing cats and dogs. The course was offered. Dorothy was LaGuardia's first deaf graduate, having entered through the paraprofessional program in 1971.

During those early years, the Program for Deaf Adults received increasing visibility, including an article in the *New York Times* and several articles within and external to CUNY. I was thrilled when, in 1987, my article "Educating Deaf Adults: The LaGuardia Community College Model" was published as "A Working Paper" in the well-known *Community Service Catalyst*. Then, in the same year, I was a presenter on deafness with Dr. Dolores Perrin in a Career Education Conference in Nashville, Tennessee. In 2016, twenty-six years after I left LaGuardia, the Program for Deaf Adults celebrated its fortieth anniversary at the college.

The period from the early seventies to the late eighties was one of rapid program and personnel growth for the Division of Adult and Continuing Education. During that period, Dean Ann Marcus, my supervisor, left LaGuardia for New York University, where she served in increasingly higher positions and played a key role in the university's expansion. She eventually became dean and professor for the School of Education. Under her administration, NYU received the largest gift ever to a School of Education, allowing Ann to also create an endowment in support of faculty development, doctoral fellowships, and research.

That period was also a very productive time for me, my area of Community Services, and the larger Division of Adult and Continuing Education that was developing and implementing programs for other adult populations, for example, the Taxi Driver Institute, the Extended Day Program for working adults, and programs for women. During the 1987–1988 academic year, the division served over 21,000 students in nondegree and continuing education courses.

However, amidst LaGuardia's successes and growth in its student population, the City University of New York (LaGuardia was one of its eighteen colleges) was faced with severe challenges, including drastic budget reductions, a two-week furlough for all CUNY faculty, and the addition of tuition for the first time in CUNY's history—all while implementing the open admissions process. Being furloughed, all employees were told to report to the NYC Department of Employment to file for unemployment. At once, my Jamaican lenses, always nearby, were in operation, and I felt uncomfortable with the idea of applying for unemployment benefits. After all, I had been working since age sixteen, work was so important to me. In my Jamaican days, applying for unemployment would probably have been quite embarrassing; that is, *if* the country had embraced an unemployment benefits plan.

So, on my way to the New York unemployment office, I hoped that no one I knew would see me entering that building. However, on entering that office space, to my surprise, I saw all my colleagues lined up, laughing and talking with each other. I felt such relief and so much better sharing this experience with them. They were neither embarrassed nor ashamed, but if there were any emotional reactions, it was more like frustration that they had to spend an hour or so to complete the appropriate forms. The furlough ended, I was relieved, and we all returned to continue our work activities at the college.

Despite the challenges of a furlough, under President Shenker's steady and astute leadership, LaGuardia survived. With approval from the Board of Higher Education, the college reverted to the more traditional departments, and chairs were then elected to lead each of the seven new departments.

CHAPTER 13

RAISING OUR FAMILY
IN NEW YORK CITY

In addition to developing my professional skills and moving up the higher education ladder in the seventies, Ismail and I were simultaneously raising our family. Prior to the birth of our second son, we needed more living space and so decided to purchase a larger apartment, since we both loved living in Manhattan. Since we were both employed, we decided to live on one salary for a year, while saving the other salary to use as the down payment on a house or an apartment. We were fortunate to find a brownstone, conveniently located in our neighborhood, moved in 1973, and have enjoyed living there ever since. By 1979 we had three sons.

Within the context of American society, and with the fact that many of our close friends had immigrated from other countries, including Barbados, Germany, and Japan, our three sons grew up in a multicultural household in which they were exposed to a range of individuals, stories, and events. Because Ismail and I also came from former commonwealth countries, India and Jamaica, we shared a few of the same values, certain items, foods, and spices, such as curry, or at least were aware of those unique to the English, Jamaica, or India. In both our cultures, we were familiar with soaps like Palmolive and Lux, were both accustomed to living with extended families, stopping by our relatives unannounced, and not having had structured play activities as children. We were fortunate too that my mother lived nearby and was delighted to look after all her grandchildren, since Ismail and I both worked in full-time positions. He was employed as an urban planner with the NYC Department of City Planning, and I was still at LaGuardia CC when our sons, Yussuf, Javaid, and Nafees, were born in 1971, 1974, and 1979 respectively.

Prior to the births of our sons, Ismail and I had several discussions around the religion in which our children would be raised. I thought a lot about my positive early church experiences as a young person. I had a place where I knew I could quietly reflect on my life and my behavior, soothe any upsetting feelings, and return home refreshed. I therefore felt it was important for our children to have those options and to believe in a higher power. However, having been exposed to a range of religious beliefs in college, my vision of religion was now more universal. I now understood the purpose and role of religion in society, how personal religion could be, and was now more flexible regarding religious choice. Although not a practicing Muslim, Ismail did not drink alcohol or eat pork, neither of which presented a problem for me. I had decided as a young person in Jamaica that I would not drink alcohol even though rum was a Jamaican staple, and pork was not usually on my menu, so together we agreed that the children would be raised Muslims. I also reasoned that we would be imparting our combined values to them, so I felt secure in our decision.

This reasoning didn't prevent me from being gripped by a sudden fear one day near to the birth of our first son, around imparting values to children. How does one really instill values? How could we be sure that we would be successful in imparting our values based on doing good, being kind, caring, and having integrity while developing an independent spirit? Ismail was his usual calm and objective self and reassured me that it's by our behavior and relationship to our children that the values are learned. Of course, intellectually, I knew that, but that was before I had to face my reality of being a parent.

Over time my anxiety lessened, we became parents, and together agreed that our sons would be raised as Muslims with the understanding that they were free to choose their spiritual/religious direction in adulthood. Although Ismail took our sons to the mosque when they were still young, those visits stopped after a few years. We developed our own traditions; for instance, Christmas brunch, a Jamaican feast, was always celebrated at my sister Hope's nearby apartment, while Christmas dinner was enjoyed with our friends Helma and Norton Reid, who provided a German meal along with a traditional German candle-lit Christmas tree that I enjoyed viewing. During January we celebrated with Chand and Subbash Raswant, our friends from

India, who treated us to a rich array of Indian dishes, while Thanksgiving, a nonreligious holiday, was always celebrated in our home, featuring the dining table covered with an attractive assortment of food and, later, desserts brought by our guests. Ismail always found such pleasure in being a host.

Thanksgiving brought many of our friends together, and so our sons were exposed early on to a healthy mix of friends from many countries and careers. In addition to the friends mentioned earlier, there were also Victoria Horsford, management consultant; sisters Alisa, Marianna, and Melissa Chiles; Nisha Chhabra and Rahul Raswant; and others, all like family and too many to name. I also maintained connection with a group of Jamaican friends like Dr. Joy Wellington, theater devotee, at whose lively annual dinners in her Harlem brownstone I was sure to meet Megan Mclaughlin, DSW and the first Black female CEO to lead the Federation of Protestant Welfare Agency in NYC. Trinidadian friend Hazel Carter, PhD, received her BA from the UWI in Jamaica and is faculty in education at the City College of New York. Our friends represented, in retrospect, a quiet support system for each other in our adopted country.

It was also important for Ismail and me that our sons have the best education possible, and because we were not intimately familiar with public schools at that time, we decided to enroll all three sons in independent schools. Besides providing them with a supportive and loving home and the best possible educational environments, I fervently hoped that our sons would have a positive impact and influence in whatever field they chose to work in as adults. I hoped for them to become change agents and to be there to inspire and help lift up others. For me personally, those were important values.

Our sons also all have Middle Eastern names. I had always been fond of those names from stories, and from some people I knew in Jamaica. I was also attracted to names that had meanings. We were both comfortable when Ismail chose Yussuf's name in memory of a beloved brother who passed away when he was about ten years old. Later, we discussed and decided on the names of our other sons, Javaid and Nafees. I liked their sounds and meanings. Javaid's name is of Persian origin but is a popular Pakistani name meaning "long or eternal life" while Nafees's means "precious."

While we worked, my mother took care of all three sons and their two cousins after school. Our sons loved and enjoyed their grandmother, found her to be hilarious, and now share numerous memories of her with much laughter and good humor, often imitating her Jamaican accent and sayings.

Nevertheless, we were raising American-born sons in NYC where customs were different. One son once questioned why he and his brother had to stay with their grandmother when all his friends had babysitters. After I explained that their grandmother obtained much satisfaction from having them with her, and was so happy to share her cooking and her stories with them, I never heard that question again. In both our cultures and during our eras, Ismail and I had experienced our families having relatives or friends nearby to assist as needed.

And of course, having three sons of mixed races, Indian and Black, in the USA necessitated many discussions around race in our household. Our sons brought home situations where, for example, they went to a bookstore in our neighborhood and were followed by security, and how this experience angered them. We listened to all their experiences and had open discussions about the racial realities in America, and possible actions to keep them safe, while also looking at their role in defusing any such challenging situation. Ismail often related that as Muslims, he and his family were minorities among the Hindu majority in his Central India district. However, a level of tolerance existed among the Northern provinces until Partition in 1947, when those Muslims and other minority religious groups fearing persecution left those provinces to settle in Pakistan, while Hindus living in Pakistan did the reverse and moved to India. The horror of the loss of hundreds of lives during that terrible period was captured in the 1982 film *Gandhi*.

Altogether, over two million people, from both sides, lost their lives during this violent transition. Ismail's experience and his reading of global history had led him to conclude that minorities everywhere survive at "the goodwill of the majority." That is his position. So Ismail understood the reality of being a minority in one's country, wherever that country may be. A civil engineer and economist by training, an urban planner with a love of literature and an interest in Sufism during his early adulthood, Ismail was a gentle and kind individual, a visionary, and a quiet intellectual with an intriguing complexity. We were astrological opposites, Virgo and Pisces, which worked well in dealing with challenges; our combined approaches coalesced to arrive at practical resolutions.

Ismail has always had a different perspective in our discussions, which expanded and enhanced my and our sons' worldview. These discussions have continued among us over the years, with each adult son taking college courses in both Islamic and African American history, and later engaging more intentionally with the history of the African Diaspora, with each one developing his own ways of addressing racial disparities in the USA, through their work in education and the business world. Ismail is a devoted husband and father. I was drawn to Indian music, and he enjoyed translating ghazals for me, and explaining their Arabic and, later, Persian poetic origins. Those were special moments for me, as the poems' echoes of pain, loss, and love were reflected in his voice. Although ghazals were sung by many poets and singers, we both enjoyed those by Ghalib, the famous Urdu poet.

My mother saw Ismail's love and care for our sons and adored him, as did my sisters. Ismail related positively to everyone with whom he came in contact and was always ready to be of assistance. As a family, we ate dinner together every night, even when I was late coming home from work; they waited for me. During dinner he would tell us stories about interesting or humorous characters from his childhood, his family interactions in Pakistan, or books that he had read. When Yussuf and Javaid left the dining table to complete their homework, Nafees, the youngest, and his father remained to continue their discussion of history or his early life in India before Partition. Ismail took being a father very seriously. When they were young, he frequently shopped for their clothing and bemoaned the fact that variety and color were lacking among boys' clothing. I was comfortable saving our older sons' clothing for the younger ones, but Ismail recalled being the middle child who did not like to wear his older brothers' clothes, so he wanted each of his sons to have their individual new clothing.

In high school all three sons were, at different times, designated drivers for their friends after parties, since they did not drink alcohol. During both high school and college, Javaid's friends would sleep over in our home. On awakening, as many as six, seven, or eight young men, and sometimes young women, were greeted at the dining table with a mound of French toast, scrambled eggs, and orange juice, all prepared by Ismail, to whom feeding relatives and friends was very important. On Ismail's retirement after fifty years in city planning, Javaid prepared a book about his father with the following introduction[1]:

> Mohammad Ismail Khan is my father. And, he will be the first person to tell you how lucky that makes him ... As we all know how smart he is, it must be so.
>   My father's profound intellect is well known by all. Engage him in conversation and you will find there is little he does not know something about—.
> . . . . . This characteristic was infused at an early age. Long before the Tiger

Mom, as a young Ismail set off to take his country's national exam, my grand-father told him simply, "if you don't pass, don't come home." And as gifted as his mind is, he is equally proficient with his hands. Ask him to show you how to make a paper airplane, or a slingshot out of a rubber innertube. Or, simply look around the house at all of the bookshelves he designed and crafted.

Less famous, however, is his comedic side. My father has a fantastic sense of humor and loves listening to and laughing at his sons' jokes. He also has a wonderfully mischievous side.

I like to describe my father as a great paradox—a simple man, who is extremely complex. . . . .Yet, his wants are simple and usually exactly as they appear: time with family, an opportunity to help anyone around him, and the hope for happiness. . . . .always in others first.

A fitting description of Ismail. In the meantime, at home, our sons under-stood that being respectful to others, and likewise to themselves, and having good manners, very important in Jamaica as noted earlier, were very impor-tant values as they developed into adulthood. Those lessons have remained with them as adults and are also visible in our four grandchildren.

I am constantly learning from our sons, who have accumulated a wealth of knowledge not only from their personal and educational experiences but have integrated learnings from immigrant parents from two distinct cultures, their Jamaican grandmother's deep influence, their individual experiences as men of mixed racial backgrounds in America, and the broader American culture, into their being. All three sons are good-natured, intelligent, thought-ful, and humorous, and each one has worked with youth programs during his high school years at Horace Mann High School. They care about equity in life and about helping others succeed.

In reflecting on my journey in life, I often wonder whether Ismail and I, com-ing from two such geographically distant countries, were destined to meet, to build a totally new life together in this third country, America, and to prepare our children to live meaningful lives, with integrity and a social justice focus.

Our Three Sons: Yussuf, Javaid, Nafees

After attending River Park Nursery school in our neighborhood, Yussuf entered Bank Street School for Children at age five. He was a very active baby and young child who talked and walked by seven months and was reading by age three. He adjusted well in his new school, so I was surprised when I received a recommendation from his teacher that we provide a reading tutor for him because he wasn't reading as expected. Upon questioning his teacher further, I learned that Yussuf had told her that he couldn't read. When I asked Yussuf why he had done so, since he was an excellent reader, he explained that teachers would call on him if they knew that he could read!

Following his Bank Street graduation, Yussuf attended Horace Mann High School, where he had a positive school experience and further developed his love for football even though he was slenderly built. He also played basketball and ran track. In addition, Yussuf holds HM's record for the longest touchdown run in the school's history (ninety-eight yards), which earned him a photo in the school's newspaper. During the summers and vacations, Yussuf worked in a neighborhood bed-and-bath shop, where his bent for business, including excellent customer relations, was so obvious that the owner often left him to manage the store when he had external appointments.

Yussuf's love for sports continued at Trinity College in Hartford, where he played football, indoor and outdoor track and was named a Tri captain and Tri MVP for track & field in his junior and senior years. After graduating from Trinity College, Yussuf completed a management training program at Chase Bank, where he worked for many years; however, having played in three sports, his heart was in sports marketing. Yussuf earned a certificate in that field from NYU and worked at ESPN and several sports-related startups over many years. He was frequently invited as a guest lecturer in college classes to talk about a range of topics in marketing and media.

Along with a relatable personality and a quick wit and humor, he also has a social conscience and used his various positions to reach out to underserved youth groups. While working at College Sports TV in 2006, for example, Yussuf invited ten Black and Latino students attending HEAF, a college prep program in Harlem, as interns in a career mentoring initiative in television media, where they learned how to film, produce, and edit material. When the film *Black Panther* appeared, he had his then-company rent a Bronx theater so its Black and brown youth could attend free of charge. In addition, the young people received a surprise welcome by Bronx Borough president Reuben Diaz. Given his service to youth in the Bronx, Yussuf received an award from the Bronx Borough president in 2019.

He also produced a film that was screened in NYC in 2018 on a Jamaican bodybuilder, Shawn Rhoden. Shawn won the 2018 Mr. Olympia contest by defeating the seven-time winner. Yussuf now teaches courses in sports mar-keting, communication, and technology at two New Jersey colleges and a NYC university. More recently he started his own digital online magazine focused on urban sports and entertainment. Yussuf received his MBA in media management from Metropolitan College of NY in 2014. He is married to Judy Figuero, an educator, and they have two sons, Dante, age sixteen, and Kaiden, age thirteen.

As a baby Javaid was playful and happy and slept well. I often had to check to ensure that he was fine, since his sleep was so long and peaceful. As a young child, he was helpful, cheerful, and independent, while displaying a unique way with words that heralded his later adolescent and adult humor and wit. He also had a special personality appeal that had strangers gravitating toward him on our walks or travels. In elementary school his teacher wrote, "Javaid is becoming a serious academic worker . . . organized, responsible and consci-entious . . . and an enthusiastic group member." His graduation speech from Bank Street's School for Children was selected to lead off all the graduation speeches in 1988. Javaid's excellent writing skills were noticed and supported by his English teachers at Horace Mann High School, where his intellectual development combined with a wonderful sense of humor was quite promi-nent. While in high school, he worked in leadership positions at Wave Hill in the Bronx, Bank Street's Liberty Partnerships Program, and LaGuardia CC Summer Science youth program. Children and youth loved being around Javaid so much that I dubbed him the good Pied Piper. As valedictorian of his high school graduating class, Javaid delivered a talk full of such good humor, wit, and intelligence that it was talked about for a long time.

At Wesleyan University, Javaid majored in sociology, played in the steel band, sang in the gospel choir, played basketball, and was often a radio host at nights. His sociology professor wrote that "Javaid . . . listens well, makes valuable contributions, draws others into the discussion, and emerges as a leader. . . . has a highly developed sense of when it is necessary to take charge, to delegate or to step back."[2] Following graduation, Javaid taught English and was director of diversity at Poly Prep Country Day School, was a group leader to New Zealand with the Experiment in International Living Program, recommended by his friend Sheldon Gilbert, and worked with the nonprofit Girls and Boys project.

Javaid received a master's degree in School Leadership from NYU and served as the upper school coordinator at Bank Street School for Children for four years before becoming director of Horace Mann's Middle School in

2019. Javaid is passionate about working with middle school students as well as his diversity work; his love for comedy and humor makes all conversations with him an inspirational and fun learning experience. He relishes contributing to someone's happiness and has also remained connected to his school friends and their families. Javaid is a faculty member with the New York State Association of Independent Schools/NYSAIS Experienced Teachers Institute, for which he was well prepared, having worked in independent schools for over fifteen years.

Javaid's love for music propelled him into becoming, like his older brother, a skilled, popular, and amazing DJ, during and after college. His record collection is musically diverse and extensive. He would often travel to distant places to purchase oldies and/or special editions records, sometimes accompanied by his father. As a youth Javaid was always full of ideas and was the planner for most of our major family trips, for example, to Busch Gardens, while still in high school. He even planned a surprise vacation for his father and me to the Bahamas once he began to work. Javaid is married to Gillian Todd, a Jamaican and director of Dalton School's First Program. They met as undergraduates at Wesleyan University and are now parents of Justin, sixteen, and Laila, eleven.

Nafees, our third son, was born when fathers were allowed in the delivery room, so he was the only son to be handed to Ismail immediately on his arrival. When arriving home after four days, Nafees was welcomed with excitement by his two brothers. They could hardly leave him, played, and developed a loving relationship with him. Ismail's ability to always think ahead led us to purchase, in 1974, an old hay barn with three sides that he termed "a handyman's delight" on several acres of land in Southfield, Western Massachusetts. He knew the importance of providing an environment where our children could play and explore safely in the outdoors. Nafees was now able to share in his family's enjoyment in the country. And that barn over time was transformed into a home that provided for many enjoyable summers with Mama, our cousins Courtney and Elsa Mair and their daughters, Tasha and Nadia, and friends who frequently spent weekends with us. We looked forward to breakfasts when Elsa, a nurse by training, prepared a full Jamaican breakfast with boiled green bananas, ackee and saltfish, codfish fritters, and other food that stirred fond memories of our growing-up years in Jamaica. Our sons loved having Elsa around because, being also athletic, she always engaged them in physical activities.

Nafees did not attend nursery school but went directly to the "threes" classroom at Bank Street School. Since Yussuf's and Javaid's adjustments to nursery school were very smooth following their positive preschool experiences at the River Park Nursery School founded by artist, progressive educator, and activist Estelle Tambak, we expected the same easy adjustment of Nafees when he began PreK at Bank Street. But that was not to happen. Perhaps he was missing the nursery school experienced by his brothers. Or maybe he had been having such a happy time with his grandmother during those early years. Whatever the reason, he was not happy on the first day of school. He cried when I left and continued this reaction for over two weeks. Ismail and I took turns taking Nafees to school, but that made no difference. His response was totally unexpected, and we had no idea what to do. Fortunately, he had a very patient and understanding teacher in Paul Schwartz, who provided the needed comforting.

I had to attend an out-of-state conference on the second weekend of his school. On my return, I took Nafees to school that Monday, dreading the anticipated crying. He walked into the classroom, and to my surprise, there were no tears. From that day onward, there was no more crying in the classroom from Nafees, and he looked forward to being in school. I was so relieved but wondered about the sudden change in behavior. I have often reminded Nafees of that story over the years. My hunch is that he probably felt that I left because he cried so much, and stopped crying so that I wouldn't leave home again. Whatever was the reason, I was a much-relieved and happy mother again.

As he developed, Nafees's interests were distinctly his own. While his brothers were engaged in sports, music, and other extracurricular activities, Nafees enjoyed watching television cartoons and nature documentaries, playing video games, visiting his close friends, and reading the *Annual NYTimes Almanacs*. He developed close friendships at Bank Street, enjoyed his school experience, and after graduation was invited by Mrs. Norma Asnes to join volunteers on the 1992 Clinton/Gore Democratic Family Bus to visit Older Americans in Philadelphia. Nafees was one of several children photographed in Marlo Thomas's book, *Free to Be . . . a Family*. His action photographs were also in a children's book of sounds, *Rat-a-Tat, Pitter Pat*, by Alan Benjamin, with pictures by Margaret Miller. His sounds were "slurp" and "burp."

Early on, Nafees displayed an intellectual bent and, according to him, collected "random facts." Like his brothers, he graduated from Horace Mann

High School, and later Tufts University, where his scholarly bent emerged as a sociology major. Upon graduation Nafees worked with a youth program for about three years at LaGuardia Community College. Then he and his three closest friends from Bank Street decided they wanted to start a charter school based on a particular social studies curriculum, but knew they needed graduate degrees. So each enrolled in a graduate program to prepare for such a major undertaking. The charter school did not materialize, but it was an incentive that motivated the friends to embark on graduate studies. Chris enrolled in law school, Rashaan and Evan enrolled in Bank Street College, and Nafees enrolled in Emory University's Graduate School of Education.

Within two months Nafees was invited by his professors to enroll in their PhD program. When he called to share that news, I was absolutely thrilled and appreciated the fact that his quiet intellect was recognized by his professors. On my visit to a class where Nafees served as a teaching assistant, his very supportive advisor and mentor, Dr. Carole L. Hahn, told me how his knowledge and intellect were initially so apparent that her team decided that he was the most appropriate candidate of several applicants who had actually applied for the doctoral scholarship award. Nafees received his PhD in Educational Studies from Emory University in 2013. A critical thinker and an intellectual activist, his dissertation focused on how slavery was represented in textbooks in the US and Brazil. He also became involved with the preparation of a database on the transatlantic slave trade and is now a consultant on slavery with McGraw-Hill Education, and a member of the African Diaspora Consortium. An assistant professor of education at Clemson University, South Carolina, until 2022, Nafees served on several committees, was especially sought after as their advisor by African American graduate students, and presented at academic conferences. He is currently working on a book with another colleague on the impact of a unique, progressive, integrated boarding school for bright, underprivileged youth in the seventies South, which positively affected the lives of the students, now adults.

Ismail and I are close to, and proud of, our sons, and I am a huge fan. I have felt that in addition to the influence of our family on their identity formation, and their development as well-mannered and responsible adults, each had a special gift that has propelled them all into being the confident, yet relatable, witty, humorous, and socially conscious individuals they have become. We are also proud of and close to our four delightful grandchildren, Justin, Laila, Dante, and Kaiden.

CHAPTER 14

Continuing Education's Community Connections

The Division of Adult and Continuing Education at LaGuardia CC continued to thrive. Now aware of trends, I was alert to the New York state education priorities and the funding available for those priorities. In addition, individuals and groups with available funding often invited us as a partner in providing college courses for their constituencies.

One such example was the National Congress of Neighborhood Women, in Williamsburg, Brooklyn. There the women invited the college to bring higher education into their community, which we did. When homeless families became the focus of attention, we collaborated with the New York Community Trust, which provided the necessary funds to develop the first college-based program for homeless heads of households in NYC. To engage homeless women for skills training, I visited several shelters to recruit them, but they were reluctant to come to the college, insistent that everyone would look at them and know they were homeless. So I invited two women to sit in a class with me and asked them to identify homeless students. They couldn't and so began to use the resources available to them on campus.

Before commuting to my work in Queens, I now had to take our two young sons to my mother's apartment, five blocks away, where she also cared for my sister Phillippa's two young children. Her experience in caring for our children was written up as a chapter entitled "Relative as Caregiver" in the book *Monday through Friday* by Jane Merrill Filstrup, and published by

Teachers College Press in 1982. Our connection to Jane Filstrup was made through the awesome Ruth Ann Stewart, whose young daughter, Allegra, was also being cared for by my mother. I was so proud of my mother's authentic description of childrearing practices in Jamaica during the interview. She was straightforward and comfortable in responding to the interviewer's questions.

Ruth Ann, an African American, was senior policy analyst for the arts, humanities, and social legislation at the Congressional Research Service. With her keen intellect, self-confidence, and natural leadership skills, Ruth Ann was a force for positive change wherever she worked. She understood the importance of policy and was soon known as a pioneer in the public arts policy area. She brought her vast experience and public policy knowledge as a faculty member to both Rutgers and New York Universities' public policy programs. Ruth Ann's many accomplishments as an inspiring leader and arts advocate were remembered at her memorial by her husband, author David Levering Lewis, an American historian and Pulitzer Prize winner for biography, and by her brother, friends, and colleagues at the Riverside Church in 2014.

Then, when the always smartly dressed Dr. Flora Mancuso, assistant dean at LaGuardia, learned about my morning routine, she offered to meet me in front of my mother's apartment around 8:30 each morning. Flora drove by Mama's building daily in taking her son to school. Sometimes I was late, but she would always be so calm, reassuring me that those were the only free and quiet moments she had each day, so she was happy to wait for me. We had many delightful conversations on our journey to Queens, solving a range of personal and professional problems during those short trips. Besides, Flora had once lived in Jamaica so we had something else in common to discuss. Flora was quite successful at LaGCC, became president at Hostos CC and, later, at another community college in New Jersey. She then decided to become a lawyer. I am sure that she remains a successful lawyer today.

A NEEDS ASSESSMENT OF WESTERN QUEENS

I was still on maternity leave in 1979 following the birth of our third son, Nafees, when Dean Kappner called. I knew immediately that I would be returning to work earlier than I had planned. I was enjoying my time with our new son and had hoped to stay home for four months this time. Sure enough, Dean Kappner, also known as Gussie, explained that the division had an opportunity to undertake a needs assessment, the results of which could assist the division and the college in meeting the needs of residents in the Western Queens community. My supervision of this project was needed, and how soon would I return to work? Although I wasn't quite ready, I understood that my service was needed, so Gussie and I agreed on a date, and I began to prepare for my return.

On my return I learned that LaGuardia and five other community colleges were invited by the American Association of Community and Junior Colleges, to participate in its Urban Demonstration Project, in January 1980. The goal was to strengthen the relationship between community colleges and their communities. Technical assistance and funding would be provided, usually powerful and positive incentives. The process leading up to the actual assessment required much coordination and was equally challenging and exciting.

With the assistance of Sister Edithann Kane, SND, and Sister Mary Gallagher, SC, both Roman Catholic nuns; the public opinion research expertise of Kane, Parsons, and Associates; participation from the college leadership, faculty, a community advisory committee; and the able assistance of Father Poulos, head of the Queens Greek Orthodox Church, we undertook the study of the needs of the Western Queens community achieving its eight objectives. This was a huge undertaking, using telephone calls, a questionnaire translated into Spanish and Greek, and in-person interviews.

Armed with data from the study, the college increased its marketing efforts to focus on career change for adults; increased the college's visibility through a variety of marketing strategies, such as attractive posters, shopping bags and so on; and initiated a number of joint college/community events, including conferences. The College for Children was developed following this extensive needs assessment. In addition to the publication of a full report in two volumes on the assessment process and outcomes, my article "A Community College Examines Its Community" was published in volume 11 of the *Community Education Journal*, in 1984.

Working in Continuing Education at LaGuardia Community College during the 1970s and 1980s involved outreach to a broad range of constituencies; as a result, I became acquainted with a large network of individuals and nonprofit programs across a variety of fields in New York City and New York State. I developed relationships with professionals from the state and local education departments, vocational education, nonprofit organizations, foundations, and program graduates.

I was invited to sit on several advisory groups, including the New York State Education Department Commissioner's Advisory Committee on Adult and Continuing Education, having been recommended by Dean Kappner, who had left LaGuardia to become (CUNY) University dean of Adult and Continuing Education. This committee was chaired by Dr. Tom Sobel, the very well liked and respected chancellor, New York State Education Department. I met educator and author Delores Lowe Friedman while serving on this committee.

Delores, an author, was a very outgoing, cheerful, and informative educator with whom I immediately connected. She was Barbadian by background and had been working with the state education department for many years. Soon after we met, Delores was hired as a faculty in early childhood at Kingsborough Community College, where she taught, wrote educational articles, and conducted staff development to improve practice in early childhood classrooms. Delores was an engaging and dynamic instructor. I once hired her as a staff developer for a group of paraprofessionals, and, sitting in on this session where she focused on supporting creativity in young children, I was impressed by her ability to simplify concepts and to make learning accessible to the range of adult learners present. Delores and I have remained friends over the years. Along with her educational publications, Delores has also published an engrossing novel, *Wildflowers*, about three girlfriends growing up in Brooklyn and their later complicated adult relationships. That story could be a powerful and culturally relevant film.

In the division I now worked closely with Dean Judith McGaughey and Dennis Berry, associate dean for budgets and administration, until he left for the US Department of Education to work with Gussie, by then assistant secretary for vocational and educational programs in the first Clinton administration. There was also Sandy Watson, a dynamic and experienced educator who developed nontraditional careers for women, the Family Institute and numerous programs for youth.

Sandy and I lunched frequently, discussing topics ranging from African American culture and history, to Caribbean culture, improving education for people of color, climate at LaGuardia, our families, and astrology, which we both found fascinating and useful in more fully understanding personalities. When I challenged her description of me as an activist, Sandy insisted that my activism was demonstrated through the programs that I developed and implemented. That was a new perspective for me to ponder. An astrologist and an activist by nature, Sandy was a very intelligent, progressive, and critical thinker, who was always focused on social justice issues. She was known as the "Conscience of LaGuardia," because if there was a hint of injustice done to any individual across the college, Sandy would be the first to speak up about that behavior.

At over six feet three inches tall, Sandy was not intimidated by individuals or their rank. She eventually became dean, reporting to the vice president for adult and continuing education. Sandy was a hard worker, thoroughly committed to implementing programs that uplifted individuals through job training or internships, and was really gifted in garnering government grants, enabling her to successfully implement transformative programs. Although Sandy reported to me, her mantra was "Fern never tried to supervise me" as the reason for our positive relationship.

Sandy retired from La Guardia a few years ago but, like me, remains connected to LaGCC through the LaGuardia Founders & Retirees Advisory Committee. I also served on the LaGuardia Archives Advisory Committee, chaired by Dr. Richard Lieberman, the knowledgeable historian, great storyteller, caring individual, and dear friend who sees something special in everyone's story and always remembers them.

CONTINUING EDUCATION: A STRATEGY FOR SOCIAL CHANGE?

The Division of Adult and Continuing Education (DACE) was the perfect vehicle for me to develop as an administrator. Its values in providing access and opportunity for underserved populations were in harmony with my personal values and background in social work. In addition to being more responsive, accessible, and low cost, continuing education programs allowed me to take risks, and to connect with and to engage individuals and communities in new ways, and were often the corridor to degree programs for students who may not have felt prepared for college. Indeed, given those incredible factors and strengths, LaGuardia's model for continuing education could serve as a most-effective strategy to advance social change and achieve equity in education.

Some of the division's programs were revenue producing; others were funded by local, state, or federal governments or foundations. The division's objective was always to achieve a balance between tuition-based programs and grant-funded programs, which were often more restrictive. DACE's advantage was that several key administrators were already on either faculty or higher education officer/HEO lines, so their positions and salaries were relatively more secure than those of continuing education programs on most other college campuses, another positive example of President Shenker's legacy.

Continuing Education at LaGuardia provided career training and preparation for entry-level jobs, personal development, academic preparation, and basic skills courses for its very diverse student populations. The staff was usually eclectic, diverse, responsive to emerging needs, and alert to the available funding sources. I welcomed LaGuardia's continuing education approaches that allowed for risk taking in developing programs, extensive outreach to nontraditional communities, and the capacity for engaging them in new and innovative ways. We held regular divisional meetings with senior staff to discuss funding and budgets, and divisional, personnel and program activities and new ideas for program development, so staff was intimately involved in moving the division forward.

It was while I still worked at LaGCC that I met my neighbor Johnsy Middleton. She lived a few buildings east from our house on West Ninety-Second Street. During the summers I enjoyed sitting on our front stoop and greeting neighbors as they walked by. I believe that we initially nodded or just smiled at each other, and then over time, Johnsy would stop to engage in a conversation. She had a friendly disposition, and a most infectious laugh, was a font of information, and loved to talk with our sons and niece Tanya Yasmin, who was a frequent visitor in our home. Soon Johnsy was part of our family, sharing in all our celebrations.

Initially from Atlanta, Georgia, and an African American, Johnsy graduated from Northfield Mount Hermon School in Massachusetts, and Princeton University, and received an MBA from Columbia University. She worked briefly as a part-time instructor at LaGCC, and then for many years as a consultant with the USAID. In this role she accompanied groups of foreign nationals who were selected by their countries for advanced learning in particular fields in the United States: higher education, business, social services, the sciences, and so on. Johnsy was a member of their orientation team. She then accompanied them to the preselected sites and organizations throughout the US. Aware that Ismail and I loved to entertain, Johnsy would often bring those visitors whom she particularly liked to dine with us, which they always appreciated. For the visitors, it was always a rare pleasure to visit someone's home during their brief but intensive sojourn in the USA.

Johnsy's intellectual breadth was impressive, and she was always reading material she came across in our home; she was a true learner. I thoroughly enjoyed her company, and we used to discuss so many topics. Johnsy came from a very intellectual, upper-middle-class family; her father had been a president of Morris Brown College in Atlanta, and her mother a sociology professor. Her brother was also a professor in Michigan, while her sister Ann worked in technology. She told me so many wonderful stories about her family that I used to encourage her to write about growing up in the South within her family. While she liked that idea, I doubt that she ever did so.

Over many years, when she was not traveling for work, I would call her on the weekend, "Hi, Johnsy. I have cooked some curried chicken [or some other main dish], along with rice and vegetables. I hope you haven't eaten yet!" Her immediate response, with that lively southern touch, was always, "Girl, I'll be right over; wouldn't miss that meal for anything!" Sure enough, within five minutes, she was seated at the table with us, enjoying and praising my cooking and keeping up a lively conversation, full of fun and laughter. My family and I loved Johnsy.

Johnsy passed away in 2015 after a diagnosis of pancreatic cancer. I have missed her rare indomitable, lively, and fun spirit. A few months after she died, I happened across an email list of her close friends and invited them to a luncheon in our home to celebrate her life. They were thrilled. What a marvelous and fun event! Everyone was so happy to be able to share her Johnsy stories in an intimate setting, a lovely way to say goodbye to a special individual who shared laughter and joy with all her friends.

Leaving LaGuardia for Bank Street College

In 1988 LaGuardia's president Joe Shenker became the president of Bank Street College, then composed of the Graduate School of Education, the Division of Research, the Center for Children and Technology, and the School for Children, an independent elementary school. In late 1989 I received a surprise phone call from him inviting me to join him at Bank Street as dean of a new division he wished to start. Joe said that he wished to expand Bank Street's reach to broader and more diverse communities through outreach programs and was convinced that a continuing education approach could achieve that goal. To work with Joe once again was a truly incredible option.

Although I had planned to eventually retire from LaGuardia, I also thought about the leadership opportunity being offered to me. I was torn about leaving LaGuardia, a place that had been so good for, and to, me. I worried quietly but didn't feel that I could discuss the opportunity with any of my LaGCC colleagues; I felt that I would be disappointing them since we had developed such positive working relationships over the years, and I was quite happy at LaGuardia.

I talked with Ismail, who was very encouraging and supported the move. Although I was thrilled at the thought of working again with Joe, I was still troubled about leaving LaGuardia. I decided to talk with Ann Marcus, now dean of the School of Education at NYU. She was very positive, pointed to the invitation as a unique opportunity, and encouraged me to accept Joe's offer. After our conversation I felt much relieved, confirmed my decision with Joe, whose delight dissolved any remaining doubt on my part, and finally discussed my decision with Dean Judy McGaughey, who had succeeded Dean Gussie Kappner when she left LaGuardia.

My farewell party was truly an extraordinary event. Continuing Education staff had always planned great celebrations, but this one was above and beyond. With input from Sandy Watson, the team created a Jamaican theme with a reggae band and delicious Jamaican food catered by an external group. My entire family and close friends were invited, along with faculty and staff; the mood was upbeat, celebratory, and delightful.

Among the special surprises was music faculty John Williams serenading me with "Lady," a song that I had heard him sing on a prior occasion and was completely awed. His singing voice was an absolute and unexpected treat. Among my special gifts was a book filled with beautiful sentiments from across the college, a treasure in itself. A special letter from Glenn Anderson, now a faculty in the Deafness and Rehabilitation program at the University of Arkansas, indicating that he had heard of my departure through "the Deaf grapevine," stated that "now is an ideal time for all of us to give you a loud applause. . . . Your guiding spirit, enthusiasm and perseverance made it possible for the Program for Deaf Adults to grow from a dream on paper to a nationally recognized program with a very fine staff and a large population of deaf students . . . it is a tribute to your leadership."

As I listened to my colleagues talk about my contributions to the division and the college at large, I was simultaneously excited and in wonder at what had been such an incredible journey since my arrival from Jamaica. I was also acutely aware that my success was linked to their willingness to join me unafraid and loyally as equal participants in all our program development ventures. And we had so much fun as we worked and learned together. When fiscal challenges arose, like the ending of a grant while awaiting the response to another award for program and personnel continuity, more often than not we found creative solutions with the help of our deans or administration.

I felt very fortunate to have had the opportunity to work in a place where innovation and risk-taking were the norm; this environment unleashed a creative side of me that was heretofore unknown to me. I only hoped that my response to my friends that afternoon conveyed the depths of my fondness and appreciation for them and for LaGuardia. This was a great ending to a happy and very productive period at LaGuardia Community College. I left LaGuardia as a tenured full professor and associate dean for Adult and Continuing Education after seventeen wonderful years.

CHAPTER 15

BANK STREET COLLEGE

We have taken multiple perspectives, values and experiences
and shaped a way of working and thinking that is inclusive
and respectful to all.
—ADRIANNE KAMSLER, Coordinator, New Beginnings Project in
Newark

In 1916 Lucy Sprague Mitchell, the first dean of women at the University of
California at Berkeley, founded the Bureau of Educational Experiments to
design a new kind of education leading to a better world and a more humane
society. Mrs. Mitchell knew and was influenced by John Dewey, and the
writings of other humanists during that period. She staffed the bureau with
a team consisting of a doctor, psychologists, a social worker, and teachers to
study how children learned and soon discovered that the children's natural
expression reflected their keen awareness of the world.

Mrs. Mitchell provided workshops in these new approaches to teaching
and learning for teachers that continued even when the bureau was granted
the right to offer graduate degrees in 1950 and became Bank Street College.
In preparing teachers for the new kind of education, Mrs. Mitchell taught
that relationships were important in the teaching and learning process and
that it was critical to view the child in relation to his or her interaction with
other children, adults, and materials. Famous for its impact on the development of responsive and creative environments that engaged, enriched,

and supported learning in early childhood education, Bank Street College remains the only freestanding—not part of a university system—graduate school of education in the country. As such, the college is unique and has been in the forefront of significant educational changes since its founding; moreover, its reputation increased under the leadership of its first president, Jack Niemeyer, hired in 1956.

Bank Street has a rich history in the shaping of quality early childhood practices during its early years. For example, the college was involved in shaping the legislation for the federal Head Start program; was consulted on several major federal programs; published the first set of multiethnic textbooks for grades K–3, *The Bank Street Readers*; and conducted important research on how schools could promote mental health in children. Later on, in the late seventies and early eighties, Bank Street was once again exciting the education world with its cutting-edge development and use of technology in education and classrooms through *The Bank Street Writer* and *The Voyage of the MiMi*, a curriculum available on TV and utilized by hundreds of schools across the nation, providing research data and information on the use of technology in education. These curricula and data were available through Bank Street's former Center for Children and Technology, intelligently led by Dr. Jan Hawkins and her team of brilliant, thoughtful, and humanistic researchers.

Over the years Bank Street has established itself as the place to obtain knowledge and experience in providing the best-quality education for young children. Many professionals have said that one can tell a Bank Street teacher upon entering an early childhood classroom; that may be related to children's engagement in learning, the joy evidenced in the classroom, the ease reflected in the teacher/child relationship, or a host of other relationships/ curriculum factors.

I began working at Bank Street College in July 1989. While walking to my office on that first day, I passed an office where an older woman was packing her books and other material, seemingly for departure. She had such a pleasant face and openness about her that I stopped by to say hello, and she graciously paused to talk with me. She also gave me a pamphlet describing her work, and then we said goodbye. I later learned that I had just met Barbara Biber, Bank Street's distinguished researcher and highly esteemed colleague. If only I had known her identity then. But how fortunate for me to have met her on her last, and on my first, day at Bank Street College.

Creating a New Program Division

Awaiting my arrival for immediate implementation was a $300,000 funded proposal from the New York State Department of Education for the Liberty Partnerships Program. The program was a collaboration between forty-seven colleges and universities, public schools, and community-based organizations to prepare youth at risk of not completing high school to graduate, enter work or college, and become productive citizens. The program required extensive outreach to several prospective partners, including Barnard College, several public schools, nonprofit programs, and parents.

After reading the proposal, I thought about the implementation process. I had no staff as yet and had to now think more consciously about the mission of Bank Street and how this mission would be manifested in the diverse programs to be developed. I also pondered my role as a dean, my desire to be an effective administrator in this new environment, to understand the culture of Bank Street, and overall to be a good, caring, and effective leader. Although I have always performed to the best of my ability in all my work situations, I also hoped that President Shenker would feel that he had made a good and wise decision in hiring me as part of his team.

Knowing the importance of building good relationships in one's workplace, my next task was to visit the offices of staff and faculty, and the mailroom and facilities staff, to meet them and to introduce myself. Soon I knew almost everyone in the building. I then hired my very capable administrative assistant, Dana Hamilton, who initially managed both budget and administrative tasks, but as the division expanded and we received more grants, the need for a dedicated fiscal staff became clear.

To coordinate the Liberty program activities, which were numerous, I hired David Penberg, a Bank Street alumnus who brought a pedagogy for student enrichment and success for all children and especially Black and brown children. David had lived and worked as an educator in South America and in China and was fluent in Spanish, so he also brought an international perspective and experience to the program. He could think both locally and globally and respected diversity in programming. In addition, our grant was focused on students who were failing in their schools, lived in challenging neighborhoods, and did not necessarily see themselves as smart. Recognizing the importance of parent participation and support for this initiative, David and I discussed a range of strategies to engage parents. With cooperation from what was then the Ninetieth Street McDonald's, we held one dinner event in their restaurant and another in a local public school. The parent participation was excellent at both events, where parents gained information on the program and had their questions answered.

In addition to the Liberty Partnerships Program (LPP) were two "I Have a Dream" programs, and the New Perspectives Program, tuition-based, weekend graduate courses and workshops for educators, waiting for the new division to acknowledge and embrace their presence. I soon connected with the two "I Have a Dream" directors, and with Dr. Susan Ginsberg, director for the New Perspectives Program; and the Division of Continuing Education was up and running.

There was one other program that began in 1988, prior to my arrival, and that was Project Healthy Choices, under the leadership of the awesome Eileen Wasow. An extraordinary, warm, and gifted early childhood educator, Eileen had been teaching the four-year-old class in the School for Children when Nafees, our third son, moved to her classroom. At our initial meeting, there was an immediate connection, and after some months of visiting the classroom, we soon became friends.

Already aware of Eileen's strong background as an early childhood professional, President Shenker had selected her to coordinate and develop a curriculum on substance abuse prevention education for grades K through 2. Funded by the Board of Education, with her staff Eileen designed an age-appropriate curriculum and conducted workshops on substance abuse prevention education for teachers, counselors, parents, and administrators in thirteen of NYC's thirty-two school districts. On my arrival at Bank Street, the program was easily absorbed within the division, and Eileen became my invaluable associate dean.

By the 1990–1991 academic year, staff from the Division of Continuing Education (DCE) were offering quality enriched, professional development services to schools, teachers, and other school-based staff as well as direct services to children, youth, and parents through fourteen programs, twenty-one full-time, six part-time staff, about forty adjuncts, and a budget of $2.1 million. We also hired Merrill Lee Fuchs as the division's budget director and, later, Elva Berger as my diligent and supportive assistant. Elva was helpful to everyone, within and outside the division. She was flexible, dependable, loyal, and pleasant.

My exposure to new experiences, people, research results, cultures, places, programs, and program impact reached new heights at Bank Street College. One result from my reaching out to the Graduate School during my first year as dean was an invitation from faculty Stan Chu to join him in meeting teachers and government officers on St. Vincent and Bequia, small Caribbean islands in the Grenadines. Teachers were exploring the history of whaling in Bequia, and Stan was guiding them in using local resources and the natural environment to develop an interdisciplinary curriculum linking history, math, and science.

In St. Vincent, my first visit there, I had an opportunity to admire the lush beauty and natural charm of the island, especially its cone-shaped Mesopotamia Valley, where farmers planted bananas, coconuts, and other ground provisions on the sides of the valley. I quietly wondered how they managed to stay steady enough to plant on the sides of the cone. We visited the Sandy Bay School for children of the indigenous Carib group, who appeared to be all of a blondish color (there are Yellow Caribs and Black Caribs). Then we drove across the treacherous Rabacca Dry River bed, where stories abounded of cars and people being swept into the ocean due to a sudden rush of water from the mountains, a flash flood, especially following a rainfall.

We met with officials in the Department of Education and visited classrooms where Stan had introduced teachers to some interesting, new, practical, and fun ways to engage children in learning; for example, instead of just reading about fish and seeing a plastic fish, they caught and dissected a fish, which was a new activity for both the teachers and the children; having teachers measure the distance from the school to the sea was an experiential math activity. Stan helped teachers to see the value and benefits in using local materials and the natural environment to engage and teach children; the natural environment was not only free but was so very accessible and available for in-depth learning. Meeting the educators and learning about their island home and culture, and seeing how Stan guided them to discover new ways to learn, and their obvious delight and appreciation, were special opportunities for learning.

A few months later, I was in the Bank Street cafeteria with a small group of educators who had also visited St. Vincent and Bequia to observe teachers in their classrooms. One educator had observed a math class and shared with the group her reaction that the teacher was not effective because she kept using a word "that made no sense at all." She was critical of this teacher's method of teaching and concerned that the children were being deprived of good teaching. I inquired about the word she had heard and she replied that the word sounded like "geezinto." I asked her to say the word in a sentence the way that teacher had used it. She was happy to demonstrate that the teacher kept repeating, "this number geezinto that number: 10 geezinto 20." Coming from the West Indies, I recognized the word and explained that what the teacher was saying, and what her students heard and understood was "goes into," but to an outsider unfamiliar with the culture and the vernacular, a misunderstanding was inevitable. I further asked whether she had asked the teacher to explain her use of the word; she had not. That was another teachable moment for all who were present.

I also appreciated the thoughtfulness of colleague Bret Halverson, who, when I first arrived at Bank Street, reached out to acquaint me with the programs in his Schools and Community Services Division. Working to improve middle school instruction in the public schools, Bret invited me to join him on his visits to programs, which I was delighted to do. On these journeys, I met several school leaders and teachers. In addition Bret talked with me about the challenges for middle school teachers, many of whom knew little about adolescent development. As a result, the curriculum was often unengaging for the students at a time when these adolescents could become excited about learning. They could be captivated by new experiences and hands-on learning.

I learned an enormous amount about middle schools from Bret, a learning that was further enhanced when Dr. Kenneth Jewell joined my division to implement the Board of Education's Middle Schools Initiative designed by its deputy chancellor, Dr. Beverly Hall, a Jamaican, a visionary leader, and an extraordinary educator. Ken developed an approach to effective professional development—learning, planning, and implementation—which was used in almost all our professional development work with schools and organizations. This involved first learning from schools, or agencies, about their individual culture, needs, and staff before designing a plan to assist them; an approach reflecting respect for their input and their story, and then meeting their particular needs.

Some twenty years later, in 2009–2010, the division's many and diverse programs served 20,520 children, youth, teachers, families, and other adults. Both Presidents Joe Shenker and Gussie Kappner's goal to increase diversity was being fulfilled through the division's programs, and the remarks often heard during this period included "we didn't know Bank Street had such diverse populations and services." Gussie succeeded Joe when he left Bank Street College.

In addition to tutoring, mentoring, elective classes, and other options, the Liberty Partnership Program provided students three-week residential programs in environmental science at Vassar and Bard Colleges, summer travel/study abroad, opportunities to explore New York City, and internships throughout Bank Street. The value of these exposure opportunities for underserved students becomes even more meaningful through the reflective discussions that follow their travel experiences. In addition, 100 percent of our LPP students who stayed in the program graduated from high school, compared with the less than 60 percent graduation rate from the public schools. Of our graduates over 97 percent were accepted into colleges and universities, while 3 percent either accepted employment or remained in the program for another semester. The significant impact was that we were increasing the graduation rates, in high schools and colleges, of predominantly Black and brown students, initially considered to be at risk of not completing high school.

Exposing our Black and brown students early to the college environment gave them ways to develop their voices and self-confidence. The college environment was also a safe space for them to feel smart, to be smart, and to become scholars. Many were overheard to tell their classmates, "I go to college" at Bank Street. Among my favorite LPP stories was that of "Maria," who had skipped most of her high school classes prior to being referred to our program. She did not connect with anyone initially, nor could the counselors engage her in program activities, yet she attended them all after school. Then the LPP was asked to send a staff member to attend a conference on another CUNY campus with a similar program. No staff was available, so our program director asked Maria to represent our program. Maria's presentation on the Bank Street program was so outstanding that the director of the host campus personally called us to sing her praises. From that day Maria seemed to have found not only her voice but her brilliance. She graduated high school with honors, received a scholarship to Mt. Holyoke College, and, after graduation, enrolled in and then obtained her PhD in neuroscience from the University of Chicago. Her story was quite popular at Bank Street.

President Joseph Shenker

Prior to my arrival as dean of Continuing Education, Joe had already been president at Bank Street for one year. He and Susan, his engaging and outgoing, knowledgeable, and very supportive wife, had already settled into the college's nearby residence and were becoming familiar with the college's community and culture. As we worked together, I felt very supported by President Shenker, who continued to encourage innovation and to have Bank Street promote and support progressive practices in the public schools. During his first year, Joe was able to significantly reduce the huge college deficit he had inherited, and to balance the budget. He also designed the urban initiative, an umbrella concept that focused on using the knowledge from both research and faculty experience to strengthen teaching, learning, and leading in the city's public schools.

The urban initiative embraced early childhood, middle schools, teachers and curriculum, parent and community involvement, and school leadership, and was an innovative strategy drawing on the strengths and expertise of faculty across all areas of the college. The outcomes from each of those areas were astounding. The teaching practices of teachers and leaders across the city and several states showed marked improvement, and many of the initiative's components still exist today, in one form or another.

President Joe Shenker was an extraordinary leader and a strategic thinker with a clear vision for the changes needed to make a difference. After he was appointed to lead Bank Street, we had a conversation in which he shared his ideas for what eventually became the Principals Institute, whose purpose was to prepare Black and brown individuals and women for senior administrators' positions. Joe recognized that the public school system needed to improve on the representation of these groups at the principal and assistant principal levels. He also knew that many current principals and other leaders would be retiring within a few years and so, were he to prepare classroom teachers as leaders, Bank Street would have made a tremendous impact on providing skilled and knowledgeable leadership while also increasing racial and gender diversity at all administrative levels in the public schools. This was a great, practical, and doable idea and plan. Joe soon hired Dr. Bernie Mecklowitz, the former schools chancellor, NYC Department of Education, to lead the Principals Institute, which was extremely successful in preparing hundreds of very diverse school leaders as principals and assistant principals in the public schools.

Joe soon realized that asking for money was not part of Bank Street's culture; however, the expenses were real and growing, so he decided to hold the first dinner as a fundraiser to support the college. Since then the annual dinner has become the largest unrestricted fundraising activity for the college. As a visionary and innovative leader, Joe had the ability to recognize the special strengths in individuals; he would then place them in positions where those strengths would manifest as leadership. I was a beneficiary of his vision to identify individuals with the potential to become leaders, even though I did not necessarily see myself as such. He helped so many of us become leaders during his years of service as president at LaGuardia Community College, his eight years at Bank Street College, and, later, at C. W. Post as provost, where he was much loved and so very much appreciated. Joe was a humane and kind leader who listened quietly and observed keenly.

As Bank Street's president, he chaired a weekly cabinet meeting with his administrative team on Wednesday mornings. These meetings with four deans, one vice president, and his chief of staff, the very cheerful and effective Jennifer Jones Austin, now CEO at the Federation of Protestant Welfare Agencies, were held in his conference room, adjacent to his rather simply furnished, very small office. The latter contained a leather upholstered couch, a small glass table on either side of the couch, two chairs, and a long, narrow desk less than a foot and a half wide built along the wall and facing the only window in the room.

For my first cabinet meeting, I arrived early and was a little anxious. Gertrude, Joe's administrative assistant, greeted me warmly and enthusiastically, while she ushered me into the conference room. Inside, I noted that the conference room, although almost twice the size of Joe's office, seemed adequate but was not at all a large room. As I surveyed the room, wondering where I should sit, since none of the team had yet arrived, Joe entered and said quietly, "Come and sit near me." Greatly relieved, I wondered how he could have sensed my anxiety; so I sat to his left on the long side of the table and fervently hoped that I would gain some of his wisdom and uncanny insight.

Joe was responsible for the advancement and mentorship of several women, especially Black and brown women as college presidents, deans, and other leadership positions in higher education. And he did this quietly and without fanfare. He was not afraid to take risks, and he encouraged and supported his administrators to do likewise. If your idea didn't work, he was there to help you understand why and then to move on. I believe that Joe's purpose in life was to do good wherever he could. Even-tempered with a quiet sense of humor, Joe was politically astute, observant, somewhat shy, compassionate, and always supportive. He used to say that he hired the best people and then gave them the freedom to do their work.

However, from my experience, he never left you alone; he was always there to offer guidance and support. I recall how he supported my idea to hold a conference on deafness at Bank Street, to expose teachers and social workers to the education and culture of the deaf population. After outlining the proposed two-day conference and the possible speakers and workshop facilitators, I submitted several proposals to obtain the funding needed for expenses, confident that I would receive the funding, since the focus was, to me, unique and was connected to special education and diversity. One week prior to the conference dates, with no proposal funded, and all commitments made, I was desperate. I had thought the topic would be appealing to funders; it wasn't. How was I going to pay all the expenses? With a sinking feeling, I went to talk with Joe about my dilemma, ready to be admonished, but really to seek his advice. He listened, then took up his phone, and made one call to a trustee. Without any explanation, Joe stated that he needed $10,000, said "many thanks," turned to me with a warm smile and said, "Fern, you have the $10,000." I could have hugged him. Joe was an extraordinary leader who set the leadership bar very high for us to emulate.

President Shenker left Bank Street in 1995 and soon joined C. W. Post as provost. He remained at C. W. Post until his retirement, and subsequent passing due to illness in 2009. In my remarks at his memorial service in 2009, I said that his "ability to listen and to distill the essence of a conversation or problem was above the ordinary," and that he always had thoughtful and practical advice to offer. For me, "Joe's leadership was an inspiring, transformative and humane one, and I will always treasure the memories of those years of knowing and working with him." It was a real privilege and a gift for me to know and to work with President Joseph Shenker and to be inspired by his leadership.

PRESIDENT AUGUSTA KAPPNER

Joe was succeeded by Dr. Augusta Souza Kappner, "Gussie," as Bank Street's new president. On arriving at the college, Gussie, who had also worked with

Joe at LaGuardia, early on, indicated to me that she would continue his legacy of bringing in new and innovative programs that met the educational and career needs of underserved groups.

Gussie was a very lively, likable, smart, and outgoing individual with a signature cheerful laugh. I recall how delighted I was to learn that her mother was Jamaican, and her father from the Cape Verde Islands. Gussie had graduated from Hunter High School, where she excelled, and later from Barnard College. With her activist background, Gussie's graduate degree was in social work/community organizing. she also obtained her doctorate in social welfare policy from Columbia University School of Social Work, was a former president of the Borough of Manhattan Community College and was assistant secretary for vocational and adult education during the Clinton administration's first term.

Gussie won many notable awards, including Barnard's Distinguished Alumna Award. With her easy-to-relate-to manner and conversational style, Gussie was well liked by Bank Street's faculty and staff, and while she continued and supported Joe's urban initiatives, she brought in impressive funding for new and innovative programs: Teachers for a New Era, the Urban Schools Attuned in the Graduate School, New Beginnings in Newark, I LEAD, the Center for Early Childhood, and other programs in continuing education, while linking the college to many new partners and friends.

Gussie knew the importance of an administrator's awareness of how policy can influence program design, outcomes, and funding, and this I learned from her. I also enjoyed working with Gussie, and my transition to her leadership style was a smooth one, because she had also been my dean at LaGuardia CC. Besides, we both had social work backgrounds and embraced those similar values around improving conditions for all people, especially the underserved. Both Presidents Joe Shenker and Gussie Kappner understood the importance and value of specially designed programs, demonstrating what was possible in making a difference in the lives of individuals and communities. This goal was achievable through the design and promotion of thoughtful educational practices tested again and again by teachers with ongoing support from their supervisors and peers, along with using community resources as needed to empower students. Social work agencies and other nonprofits also work towards having an impact by achieving positive outcomes for their clients through effective program design and implementation.

Given her activist background and her belief in social change that benefits society, Gussie was responsive to a request from Marymount Manhattan College's then-president, Dr. Regina Peruggi, that Bank Street become a supporting member of a college consortium bringing academic programs to women in the Bedford Hills Correctional Facility, a maximum-security prison located in Westchester County, a suburb north of NYC. Regina, who had previously worked with Gussie at the Board of Higher Education, was responding to an urgent plea from Mrs. Althea Jackson, former deputy commissioner, Department for the Aging, that the women in Bedford Hills, where Althea volunteered, were restless and bored, not a good sign in prisons. Since Pell Grants were no longer available to inmates for education, an alternative approach was needed: get colleges involved. About twelve private higher education institutions initially responded to the call for action.

Bank Street agreed to contribute instructors as well as funding for the consortium to hire faculty as needed. Despite its initial challenges as a new program, coupled with the restrictions and rules within the prison, many inmates were excited and motivated to learn, and the faculty was likewise extremely encouraged by students' eagerness to learn. Assisting us in the education-in-prison process were two dynamic and caring inmates who had earned MA degrees from Teachers College during their incarceration, Judith Clark and Kathy Boudin. Both women played important roles in teaching classes and preparing new inmates to survive while incarcerated, which was critical since the least infraction could result in their being sent to Albion,[1] or another facility far away from their families.

They were also among the key researchers, including Iris Bowen and Migdalia Martinez, in Dr. Michelle Fine's monumental study on the positive impact on incarcerated women of a college education while in prison; they always gave the loudest cheers at the annual graduation of students completing their degrees and diplomas. In addition to college credit courses, Bank Street offered a childcare certificate course to improve the knowledge and skills of female inmates working in the Children's Center, so they could be employable on release. Coordinated initially by the DCE's Maureen Hornung, inmates learned about child development, learned how to tell stories to children, and wrote their personal stories. In the music and movement workshop, one student wrote, "It let me express the little girl within me."

Success in the Bedford Hills program was evidenced through several measures. In addition to the increased numbers of students earning their high school diplomas, and associate and bachelor's degrees through the higher education program, the study undertaken by the City University of New York's faculty Dr. Michelle Fine showed that the recidivism rate for inmates who had participated in the higher education program was zero. Even after taking one course, participants developed a new understanding of themselves, their strengths and abilities, and their communities through the course and the support of their professors.

The program served as a model for other prisons such as Taconic Prison, while Sing Sing offered its program for male inmates. Bank Street supported the Bedford Hills program until 2012; however, several colleges have continued to educate and elevate the aspirations of their students under the leadership of Marymount Manhattan, Mercy, and Bard Colleges. Dr. Fine's study demonstrated that higher education in prison reduces crime and recidivism and saves taxpayers substantial dollars. Best of all, the graduates have gained or regained self-respect and enhanced self-esteem through education.

My experience in visiting Bedford Hills prison and talking to the women provided insights that I could have gained only from being there. I learned to be prepared for changes from one visit to the next, from the process of gaining entry to leaving the facility. In addition, so much depended on a warden's orientation and belief system about incarceration and the individuals who are incarcerated. The first warden with whom we worked was a social worker by background and so brought a certain flexibility around programs, rewards, and punishment, and a more humane approach in managing the women even while she adhered to the rules and regulations coming from the New York State Department of Corrections in Albany. The wardens following her retirement were quite different, and we found tighter rules to enter the facility. We also learned that a few guards resented the educational advantages being given to the inmates, since they were not receiving similar educational benefits. Yet I recall one instance when they were invited to sit in on a writing class and heard the stories written and read by the women, how emotionally moved they became. One guard commented that he'd had no idea of the life challenges faced by the women who read their stories. Whether this enlightenment resulted in a change in his attitude and behavior toward the inmates thereafter, I have no idea but hope that it did.

I saw the immediate and long-term benefit of bringing higher education into the prison system. In addition to the reduced recidivism rate, the women soon recognized that they could handle the academics by working hard, and developing the confidence to master new skills. Some inmates felt for the first time that they were really smart. Then, the fact that their professors believed in their potential and were delighted to be teaching them proved that they were indeed worthy and were capable of achieving an education. They could learn and would succeed. The faculty also benefited from their work with the women. They saw individuals who, often turned off from school and education, were now eager to absorb new learning, participate, and reflect on their experiences during classroom discussions. Writing about their life experiences provided an opportunity for reflection, which had a profound impact on the students as they released hidden fears, recalled broken dreams and relationships gone wrong, and the lack of positive role models. As faculty saw the positive impact of their teaching and learning on their students, they became even more inspired and committed to continue this important work.

Attending several graduations, and sitting on the platform with the dignitaries, I was able to see the satisfaction, pride, and joy reflected on the faces of the students, whether they were receiving high school diplomas, associate's, bachelor's, or master's degrees. There were also inmate attendees; many hoped to be members of a future graduating class. The room was always filled with a happy buzz; everyone was smiling and offering congratulations to the graduates. Tables placed along one wall were packed with a variety of food, salads, and drinks, and balloons floated from the rafters. Faculty from all the partner colleges, a college president, officials from the NYS Department of Corrections, an inspirational guest speaker, and others were all present to congratulate the graduates. However, amidst this joyous occasion, as guests we were also conscious of being in a maximum-security facility by the sudden interruption by guards if the count did not match; that is, inmates entering the huge gym where graduations are held are counted upon entering; then there is a random count again, and if the numbers do not correspond, the ceremony is on hold until they do. Then the ceremony could proceed. That was an aspect of life in prison.

The education of the women in Bedford Hills was a program that tested one's commitment because of the many restrictions but also one offering the greatest personal rewards, because the outcomes are visible and so tangible: the lives of the women and their children are changed positively by the mothers' achievement of an academic education. I was grateful to have played a small part in this unique and effective intervention program.

My directors and their staff understood the college's mission. They undertook innovative and important work that helped to improve the social, educational, and emotional conditions for teachers, paraprofessionals, and students in their schools and communities. We received feedback on the impact of our intervention through a combination of formal and informal evaluations, comments from teachers, social workers, and parents, and then seeing students more prepared to enjoy learning. Relying heavily on grant funding, we were frequently writing proposals with short turnaround deadlines while simultaneously implementing the activities on existing projects; however, that was never a deterrent. We were typically alert to grant opportunities.

The DCE directors deserve much of the credit for the impressive results that were attributed to our division. Our success in identifying and serving our target populations, including educators, in innovative and respectful ways enhanced the division's visibility and reputation and in the process significantly extended Bank Street's reputation for high-quality work. Our divisional successes were also due to the ongoing support and acknowledgments from both Presidents Joe Shenker and Gussie Kappner. Gussie retired from Bank Street in 2008, after thirteen years as president. Gussie was succeeded by President Elizabeth Dickey, formerly of the New School, and, much later, by Shael Polakow-Suransky, former senior deputy chancellor for the NYC Department of Education.

MY EARLY CONNECTIONS TO BANK STREET

Interestingly, my connection to Bank Street College began years before I assumed a full-time position there. While the college was still at 69 Bank Street, someone whom I do not recall had connected me with a Bank Street senior administrator about becoming an advisor for its counseling program, which no longer exists. I was hired to supervise three professionals working to obtain their master's degrees in school counseling. Their field placement was in the Henry Street Settlement on the Lower East Side. My responsibility was to observe their interaction with the children and then write a report at the end of the session. I developed a very positive relationship with my advisees; we met frequently to share their observations about the children with whom they worked. They were thoughtful, insightful, caring, and able to objectively assess, without judging, the behaviors they observed among the children.

That was my first connection with Bank Street. Much later, through my friend Dr. Janet Lieberman, I met Rebecca Strauss, then-director of the School for Children, who encouraged me to apply to the school when I had children. With the arrival of our first son, I called Rebecca to indicate that I was looking at schools for him. The college had now moved from its original site on Bank Street in Greenwich Village to West 112th Street in Manhattan's Upper West Side. On entering this new Bank Street building, I was immediately struck by the surprising but very appealing presence of a tall tree situated within a large opening in the middle of the entrance hall.

Surrounding the tree was a circular wood and metal frame with attached cushioned seating. Through the open area, I looked down to see that the tree's beginning was located in a wide circular planter inside the cafeteria. I hadn't seen such a creative design in the few schools that I had visited previously, and I felt an immediate connection to Bank Street. Our application was accepted, and I chose Bank Street among other positive responses.

Exposure to Board Work at Bank Street

While our children were in the School for Children, I was elected as a parent trustee on Bank Street's board of trustees. There, I had the unique opportunity to meet, work with, and observe trustees as they fulfilled their individual and collective roles and responsibilities in the interest of the college's mission. While serving as a parent trustee during Dr. Dick Roup's presidency, I was invited to join Bank Street's board as a statutory trustee and to serve as a member of the program committee. However, hired as an employee by President Shenker in 1989, I had to resign my trustee role; nevertheless, the transition from trustee to employee was a smooth one. The three deans and two vice presidents attended all board meetings anyway, and each of us was the liaison to a major committee where discussions were held on finance, programs, fundraising, or membership.

President Shenker assigned me as staff to the membership and program committees, where the chairs and I facilitated discussions around trustee responsibilities, planning board presentations, trustee recruitment, and vetting new trustees for full board approval. These were again invaluable learning experiences, working with caring individuals who were enthusiastic about, and inspired to be part of, the governance body at Bank Street.

It was also during this period that Dean Ann Marcus invited me to cochair NYU's School of Education's Alumni Association. Serving with Sandy Poster, faculty at the Borough of Manhattan Community College, we sought ways to engage with alumni by first developing a list of alumni names, planned and offered special events, and greeted graduates on stage at Graduation. Our service ended when the university decided to focus on a university-wide alumni association. I have maintained my connection to Ann and have attended the special symposia that she has organized to focus on critical topics in higher education.

Among some memorable experiences in my role as trustee was an invitation to participate in a School for Children reception to welcome new parents. I happened to stand next to a gentleman with whom I began talking. Using American Sign Language as we talked, he told me that he was a new parent. Naturally, given my LaGuardia experience with the deaf population, I became quite excited and responded with a question about his knowledge of sign language. Yes, he had learned ASL for his work. As we talked and signed, I noticed that Betsy Hall, coordinator of the event, and the school's admissions director, was signaling excitedly to me.

On concluding my conversation with this interesting parent, having naturally informed him about LaGuardia CC's Program for Deaf Adults and inviting him to visit, I walked over to Betsy and wondered what she wanted to share. She was quite excited and asked if I knew the person with whom I had been speaking. I said, "No, but he was so very interesting. He knew sign language. Who was he?" Very amused and still excited, she revealed, "That was William Hurt, the actor. He acted in the movie *Children of a Lesser God*. My reaction was, "Oh, so that's why he knows sign language. I am so glad that I didn't know his identity; otherwise, I would not have been so effusive."

Another cherished memory was with a group of early childhood teachers from South Africa who were visiting selected NYC programs. They had completed their classroom observations and visits to the NYC childcare centers. I invited them to a dinner of curried chicken with basmati rice in our home, which they really enjoyed. But the delight they displayed when I served condensed milk with their tea was absolutely thrilling. They commented that this small act made them feel so much at home and wondered how I knew that condensed milk would make such a difference. With a smile, I revealed my Jamaican background, where condensed milk was a staple in our homes. Another commonwealth connection.

CHAPTER 16

THE LONG TRIPS

During one of our board meetings, I met Carol B. Hillman, then the alumni associate trustee, author, farmer, and a wonderful friend and colleague. Carol told me the story of Bank Street's Long Trips, begun initially in the thirties by Lucy Sprague Mitchell during a time of significant social reform in America. Mrs. Mitchell, a geographer and Bank Street's founder, used these trips to expose teachers to new learning, new environments, and new people to enrich their personal and teaching experiences.

Her intention was to move those teachers from their comfort zones so they could experience the reality of everyday living for diverse citizens and communities. The trips ended in the 1950s, for a variety of reasons, including politics of the time, and Carol was interested in reviving them. I loved the idea, and since I was always open to new ideas and opportunities, I was ready to embark on this adventure.

Carol and I have since planned and coordinated fifteen of nineteen Long Trips, and I have participated in eighteen of those trips over twenty years. Each trip has provided me, as well as our participants, with powerful cross-cultural learnings and opportunities to connect with diverse people and their environments, broaden our understanding of the world, develop relationships with each other, and make new friends. The trips truly embodied the Bank Street approach to learning, which is through direct experience. Each trip began with the story of the first Long Trips in the 1930s, told by Sal Vascellero, historian and social science faculty in Bank Street's Graduate School. Sal had written his dissertation on the initial Long Trips after interviewing participants who had gone on those trips. A recurring response theme was how the experiences had changed their lives, forever.

In addition, each of our Long Trips had a particular focus, and there were so many serendipitous opportunities that added a heightened sense of adventure or pleasure. According to Carol, the trips provided for her, "a time for experience and deep reflection and broadened [her] understanding of the world."

Our first trip was participation in the 1996 Storytelling Festival in Asheville, North Carolina. It was a memorable trip in so many ways. In addition to associate dean and educator Eileen Wasow were some distinguished Bank Street professionals, including Joan Blos, writer and the niece of famed researcher Barbara Biber; and Sally Kerlin, a trustee and alumna who had participated in the first Long Trips. Sally was also the trustee who recommended me for appointment to the Wave Hill board, and had once been chair of Bank Street's board. Joan had also invited Connie Regan, a famous storyteller and a participant in the festival, to meet with us in our hotel and to share some regional stories. Before she began to speak, Joan placed a strand of beads belonging to Lucy Sprague Mitchell on a low table in the middle of the group. There was a stunned silence. That was an inspirational and magical moment. Although I had never met Mrs. Mitchell, I had read her biography by Joyce Antler. She came across to me as an awesome woman, knowledgeable, strong, a force of nature, a change maker, and someone who did not tolerate mediocrity. I would have liked to have met her.

Another highlight was meeting our volunteer "guide" Julie, who had attended Bank Street but had lost her dissertation on a train and was too discouraged to continue on toward graduation. She now resided in Asheville. We felt compelled to change such an unhappy story. So we reconnected her to the appropriate faculty at the college. She received the needed guidance, followed through on our suggestions, and completed all the requirements for a master's degree. Several of us watched her walk during graduation the following year. We were so happy for her.

In 1998 fifteen educators participated in the Long Trip to Santa Fe, New Mexico. The theme was "Connecting Storytelling, the Arts, and the History of Santa Fe and the Southwest." Prior to this trip, I contacted an alumna, Yvonne Spitz Wilson, living in Santa Fe, who was delighted to assist us in planning the agenda. I soon learned how happy Bank Street alumni in general were to reconnect with their college and so were always willing to assist us. They usually ended up joining our group. Santa Fe, said to be the oldest capital city in the US, offered a unique mix of Native American, Hispanic, and Anglo cultures and histories.

En route from the Albuquerque airport to Sante Fe, I observed the dry air and earth, and balls of tumbleweeds as the main vegetation. Without any other companion shrubbery, tumbleweeds seemed lonely and a bit bored. Maybe they tumble seeking other native species as companions. Watching them I recalled a song about "tumbling tumbleweeds" popular during my youth in Jamaica.

On the first evening we were entranced by the words from Elena Ortiz, native storyteller. In addition to English, she speaks the Tewa language and is the daughter of a famous anthropologist, Alfonso Ortiz. Our visits to pueblos and churches enhanced our knowledge about the connectedness of Native Americans to their sacred traditions and to their land.

Knowing that our visits included two early childhood schools, the charming Little Earth School and the Rio Grande School, Carol and I had packed educational books and Bank Street bags as gifts for our respective hosts. Our group was charmed by the Little Earth School, a fascinating adobe structure with low ceilings and cozy, colorful, and well-utilized classrooms, and a large traditional clay oven in the open yard. As we toured the classrooms, Zeni Muslin, the Spanish teacher in Bank Street's School for Children spent time in the Spanish class that had a very new teacher. Zeni provided some much-appreciated strategies to assist this new teacher in gaining the attention of her children.

At the Rio Grande School, its head, Linda Harris, a Bank Street alumna, saw the college as "a bright spot" for herself and for her husband. Her students were engaged in experiential learning, clearly demonstrated in the school's culture of fun, social interactions, and exploration experienced on a daily basis. As a progressive educator, Linda had called on Bank Street's faculty Elaine Wickens when she needed help with curriculum. All students now perform community service, including kindergarten children who work with homeless shelters. Linda also mentioned that she had spent two years in the Peace Corps as an educator training early childhood teachers in Jamaica. This is such a small world.

On visiting the Museum of the American Indian, we joined other visitors in listening to a presentation, "Here, Now, and Always." Members of our group asked a few questions that intrigued Ed Ladd, a museum staff member also present. Greeting us after the lecture, Ed, a Zuni, invited our entire group to return in the afternoon when he would share more information about the Zuni culture with us. We returned as promised and were invited into an intimate conference room where we heard a story about the nineteen tribal groups, the eight different languages existing in New Mexico, and the markers in the history of the American Indians.

Our learning while in Santa Fe covered several aspects of the culture. We visited museums, a pueblo, a community college where we participated in a seminar on early childhood education, and several Spanish missions many miles away from Santa Fe, and were fascinated by the changing landscape boasting tall pine trees as we traveled north.

We also became engrossed with the spirituality that has been such an important part of this southwestern culture, such as the annual Easter week pilgrimage from Albuquerque to the "miraculous" Santuario de Chimayo. In this church with its incredible golden altar, we saw on display wheelchairs, crutches, and other prostheses left behind by believers who said they were cured by the existing power of healing. I was intrigued by this information. Visiting the homes or studios of artists, we saw the beautiful retablos, complex, usually wooden structures with carved holy images placed within them, and carved wooden santos, images of saints. I was particularly struck in learning about the Penitentes, a secret sect now outlawed, that practiced flagellation as penance for their sins. One guide explained that life was based on tradition in this culture where church, family, and community were important; hence, tension existed between an individualistic society, the Anglos, and a more community-oriented one.

Santa Fe was a culturally rich experience for our group and for me. Meeting and learning about the lives of its residents and how the three distinct cultural groups coexisted was indeed enlightening. As one educator later wrote, "We learned in a social context, discussing what we had experienced, pondering the meanings, vigorously discussing our semiconclusions and then reformulating our questions and answers. Not a bad experience for teachers!"[1]

The Long Trip to the Penn Center on St. Helena's Island, South Carolina in 2000, and to the Highlander Folk Center in Tennessee in 2005, tremendously expanded our knowledge of African American lives and culture, past and present, with an emphasis on the civil rights period. those two centers were the only safe places in the South where Dr. Martin Luther King and his colleagues, many of whom were white, could meet as they planned the Civil Rights Movement.

The Penn Center was the first school established in 1862 to educate formerly enslaved individuals. Known as the Port Royal experiment to determine whether the now freed population could learn, the school was supported by the Quakers of Philadelphia, with Laura Townes and Ellen Murray as the first teachers. They were later joined by Charlotte Forten, the first African American to teach there. Joan Blos informed us about Charlotte's familial relationship to the Grimke sisters, both white abolitionists.

We were encouraged to visit the Penn Center by trustee Kate Whitney, who, as a member of the Sankofa Circle,[2] founded by Lucia Jack, was already familiar with the institution. Every institution needs an individual who is or becomes the conscience for that place. At Bank Street, Lucia Jack was that conscience. She was fearless in working toward equalizing experiences for everyone, and especially for African American children, youth, and adults. Lucia and her husband, Edwin Jack, were influential in linking the college to new ideas, new people, and new activities, for example, being a founder and first leader of the Pemberton Society. Lucia also talked with me about the Gullah/Geechee people, their language, and their close cultural relationship to West Indian people.

At the Penn Center we learned more about the Gullah/Geechee culture from Emory Campbell, executive director, and the sustained efforts to preserve the land for the Gullah people. Our learning continued to expand as we saw examples of sweetgrass basket weaving and gained more information about the former enslaved people's outstanding work as skilled builders, carpenters, and artisans; we also attended enlightening presentations on African American history and culture at Armstrong Atlantic University and the Avery Research Center, originally a private school for middle-class Black children. We were joined at the Avery Center by Bank Street alumnus, intellectual, and retired educator Jim Campbell, a real treat for us.

Many close relationships developed among our group at the Penn Center. We were hosted in different houses, all built by Penn students in earlier times; we often gathered on one verandah during free moments to talk. And there was so much to talk about and to bond around, especially acknowledging how little we all knew about African American history and culture. I felt privileged to have seen firsthand the many contributions of African

Americans to American history and culture and to have met the guardians of their culture.

This trip illuminated for me not only the richness and the enormous contributions of African Americans to America but also the omissions of their achievements, voices, and narratives in the social studies, history books, and popular magazines. Of course, there were African American magazines like *Ebony*, *American Legacy Magazine*, or *The Crisis*, the oldest Black magazine, founded by W. E. B. Du Bois and published by the NAACP, but these are not generally introduced in the public schools. Where, then, would the general populace learn about the Gullah/Geechee culture and the challenges facing them regarding preservation of their land? Only if they had watched *Daughters of the Dust*, the 1991 film produced by Julie Dash, or the *Gullah Gullah Island* TV series for children in the mid- to late nineties.

The year following this trip, Emory Campbell received an honorary doctorate from Bank Street. In addition, our commitment to the work being accomplished at the Penn Center inspired me and my fellow travelers to hold a modest dinner fundraiser at Bank Street for the Penn Center. We presented Emory with a check for two thousand dollars as our contribution in preserving the legacy of the Penn Center.

Jamaica, in 2002, provided us with a glimpse into its past through a visit to historic Falmouth, with its Georgian architecture, the Harmony Hall Art Gallery, and the production of sugarcane at the Long Pond Factory. We were exposed to Jamaica's rich cross-cultural history, art and architecture, economy, music, education, and stories. The first Caribbean country to gain independence from Britain, Jamaica is rich in natural resources, like bauxite, with breathtaking views throughout the island, especially its interior. The visit to the infamous Rose Hall Estate, with its violent past, was challenging for three of our members, who felt the negative energy within the rooms and had to leave the building. The story of the evil Annie Palmer, former owner of Rose Hall Estate, was made famous through the novel *The White Witch of Rose Hall*.

One unplanned activity was the special cooking lessons for our group at the Fisherman's Inn, in which several individuals participated, and then it was storytelling time the Jamaican way, by acting it out. We later toured a sugar factory, and we learned how to drink coconut water from the coconut on visiting the home of Mr. Spence, manager of the sugar factory. We also received a warm welcome and lunch at the Sam Sharpe Teacher Training college in Montego Bay, where we were able to participate in a mini-conference on campus. Sam Shape, whose ideas about freedom and justice inspired his followers to participate in the 1832 Western Liberation Uprising, is now one of Jamaica's national heroes.

Our group of educators traveled to Finland in 2003, to learn about its education system and culture. We landed in Helsinki, the capital, all bleary-eyed after a sleepless night of air travel from New York City. That afternoon all twenty-two of us were welcomed in the home of Leila Mustanoja, whose father had worked with the Fulbright Foundation. There we met with several of her friends, who talked with us about life and customs in Finland, while we ate pulla and drank coffee, a custom in Finland. We learned from Leila's friends that children start school at age seven and that adults and children are deeply connected to the natural environment.

During our tour of the city, we saw the musical sculpture carved by Eila Hiltunen, a female artist, in Sibelius Park; participated in the baptism of a Congolese baby in the Rock Church, or the Temppeliaukion Kyrka, actually built into a granite rock; and learned that shipbuilding, paper, and high technology were among the country's major industries. I will always remember our visit to the Kiasma Museum, where I first saw Yinka Shonibare's unique, bold, and compelling artwork. A British-Nigerian artist, he "inserted" his photographs into famous British paintings as the "outsider within." In a sense he became a "disrupter," because, as Suzanne Landau and Jean Fisher wrote in *Yinka Shonibare: Double Dress*, "connecting to the centres of power has not been an easy matter for black British artists whose work has tended to be accepted not for its artistic merit but for the extent to which it could be disengaged from mainstream art."[3] Shonibare also designed Victorian-styled clothing using African textiles, another extremely creative and much-welcomed activity that I have often thought about with admiration. Shonibare's creations were so out of the box and so startling that I hope they will continue to be inspirations for future artists, especially Black artists.

From Helsinki, we flew to Mariehamn, capital of the Aland Islands, where we were warmly greeted by Johanna Grussner and her family, and where Swedish is the language spoken. I had met Johanna in New York City through Margaret Bartelme, a regular Long Trip participant and friend. Margaret had hired Johanna as a teaching artist for her Bronx public school classes, but she was back in Aland for us, and to see her family. Johanna actually lived in Sweden. Joanna accompanied us on visits to both academic and vocational schools where we met with teachers and students and learned about the many challenges facing youth and families, and that 62 percent of the children came from unmarried and single parents. Admirably, there was no judgment attached to the families or their children. Our meeting with the department of human services shared information about the current social problems, including alcoholism. Later we were interviewed for an article that appeared in the local papers the following day with a photograph of our group.

Following a special and awesome organ recital in the eleventh-century St. Michael's Church, arranged just for us, we were dinner guests at Johanna Grussner's parents' landmark farmhouse. We left Finland with new knowledge about its people, place, and culture: its education system, where all teachers must have a graduate (MA) degree; that children learn three languages; that the union supports teachers to continue their professional development; that there are good benefits for families, for example, eleven months' maternity leave; and that no foreigner can buy land in Aland. This was an absolutely amazing and most gratifying learning experience. In Aland, from my perspective, we saw a government working to benefit its people.

The 2004 Long Trip to Costa Rica was focused on the rain forest and the natural environment. Following our welcome at the Peace University in San Jose, where we learned that Costa Rica has no army, we traveled through forest and alpine vegetation to La Fortuna and Arenal, site of an active volcano, and famous for the hot springs at its base. After relaxing in the geothermally heated pools, we left the following day for Monteverde, where we observed small-scale agricultural projects in the St. Luis valley and provided materials to equip the one-room Community Kinder, along with sufficient funds for the teacher to obtain her certification, purchase a computer, and complete some personal dental work. We were fortunate in meeting, and visiting the home of, Lucky Grundion, the last surviving family member of the fifty Quaker families who left Ohio in the fifties because they were pacifists.

Walking and waiting patiently in the rainforest, we were able to see the exquisite Quetzal bird; everyone was excited and took as many photos as was possible before she flew out of sight. Prior to leaving Costa Rica, I heard of the renewed interest of some Costa Ricans in reviving and promoting their cultural connections to Jamaica, especially through music. I even listened to a tape of the calypso music being sung by an older calypsonian, a second- or third-generation Jamaican. That was interesting to me because as a young child in Jamaica, I had heard of Jamaicans leaving the island to work in

Panama and Cuba, but I did not recall Costa Rica as another place for work opportunities. I learned that they worked on the banana plantations and lived on the Caribbean side of Costa Rica. However, we were not scheduled to visit Limón, so I missed interacting with the Jamaican cultural group. My final event in Costa Rica was experiencing a spectacular performance by pianist Manuel Obregón in an outdoor space.

The Long Trip to Tennessee in 2005 was focused on civil rights and social and environmental justice. Staying at the Highlander Center, we learned about its broad-based movements for social change, including work on popular education, labor, civil rights, immigrants' rights, and empowering people for action. This was Bank Street's second trip to Highlander. In 1948 student teachers led by the college's Eleanor Hogan visited the Highlander Center, where they met with Myles Horton, Highlander's founder. There is a wonderful photograph from the archives showing Miles Horton talking to the group of student teachers seated outside on the grass. Eleanor Hogan stands nearby.

On our visit, we met and sang with famous authors, singers, and friends of Miles Horton, Guy and Candie Carawan. This delightful couple regaled us with stories and songs of the labor and Civil Rights Movements. It was Guy who encouraged the singing of "We Shall Overcome," which became the anthem of the Civil Rights Movement. While Candie described the preparation of Rosa Parks for participating in the bus boycott, it was also interesting to hear about the less serious side of Ms. Parks when Candie fondly recalled that Rosa Parks "was always up to something."

On leaving that remarkable space, where singers like Woody Guthrie, Pete Seeger, Bernice Reagon—founder of the a capella group Sweet Honey in the Rock—and others all had a presence, we visited the Norris Dam, the first dam constructed by the Tennessee Valley Authority, and Alex Haley's farm, with its Maya Lin–designed ark-shaped chapel, before we drove to Nashville.

During the ride I stared in wonder at the lush, calming, and beautiful Smoky Mountains; they were indeed a surprising pleasure. On arriving in Nashville, we soon located the public library, then climbed its unexpected and magnificent sweeping staircase leading to the Civil Rights Room; there we sat at the impressively recreated lunch counter. Stories with pictures from the sit-ins were encased under glass for protection. We read the stories in silence. Then the librarian shared with us more compelling stories from the civil rights era, about key players like Septima Clark who taught literacy to African Americans so they could vote. I was inspired to learn about her.

My favorite story that day was about students being trained together in nonviolence and peaceful sit-ins in Nashville. White and well-dressed Black students would enter a restaurant. Upon arriving, the white students scattered around the room without attracting any attention, while the Black students sat at the lunch counter waiting to be served. When the Black students were arrested, the white students, who had pockets full of dimes, would call headquarters so another group of Black students could immediately arrive to take their places. After several such repeated actions over several months, these brave students' actions led to the desegregation of lunch counters in Nashville following a meeting with the mayor.

I found the story to be so inspiring. Vanderbilt University, years later, honored James Lawson, who also taught there. We also met with Avon Rollins, cofounder of the Student Nonviolent Coordinating Committee (SNCC), executive director of the Beck Cultural Exchange Center, and a very prominent social justice activist in Knoxville. Mr. Rollins in his presentation told us that one of his real regrets was the absence of Black women on the platform in DC during the March on Washington. He wished that he had done something to change that situation, since the women were major contributors to the planning and execution of the march. I was pleased to hear his reflection on the critical role of women in that significant event. I learned years later that Mr. Rollins passed away in 2018.

In April 2006, our group headed to West Virginia, another site of the original Long Trips, where our focus was now on the effects of coal mining on the environment, and social justice. Our guide was Bill Price, an activist from the Sierra Club. On our first evening, we were treated to the music of Appalachia by famed fiddler David Bing. Over the next few days, we saw the destructive impact of mountaintop removal on the health of individuals, families and communities, their schools, and streams. Group members noted sadly that miles of once-beautiful mountains were now denuded. In sampling ramp onions, a staple in West Virginia, we learned that the mountains were pharmacies and supermarkets for residents. We admired the strengths of the people, for example, the "Dust Busters," two women who had organized their community to challenge the coal companies and to create healthier environments. For them, it's not what the law says but whether the law is enforced, which more often than not is not enforced.

In Beckley, we spent about forty-five minutes underground in one mine and shuddered at the dampness, low ceilings, and cruel conditions that miners had to endure when the mine was active, while being paid twenty cents per ton of coal. We met many remarkable residents, listened to local storytelling, heard ballads, and were introduced to mountain-style dancing. In West Virginia my group saw and heard from several community members about the severe health and environmental damage caused by mountaintop removal, an environmentally destructive way used by coal companies to extract coal by blasting off the tops of mountains and using tractors to dig for coal. The resulting waste was then pushed into the streams and rivers, which soon destroyed the fish life and polluted the waters. My group and I actually visited one of the denuded mountain sites and a polluted stream where the destruction was truly shocking and very sad. We were all so moved by the sight before us: utter devastation, not a mountain was visible. The scene reminded me of the devastation of numerous acres of once-lush vegetation left barren in Jamaica as a result of bauxite mining. I bought a CD recording, *Moving Mountains: Voices of Appalachia*, the story and grief of mountaintop removal coal mining. The songs are plaintive and evoke moving images of what losing their mountains meant to the community. In one song, the mountain is personalized and tells how as a West Virginia mountain, "I am nervous, I am wondering if I am gonna lose my top."

Mountaintop removal ruined the health of residents and devastated the once-beautiful mountains. My group and I felt much empathy with the awful experiences of this West Virginia community, but we also admired their strength, as residents pursued legal recourse to stop the coal companies' actions, and as they also continued to advocate for, and be hopeful about, justice to improve the environmental and community conditions. A real David-and-Goliath story.

Later that year Bill visited Bank Street and spoke to students in the School for Children about ways to protect the environment. Then-faculty Ann Porter, who cared about social justice, joined the Pennies for Promises campaign and delivered several huge bags of pennies on the doorstep of the legislature in West Virginia to build a new and safe K–5 school for the Marshfork community.

We were motivated to visit Iceland in 2007 because Bank Street's esteemed faculty Harriet Cuffaro had introduced the use of blocks in that country's early childhood curriculum. During the bus ride from Keflavik Airport to our hotel, I was struck by the unbelievably surreal environment featuring an almost barren landscape with numerous round stone sculptures along the highway, no evidence of grass, snow-capped low mountains in the distance, and black volcanic soil. The sky was gray and overcast. There was little or no vegetation, and no trees anywhere, but once in a while clusters of houses appeared, quite far apart from each other. I learned that two-thirds of the entire population live in Reykjavik, the capital.

Prior to our appointment with the Department of Education, we explored the National Gallery of Iceland and the Culture House. In the latter I learned about Iceland's history and culture through manuscripts on the eddas and sagas on display. These were captivating twelfth-century handwritten manuscripts, illustrated with fine drawings and so exciting to behold. Later, at the Department of Education, we learned that the mayor controls the schools, and that schools were now working on strategies to successfully include children whose parents immigrated from the Philippines, Russia, and Lithuania. This appeared to be a new challenge for Icelandic teachers, who were still figuring out how to integrate the children so that they would be comfortable and would soon develop a feeling of belonging in the classroom.

Our visits to four preschools were enlightening. We observed how young students interacted with each other and were trusted by their teachers to work independently; they were also free to move among the various classrooms. We were surprised by how quiet the teachers were; their voices were rarely heard, and children were encouraged to resolve conflict by talking together. The classroom walls were devoid of paintings and postings, which added to the calm within rooms. We couldn't help comparing the overall calm and quiet of Icelandic classrooms with NYC early childhood classrooms overflowing with paintings and other materials on the walls and teachers' voices ever present. When one member of our group inquired whether children go outside in bad weather, the Icelandic teacher responded, "Yes, they do; there is no bad weather, only bad clothing!"

We had an opportunity to soak in the geothermally heated Blue Lagoon, gaze at the awesome Gullfoss waterfall and, later, the magnificent Hallgrimskirkja (church) structure. In addition, I was inspired by and fascinated to read the novels *Iceland's Bell* and *Independent People*, both written by Iceland's Nobel Prize–winning writer Halldor Laxness. I was fascinated by learning so many unique pieces of information about Iceland. For example, the world's first and oldest parliament was Iceland's Althing, founded in 930 in the Thingvellir National Park; judges meted out punishments from the top of the high rocks at Thingvellir to the accused, who waited at the foot of the rocks. Other notes of interest were that Icelanders refer to the weather as "he," that mountains are sacred to the people, and that Denmark ruled Iceland from 1400 to 1600.

In 2009 our group traveled to New Orleans, Louisiana, also known as NOLA. We participated in a panel discussion hosted by faculty from Dillard University, Delgado Community College, and the city's Office of Recovery, focused on the ability of sunflower plants to remove toxins from contaminated soil; the toxin remained in the roots of the sunflower plant. Given these results, the Office of Recovery initiated the Sunflower Project, converting remediated lots into much-needed sustainable vegetable gardens providing residents access to fresh and safe food. We learned from local activists about the devastating impact of Hurricane Katrina on the African American, Houma, and Vietnamese communities. The many community activists with whom we met were focused on changing deliberately crafted unfair societal systems and rebuilding communities after the hurricane that devastated NOLA but especially the Ninth Ward, where most African Americans resided. The activists told us that volunteers from New York City were the best helpers, and their help was much appreciated. They also explained that their local politicians did little to help them and frequently thwarted their recovery efforts.

Lunch at Café Reconcile, a nonprofit restaurant, exemplified how strategic partnerships can help youth in under-resourced communities get the training needed to become self-sufficient, while our visit to the Juvenile Justice Project of Louisiana (JJPL) left us feeling deeply hopeless about sharply reducing the very high numbers of African American children in detention facilities. A nonprofit, the JJPL is working to reform the state system; we learned that the rates of suspensions, expulsions, and incarceration of youth throughout Louisiana are the highest in the country. These youth were arrested for the slightest infractions, which seriously affected their futures as capable and contributing citizens, not to mention the loss of just being adolescents and the suppressing of their natural talents. I am still saddened by the juvenile justice system's unfair treatment of African American youth. Little or no counseling is available for youth, which could have been a deterrent to suspensions. An awfully sad situation.

Moreover, our group heard a lot about activism, women as activists, and self-help as tools for social change in New Orleans. But the struggles continue with the ongoing oppression of Black and brown people and the persistent systemic barriers that they regularly confront.

However, our visit to NOLA would not have been complete without coffee and beignets at Café du Monde, and a concert at Preservation Hall.

In Patzcuaro, Mexico, 2010, we observed and were deeply moved by the Procession of Silence, the silent walk of nuns and other congregants with candles during Easter, and the general reverence with which this activity was observed. Along with this extraordinary activity, we were hearing the history of the ancient empire of the Purepechans, the current arts, culture, and ceremonies of the city, and being amazed at the complex design of the pyramids we visited. The spirit of a harsh historical past was ever present in Patzcuaro with its cobbled streets; we heard the stories of the brutal colonization of indigenous peoples, saw the awesome pyramids, and visited the health clinic that used herbs and traditional medicine to heal. We also watched with fascination young men using masks, canes, and costumes perform "The Dance of the Old Men."

After showing us the film *El Sistema*, our hotel owner was so thrilled at how engaged we were in the discussion that ensued that he labeled us as the hotel's best guests ever. Patzcuaro was quite another spiritual experience.

In Seattle, Washington, 2011, we focused on the cultural connections, challenges and community involvement among First Nations peoples, visited their Daybreak Cultural Center, and learned from storyteller Roger Fernandes that the Duwamish is Seattle's native group and one of twenty-nine recognized tribes in the state. He shared that Seattle was named after an Indian chief, and the importance of salmon to the survival of First Nations people, since "the salmon brings life to us." Lunch at the Lummi Youth Academy, a residential school and drug treatment center for their youth, provided insight into the successes and struggles within this extraordinary self-help group. The movement then was around tribes taking control of their education from the dominant majority group.

The Wing Luke Museum, named after the first Asian American elected to the city council, illuminated the sad stories and struggles of the early Chinese immigrants through its Tradition and Change exhibits. Themes of social justice were evident in several exhibits throughout our tour. Visits to the Japanese Garden and the Hiram M. Chittenden Locks, critical to Seattle's marine industry, were additional treasures to behold in this beautiful place.

Then on to the historic Panama Hotel, where the personal possessions of Japanese families who were sent to various relocation camps between 1942 and 1945 could be seen through a glass window secured within the middle of the floor. I had read about this hotel in Jamie Ford's book *Hotel at the Corner of Bitter and Sweet* and so planned a special visit there to see the exhibit, reflect on that period of history, and, later, indulge in dessert and coffee in its current iteration as a tea and coffee house. Our visit to Seattle ended with a tour of her bookbinding workshop, a delicious dinner, and lively conversation in the home of Claudia Cohen, Carol's friend.

In Havana, Cuba, during 2012, we visited schools; exceptional arts programs; an exquisite ballet performance with dancers of varied skin colors, which was a pleasure to see; the Fuster community, where every building was a work of art; a planned ecotourism community, Las Terrazas; and Ernest Hemingway's home. Walking through the Plazas of the Cathedral and the Revolution, I could imagine the former grandeur of the magnificent old buildings surrounding the plazas, many of which were now in grave disrepair. I learned that prior to the revolution, often just one family owned and occupied many of those elaborate and extraordinary buildings. That was hard to believe, given the size of those buildings.

At the University of Havana, a graduate student led us to a grand building with amazing murals on the ceiling. We learned that the faces of the women on the ceiling were actually daughters of wealthy donors. A visit to the Upmann Cigar Factory revealed that 25,000 cigars are produced daily. We saw workers rolling cigars of different sizes, colors, taste, and flavors; we ate well and enjoyed the cuisine in both the government restaurants and the privately owned Paladares. In Cuba we did not get to talk with the citizens except the brief dialogues with teachers and with the graduate student who guided us at the university. However, our tour guide, who had left his teaching position to earn more money leading tours, felt comfortable with our group and so provided us with additional inside information.

In our 2013 visit to Panama City, Panama, we observed the canal in operation, endured a rocky canoe ride to lunch with the Emberá people upstream, and visited the Frank Gehry–designed BioDiversity Museum. We saw the beautifully decorated modes of transportation wherever we traveled, and the food we ate was delicious. Panama City was a study in strong contrasts: tall, very modern office and apartment buildings alongside old, poorly maintained, dilapidated buildings. We also visited Colón, which has a Free Zone where visitors can shop for duty-free merchandise. Colón was also the city where West Indians lived as they worked on the Panama Canal. I recalled a mento or calypso from my younger days in Jamaica about "One, two, three, four, Colón man a come . . .

[repeat three times] / Wid him brass string him nak him belly boom, boom, boom." We also discovered the Museum of the West Indies located in a former wooden church building, and saw the special items the West Indian workers who came to seek work on the canal had brought to Panama to keep their home culture alive. A common thread among the places visited where social justice was an issue was the past and current harsh and cruel treatment of people from the African Diaspora. The only places where hope for positive change seemed possible were the Penn Center in the South Carolina Sea Islands, and the Highlander Cultural Center in Tennessee. Jamaica could occupy third place, but it has to be more intentional in specific areas.

Copenhagen, Denmark, on the 2015 Long Trip, offered our group opportunities to explore education in a forest school and to spend a morning visiting classes in an independent school; to be transfixed by the sea of bicycles flooding the streets; and to be fascinated by the Christiana autonomous community, a commune on eighty-five acres, where there were beautiful murals all around and the blacksmith shop was owned and operated by women. A few of us traveled by train to see the Louisiana Museum and to lunch in its tranquil surroundings.

In visiting Mariendal Friskole, a private school where some of the tuition is paid by the state, we observed several classes and were then invited to attend the school's regular assembly. We were told that the focus was on developing a child's mind, heart, and body using themes from philosophy, singing, storytelling, or games. Faculty usually prepared a script with a presenting problem, such as bad manners, which they then role-played. We saw how the school integrated critical-thinking processes using the scenario presented to the children onstage by two teachers. The students then worked out their solutions together by careful examination of the issue.

Later, we learned from a student that the scenario presented in the assembly would be discussed in his philosophy class. The function of the assembly is community building, so that children will feel safe in their environment. Following graduation, students attend a Danish gymnasium—similar to a US academic preparatory school—that over three years prepares students for university entry, through an exit examination. Later that evening we experienced the joy of being guests for refreshments in the home of one of the teachers we met at this charming school.

Moreover, we traveled by train to Norrebro, a neighborhood in which many immigrants lived, and enjoyed lunch at Send More Spices, a restaurant run by a diverse group of immigrant women; we also walked to Osterley to experience a different neighborhood and took a guided minibus tour of the city. Different from our other Long Trips was the amount of walking we accomplished in Copenhagen; there was so much to see, including the opulence and grandeur of the Christiansborg Palace and a canal ride for another perspective.

Our Long Trip to Scotland in 2016 began in Glasgow, reputed to be the third-oldest city in the UK. Our group of eleven educators and friends of Bank Street desired to see other models of forest schools. We visited the Secret Gardens Forest School, where children were immersed all day in exploring and learning about the forest and nature. Their natural curiosities and imaginations were enhanced as, using available material, they studied and role-played in the forest. The curriculum was more eclectic at the Mindstretchers Forest School, whose philosophy is "inside, outside and beyond," with "beyond" representing the nearby forest, where children explore "nature on nature's terms." Unlike the Secret Garden, Mindstretchers has a small building and an open shedlike structure. The children's learnings are documented in different formats, and portfolios are prepared on each child connecting his/her development to Scotland's curriculum.

On our tour of the city, I noticed that many of the streets bore Caribbean names, such as Jamaica Street and Trinidad Street, and on inquiring learned that Glasgow's former immense wealth came from the trading of sugar, tobacco, and other products from the West Indies during the eighteenth and nineteenth centuries, and was linked to the slave trade in Jamaica, with its thriving sugarcane plantations and the production of sugar. Of current interest is a recently signed memorandum of agreement between the University of the West Indies and the University of Glasgow to study the effects of slavery and programs for reparations.[4] This event occurred on July 11, 2019, and was attended by UWI vice chancellor, Sir Hilary Beckles, and the University of Glasgow chief operating officer, Dr. David Duncan.

Today, shipbuilding is a major industry in Glasgow, and the River Clyde has been critical to the city's economic development. Our hotel, the Grasshopper, was nestled between two nondescript buildings and did not stand out until I was in my surprisingly calm and inviting room, with cool gray and white colors, and facing Glasgow's historic railway station. At the Glasgow Women's Library, by chance, we met Sharon Thomas, artist wife of city council member Matt Kerr. Sharon arranged for her husband to give us a tour of the council's historic structure.

Our walk up the wide and impressive marble staircase was slow as we marveled at the grandeur and elegance of the interior. Matt also pointed to the bust of Nelson Mandela that was prominently displayed in the council's lobby. He explained that Mr. Mandela received the Freedom of the City award in 1981, and that Glasgow was the first city to support Mr. Mandela while he was in prison. Glasgow renamed its famous St. George's Square as Nelson Mandela Place, and two years after his release from prison, Mandela visited Glasgow to thank its citizens for their years of supporting and advocating for his release from prison.

After listening to the daily lunchtime organ recital at the Kelvingrove Gallery and Museum, we were off to the Scotland Street School Museum designed by Glasgow's celebrated artist Charles Rennie Mackintosh and opened in 1906. Built for children of the then-thriving shipbuilding industry around the River Clyde, the school closed in 1979.

The next stop was Edinburgh. With its stately architecture, the city appeared much lighter in color than Glasgow. After visiting the awesome Edinburgh Castle at the top of the Royal Mile, and the Canongate Church, which Queen Elizabeth attends when she is in Scotland (and sitting behind her pew), and its historic graveyard, and receiving a gracious welcome by the vicar, we next viewed the gardens and art exhibit in the Inverleith House. Memorable for me was afternoon tea at the Colonnades at the Signet Library; that's not to be missed after visiting the fascinating Edinburgh Castle. There was so much to see and history to learn in Scotland.

In Aland I saw a place where the government took care of its people; in Detroit, Michigan, on our 2017 Long Trip, I saw a local government that not only neglected its African American citizens but intentionally ruined their lives. Our experience in Detroit began by attending a most inspirational Sunday morning church service at the historic Second Baptist Church, where we were warmly welcomed by Rev. Dr. Kevin Turman, the African American pastor and Harvard Divinity School graduate who invited our new coordinator, Abby Kerlin, to describe the purpose of our visit for the congregation. Although our group contained members of several different faiths, everyone felt included and inspired by his keen awareness and acknowledgment of the challenges around the globe. He was masterful and thoughtful in his use of inclusive language, giving something special to each person present. With such an auspicious beginning, we headed to our next major meeting at the James and Grace Lee Boggs Center to Nurture Community Leadership.

There, we heard from various grassroots activists about the different schemes used by the city's decision makers to drive African American families from their homes; we toured devastated communities where houses that were once beautiful and intact were now shells due to the city deliberately combining excessive water rates with their mortgages that residents could not pay and so lost their homes. In education their public schools were losing to increasing numbers of charter schools, and the lack of adequate public transportation in communities with Black residents remained a persistent challenge in navigating the city.

However, our meetings with activists from the James and Grace Lee Boggs Center to Nurture Community Leadership and lunch at the Earthworks Soup Kitchen operated by the Capuchin Brothers gave us hope. Speakers at the Boggs Center offered up new ways of thinking about sustainable activism, grassroots efforts to reimagine work, rebuild devastated communities, and care for each other. We learned about and saw revolutionary art, industry, and innovation at work, and thoughtful individuals joining together to reframe the conversation around social and environmental injustice. Pony Ride, a nonprofit space, trains women living in homeless shelters to sew special coats for homeless individuals. The coats serve as a sleeping bag or shoulder bag when not in use. This was innovation at work.

We observed teaching and learning approaches in classrooms at the Boggs School, which uses the environment as a foundation for student learning; at the Wayne State Early Childhood Learning Center; and the Spain Elementary School, a performing arts school. Tours of the Detroit Institute of Arts; the Heidelberg (art) Project featuring discarded items; Motown, which produced and turned local singers into national and internationally famous musical artists, all accomplished in a relatively small and modest building; and the Museum of African American History further enhanced our knowledge about the African American experience in different spaces, as well as the transatlantic slave trade. In the museum the visual manifestation of the Africans packed like sardines in the ship holds was both startling and moving. As we moved past the horrific reminders of the suffering of so many souls, we were confronted, just a few steps away, by the "door of no return." On exiting the museum, most of us needed a few minutes of silence to reflect and recover.

Before leaving Detroit we returned to the Second Baptist Church for a tour and important history lesson. "Midnight" was the code for Detroit on the Underground Railroad, less than two miles to Canada and freedom for enslaved people. This church was a critical stop on the Underground Railroad. Visiting Detroit was a history lesson for all of us. Detroit represented all the injustices with which African Americans were confronted, yet their determination and continued resistance to oppression were also evident in the music, art, and continued activism to bring about change for societal betterment.

In 2018 we traveled to Selma, Alabama, where we walked over the famed Pettus Bridge, met and listened attentively as the original "Foot Soldiers" shared their stories about that horrific and brutal experience when policemen on horses cornered them on the bridge and were merciless. Our storytellers, now retired adults, were children at the time of the event but were participants in that unforgettable experience. Listening to their stories was simultaneously heartrending and empowering. They had succeeded against all odds and were now involved in meaningful social and educational activities to benefit and strengthen their community.

In reflecting on all those trips, what stood out for me was how moved and appreciative were the people with whom we met that we were interested in knowing about their lives, histories, strengths, and challenges. They were proud and delighted to share their stories with us, and sometimes to dine with us. Mr. Charles Maulden's story that "being inquisitive was a threat" in Alabama, and so Black children did not ask questions, resonated with me, since I was always inquisitive as a child. I could hardly envision accepting and not inquiring "why" in Jamaica, yet adults and children alike would be risking their lives to raise questions in the South. They could be killed or parents could be punished by losing their jobs or being jailed on some trumped-up charge. Mr. Maulden credited Stokely Carmichael, from Trinidad, and his SNCC movement for inspiring him to "break loose from intellectual incarceration." He began to read books, expanded his vocabulary, and joined the movement. He told us that the Civil Rights Movement provided youth in Alabama and elsewhere in the South with an opportunity to expand their vision and be involved in some activity that benefited their community and provided a sense of personal satisfaction.

Our group always left something behind for our new friends, as concrete as books and supplies for children in the empty classroom in Monteverde, or my and others' ongoing financial support of the Penn and Highlander Centers. Except in Cuba, meeting the local people was very important for us, and we all left with fond memories and a mix of emotions from these meetings. In planning the Long Trips, our relationships usually began with the first phone call to a key individual living in the place to be visited. Once he or she learned of our wish to come as learners, the excitement was obvious as together we planned the itinerary. We have yet to be disappointed as we fulfill Mrs. Mitchell's vision to broaden and enrich the experiences of educators by exposing them, and us, to new people and environments.

While our cultural and racial awareness, histories, and knowledge of geography were significantly increased on these journeys, we were also introducing Bank Street abroad to many new educators and community activists, thereby increasing the college's visibility and excellent reputation. Although some faculty from the Graduate School and the School for Children had already developed partnerships with schools abroad, for example, Rato Bangala School in Nepal since 1991, the Long Trips introduced larger groups of US educators and other professionals to new experiences, to new learning, and to each other, contributing to our own continuing education/lifelong learning.

The Long Trips have led to the development of many lasting relationships for participants. For me, one of these relationships is with Dr. Torbjorn Sandel, or Toby, a director within the Abo Akademi in Vasa, Finland. When Toby desired to visit schools in New York, his friend Johanna Grussner connected us. I arranged a special schedule for Toby and his two colleagues to visit and meet educators at Bank Street, Midtown West School, a high school in Harlem, and other educational sites that had supportive environments and progressive practices. They were delighted and very impressed with the resulting conversations with fellow educators, and especially appreciative that they were able to continue these conversations at a dinner in our home at the end of their visit. Since that time, Toby and I have kept connected through our annual Christmas correspondence, when we share family and school happenings. Toby also wrote about his experiences with us in his book on education, a Swedish publication.

Another important personal benefit for me was getting to know my fabulous and fearless cocoordinator and friend Carol B. Hillman. Besides being an enlightened and highly respected educator, Carol is an inspirational author, farmer, visionary, and philanthropist. For me, she is forever a reflective practitioner and a true humanist. Besides having been a very supportive friend of my division, Continuing Education, Carol is thoughtful, respectful of the gifts within each individual, and attuned to the effects of climate and geography, as well as the social and economic conditions affecting citizens in each country, state, or city we visited.

In her writings and conversation, Carol advocates for environments promoting discovery and developing curiosity in young children. She feels strongly, and rightly so, that we should "model the kind of person we would like them [children] to be." Carol's writings, whether in her books or on the Long Trips, are educative, and sheer poetry. In her review of Carol's book *Teaching Four-Year-Olds: A Personal Journey*, educator Arlene Uss wrote that Carol's work envisions "a classroom that nurtures children to be friendly and helpful, curious and alive, exploratory and risk-taking in the service of discovery, and most of all, a safe haven to love, laugh, and learn."[5] Arlene anticipates that this book will become "a classic."

While Carol is all of the above, she is also especially gifted with a quiet sense of humor, thoughtfulness, and with a warmth and ready connection to the people we met and places we visited on the Long Trips. I have benefited from her thoughtfulness and sensibilities, both of which were evident in her reflection on our 2017 Long Trip to Detroit. Carol wrote that she was filled with "a reverence . . . as we explored neighborhoods, witnessed crumbling factories and abandoned houses, talked the talk with community organizers, teachers, an urban farmer, listened to jazz and felt an overarching air of dedication, from all those that we met, to their city in transition, and hope to improve the human condition." Those thoughtful qualities are also just as visible in the gifts, always connected to the place just visited, that she sends me following each and every trip. And I am always pleasantly and honestly surprised, excited, and delighted on opening those totally unexpected gifts.

CHAPTER 17

CONNECTIONS AND PARTNERSHIPS
WITH NONPROFITS

In my board work at Bank Street during the nineties, I worked with the chair of the program committee to orient trustees to new program developments, to plan site visits and prepare program presentations at the full board meetings. However, I soon became aware that trustees desired to hear about the challenges and key issues that each program area was confronting, and either how they could be helpful and supportive or how these challenges were being addressed or resolved as opposed to just hearing reports on programs.

My first invitation to become a board member in other nonprofits came from two of Bank Street's very active and involved trustees, Betty Pforzheimer and Sally Kerlin. They invited me to serve on boards with which both trustees were affiliated, New Alternatives for Children (NAC) and Wave Hill, respectively, and almost at the same time. Both places were engaged in important work to positively enhance the lives of children and families. As a social work agency, NAC provides comprehensive services to medically fragile children and their families, and Wave Hill is a magnificent cultural institution offering a breathtaking vista, alluring gardens to inspire and uplift the human spirit, art, and educational programs focused on environmental science.

Moreover, as the work and outreach activities of the Division of Continuing Education expanded beyond schools to afterschool programs after the mid-nineties, my connections to the nonprofit world blossomed and expanded tremendously. Bank Street's name was well respected in the education field, so many program administrators were delighted to partner with the college. Our partnerships increased significantly.

One such dynamic partnership was forged between Bank Street and Stevens Institute of Technology/SIT in 1998. The connection was made through President Kappner after she met and had a conversation with Dr. Edward Friedman, physicist and dean, Center for Improved Engineering & Science Education/CIESE in New Jersey. The internet was becoming a useful tool in education, and Dr. Friedman understood the importance of helping teachers understand how to effectively use the tools that were emerging, in other words, to become "facilitators of learning." He and his team first developed the Savvy Cyber Teacher (SCT) a curriculum that trained school teachers to integrate "unique and compelling" use of the internet into their classroom courses in schools with a goal to strengthen the teaching of math and science courses.

As a visionary, Dr. Friedman saw how the internet could be used to excite and enhance learning in these subject areas through collaborative learning and real-time projects. The Savvy Cyber Professor soon followed to help community college faculty integrate "unique and compelling" use of the internet into their science and math courses."[1] The focus was now on preservice students in education. In our partnership Stevens had the content and scientific expertise, while Bank Street brought a developmental approach and an understanding that children learn best as they interact with the environment, with adults, and with their peers.[2] The latter is also true for many adults. Our combined strengths worked well for our eventual professional development work together in training several hundred classroom teachers in New Jersey as well as community college faculty in Miami, Cleveland, and Phoenix whom I met on our visits to promote the program. The partnership with Stevens was a successful one, with learning occurring on all sides, soon creating a community of learners.

The division's collaboration with the New York Times (NYT) was another partnership that worked well and benefited classroom teachers using technology as a tool. Working closely with the thoughtful, patient, and supportive Rev. Craig Dunn, then of the New York Times, Bank Street became curriculum advisor for the New York Times Learning Network, an educational support available online for parents and teachers. The articles to be converted as online curricula were selected by the NYT; however, using a collaborative approach, Bank Street and the NYT teamed with other writers to create the theme-related curricula. Bank Street and the NYT also hosted institutes to acquaint and prepare teachers in the use of these enhanced online tools.

One of several individuals taking a personal interest in the DCE programs was Jerry Blitzer, brother of board member Bill Blitzer. Jerry, a Bard College graduate, was involved with a Rikers Island program for incarcerated youth as well as with the West Side Middle School, an alternative school for students unable to function in the regular school setting. With his deep commitment to social justice, Jerry admired the division's work with youth at risk and so connected me with the principal of the West Side School, who became another partner requesting professional development for her teachers. Jerry frequently visited the division to receive updates on the Liberty Partnerships Program and made an annual financial contribution to the division's budget. When Jerry passed away, he generously gifted ten thousand dollars from his estate to continue the DCE's work.

Dr. Verne Oliver, an outstanding educator and a friend of school libraries, served on the DCE's Friends of Continuing Education Advisory Committee, imparting wisdom, friendship and financial assistance. Verne had been college faculty and an administrator in independent schools for many years. She continued to promote literacy education as director for the Gilder Foundation and became thoroughly involved in building libraries in schools. Verne was a marvelous, wise, tireless advocate and supportive colleague with a wealth of knowledge and experience about education that worked for children and youth, especially Black and brown children and youth.

In the early nineties, another divisional friend, Mrs. Norma Asnes, along with trustees Kate Whitney and Peggy Stevens, invited about a dozen formerly homeless women in one of my division's projects to a "Belated Mother's Day Celebration," in her charming Fifth Avenue apartment. Norma, a most gracious hostess, wished to celebrate and acknowledge the success achieved by the mothers despite their earlier hardships. The mothers, many now living in neighborhood revitalization apartments offering comprehensive supportive services in the Bronx, were thrilled and had an unforgettable evening, meeting new people, being celebrated, and enjoying the festivities. Their appreciation for this special recognition was expressed by all the mothers prior to departing that evening. During the planning for this event, a white male consultant to our fundraising efforts wrote me a long letter, stating that by exposing these low-income mothers, most of whom were Black, to such a wealthy environment, I was inappropriately raising their aspirations.

According to him, they would never achieve the success of their hostess, and therefore I was treating them unfairly. Once my feelings of surprise and annoyance subsided, I recalled the reason that the planning team, which included the hostess, decided to celebrate the women and was even more determined that the event was not only appropriate but would be a morale booster for our parents. And it was. The event achieved its goal of validating the women as worthy of a tasteful, celebratory, and enriching experience. I invited his participation; he attended but remained quiet throughout, did not offer any comment. I did not ask for any, and I very soon ended the consultative relationship.

His behavior reminded me of a similar reaction when I developed a comprehensive education and career training program for homeless heads of households residing in a shelter in another NYC borough. The women had access to a range of resources, including a high-quality Head Start program for their children, and counseling for themselves. The manager of this shelter complained that "these women" were undeserving of so many resources and utilized a number of strategies to close the program. His actions involved harassment of the program staff, and sending false reports on the program to the State Department. He was finally fired, but that was after I decided that we would no longer tolerate his negative behavior and found another site that supported Bank Street's vision for the women and children. The Bank Street Head Start program, over twenty-five years later, still exists and is thriving today on NYC's Lower East Side.

Dr. Pola Rosen, founder and executive director of *Education Update*, a very informative monthly newspaper for educators, featured several articles on the division's activities. Its February 2004 headline by writer Sybil Maimin was: "Fern Khan: Bank Street Dean Forges Social Work, Community Outreach & Continuing Education into Powerful Force for Change." The article clearly described the division's work and was the most fitting description ever written about the multifaceted work of the Division of Continuing Education at Bank Street College.

In addition to their work improving practice with classroom teachers and leaders, my divisional staff was involved in providing professional development for many afterschool programs. They helped afterschool staff to develop and use themes to engage youth like "Creative Curriculum for Afterschool Programs," "Understanding Adolescent Development," and "Engaging Youth through Art or Music." By participating in discussions in the field, I met many key leaders and supporters of afterschool education, like Janet Kelley, John Bess, Lucy Friedman, Rich Buery, Bill Newlin, and other influential professionals. Soon I was recruited for membership on the boards of the Partnership for Afterschool Education/PASE, a trainer for afterschool program staff using grassroots experts from the field, and the Harlem Educational Activities Fund/HEAF, a college prep program for underserved students, sixth through twelfth grade and then through college graduation. Through PASE, I met the amazing Alison Overseth, PASE's founding board president and its current visionary and inspirational executive director, and Ken deRegt, board member, philanthropist, and a former managing director at Morgan Stanley.

The relationship that soon developed between Alison and Ken is among my very favorite love stories. My intuition convinced me that Ken fell in love with Alison when he first met her. As their relationship blossomed quietly over the years, it was also apparent to a few of our fellow board members. I recall talking with colleague Bill Newlin and was surprised that he too had noticed, since Alison and Ken were very discreet and quite the professionals. Bill laughed and commented that their fondness for each other was quite apparent. Alison soon shared her story of their relationship with me, and with her approval and as PASE's board president, I informed the board, to ensure that there would be no conflict of interest. There was none. Ken and Alison are now happily married, and Ken remains an active board member.

Ken's thoughtful personality and his kindness were known within and external to the financial industry, and there are many stories about his humanity and generosity. My Bank Street programs have benefited substantially from both on numerous occasions. A few years after joining PASE's board, some of our board members were guests at a reception at a Manhattan East Side location. I was talking with a few colleagues about my Bank Street academic program at the Bedford Hills prison, and the positive effect the program was having on the female inmates. Ken was listening quietly. Then he asked, "How much do you need to implement the program?" I didn't think I had heard the question correctly, since very few individuals were so direct in offering funds for programs, so I kept talking until Bill Newlin, obviously amused, asked, "Fern, did you not hear Ken's question?" I looked at Ken, who with obvious earnestness repeated the question. Seeing he was serious, I asked, still in a state of semi-disbelief, "Could I get back to you on that question?" Ken replied, "Sure, just call or email me with the amount."

On returning to my office the next morning, I looked at the budget I had prepared for that semester and sent it on to Ken. Within two days, I received a check in the mail for the exact amount I had submitted.

As a board member of HEAF, I met Dan Rose, real estate developer, philanthropist, author, and HEAF's founder. With his wife, Joanna, he has financially supported and remained active with the organization since the early nineties. Dan speaks passionately on, and writes numerous essays about, a wide range of social, global, educational, political, and personal identity topics to which he has given serious thoughts. A collection of his essays and speeches was published in his books *Making a Living, Making a Life* (2014) and *The Examined Life* (2019). Dan is also a founder of the *Harlem Times*, an informative newspaper serving the Harlem community, and since 1993 has been involved in several projects in Ghana through his Helping Africa Foundation. One of these projects is the renovation of the W. E. B. Du Bois Memorial Center in Accra, which had fallen into disrepair.

I also reconnected with Dr. Danielle Lee, educator, writer, administrator, advocate for social justice, and HEAF's former CEO. It was Danielle who recruited me for the HEAF board. Danielle was already showing leadership skills when I first met her as a teenager. Since then she has mentored and helped hundreds of youth, especially Black and brown youth, to achieve their personal and educational goals. Danielle is currently executive director for the Oliver Program, whose aim is to prepare and support youth for college and for life.

And then there is the knowledgeable, warm, and generous David F. Walker, who knows almost everyone in the nonprofit and funding worlds and is comfortable in sharing his wealth of knowledge with anyone who needs that information. David, a true connector, who for many years worked at the United Way of NYC in development, now consults with nonprofits and does much pro bono work. He is also known for preparing novelty and exciting meals for friends at a moment's notice.

By the time I retired from Bank Street in 2012, I was serving on six boards, including PASE, Goddard Riverside Community Center, New Alternatives for Children, the American Caribbean Maritime Foundation, HEAF, and Gray Matters, the latter an organization that helps nonprofits with their needs or challenges, for free. These organizations are all focused on providing a diversity of programming for underserved populations. Their individual missions have resonated with my interest and lifelong purpose to be of help, to connect individuals with mutual interests, and to make a positive contribution where possible.

After being involved with the field of afterschool education for many years, I realized that staff members across community-based programs often approached me to discuss their future career moves. I also became aware that a significant number of African American and Latino males were employed in these community-based and school-based programs. Some had a college degree; others had high school diplomas. Many were undecided whether they should become teachers or social workers. Following a discussion with Lucy Friedman, executive director, the Afterschool Corporation/TASC, about the significant numbers of African American and Latino men in community-based programs, we jointly applied for and received a small grant from the Mellon Foundation to identify and enroll a sample of four men from the above racial groups in a credit-bearing seminar and provide intensive advising, tutoring as needed, and counseling to assist them in determining their career goal, teaching or social work.

One man actually enrolled in a graduate school of social work, one was still undecided, and two decided on teaching by the seminar's end. The one factor that all four commented on was the personal interest and attention, support, and respect for their experience and knowledge that they obtained from their Bank Street advisor. They had never had those experiences in their previous educational lives.

Observing a similar dilemma of education or social work within the wider group of afterschool workers, I then informally surveyed a group of nonprofit directors about their willingness to encourage or support their coordinators to obtain graduate degrees. Given their positive responses, I prepared a white paper, "Bank Street's Role as a Provider for After School Education," and later talked with selected Bank Street faculty about their interest in the design of a master's degree to meet this constituency's needs. I then brought both groups, Bank Street faculty and afterschool leaders, together to have a conversation around the need for, and the development of, a degree program for the field. Their enthusiasm was most encouraging. Following an internal faculty discussion led by former associate dean Penny Spencer, faculty supported the development of a graduate degree, which they entitled Leadership in Community Based Learning/LCBL. Faculty renaming the program was a positive sign; it showed ownership of the program, which became a reality, and with New York State Education's swift approval, the first course was offered in 2009.

Alison Overseth, PASE's executive director, and faculty Rima Shore were the first to teach in this important program that attracted a reasonable number of graduate students in the first two classes. The students were excited to be enrolled, were learning new ways to engage young people, and were further inspired by their faculty. Unfortunately, the program was temporarily suspended after the first year; however, I still believe in the need for, and the potential of, the LCBL to reach practitioners in community-based organizations and other nonprofit programs to obtain graduate degrees, and to enrich and stimulate more research within the field.

Alison Overseth, an excellent communicator and visionary thinker, a collaborative leader adept at bringing diverse people and communities together, and a wonderful friend and colleague, is well received wherever she goes. Her intelligence and enthusiasm in either meeting new people or listening to their ideas are infectious. She has maintained her interest in Bank Street and the LCBL, and was given Bank Street's Ida Karp Award in May 2019 for her extraordinary service in the field. As the founding board president of PASE, Alison was hired as its executive director beginning in 2010. In that role, Alison has continued to provide the kind and quality of leadership that is strategic while inspiring not only her staff and board members, but the larger community of grassroots leaders in the field. She has thoughtfully expanded PASE's board of directors, PASE's vast network of youth-serving agencies, and the number of partners. Best of all, during my seven wonderful years as PASE's board president, Alison and I worked closely and collaboratively as partners in fulfilling PASE's mission. Our regular meetings were always delightful, even while we discussed staff challenges, governance matters, or her creative ideas for promoting PASE programs and their notable impact in preparing new leaders for the afterschool field. Aware that harmony between board presidents and executive leadership was not a given, I valued and enjoyed the trusting relationship that existed between Alison and me.

CHAPTER 18

A MOMENT FOR REFLECTION

Infusing high quality in education through innovation and collaboration and using results from research and practice in effective ways were central to the Division of Continuing Education's work. The division was also a catalyst for change within the college, as evidenced through its unique social impact programs, such as Head Start or Liberty Leads, both programs designed to improve life opportunities for low-income children, youth, and families, the majority of whom were African American and Latinx.

Prior to the closing of the adolescent education degree program, Graduate School faculty often invited LPP students, now Liberty Leads, to talk with graduate students about their experiences growing up in their particular neighborhoods. Graduates have remarked on how much they learned from the students about the real and often dangerous challenges they faced in even getting to school. For the LPP students, these opportunities to interact and share their experiences and ideas with future teachers were solid con-fidence builders. In addition, division staff became natural ambassadors for the college, given their extensive outreach work. They were instrumental in recruiting students into the graduate programs, as occurred in the New Beginnings in Newark program. At least seven teachers from Newark's New Beginnings program received graduate degrees from the college. Over the years, many teachers and other practitioners who initially enrolled in our New Perspectives/Continuing Professional Studies weekend program often continued their education within the Graduate School. On our Long Trips, a core group of faculty usually participated, thus enriching their perspectives through their meetings with new regional and cultural groups as well as with our non–Bank Street colleagues who joined the Long Trips. Our individual continuing professional and personal education goals were being achieved through those experiences.

Finally, our collaboration with the Graduate School and the School for Children enriched all our experiences as we worked together and learned from each other. The external community began to see more Black and brown faculty and staff, which demonstrated that the college valued diversity and was therefore open to new opportunities and a diversity of ideas. The openness to diversity, and the inclusion of other voices and perspectives, enriches conversations and emboldens actions leading to real change. This inclusive approach to shared decision making has blossomed under the current leadership of President Shael Polakow-Suransky.

Through the design and implementation of socially responsible, culturally sensitive, and researched enriched education programs, my staff and I were fulfilling Bank Street's mission and its then-priorities to increase diversity, improve and enrich education in high-needs schools and communities, and capture the learning through research, documentation, and dissemination.

Young children and youth received the highest-quality care, education, and support from caring adults in our Head Start, Liberty Partnerships, New Beginnings in Newark, and other programs, including Arts and the Garden, a summer program for children in Harlem developed by Paul Coppa, a resident and lawyer. The positive personal and academic results in the New Beginnings program are accessible in the book *Putting the Children First: The Changing Face of Newark's Public Schools*, published in 2003 by Teachers College Press.

New Beginnings in Newark Public Schools

In 1996 Bank Street College was invited by Dr. Beverly Hall to improve teaching and learning in the Newark public schools. Having worked with Dr. Hall over several years, I was always impressed by her dedication to improve the learning environments for children. She was a professional in all her undertakings and set very high standards for herself, teachers, children, and the general school staff. She also expected her teachers to provide and equip all students with the critical thinking skills and appropriate yet rigorous content to prepare them for success in school and in life.

During our first two years in Newark, about twenty-three DCE staff and Graduate School faculty worked as a team to provide a varied menu of professional development activities for Newark's educators through listening and learning, modeling effective classroom teaching, organizing local trips, seminars, and conferences, and working with parents. Dr. Hall knew that to change the trajectory for Newark's children, "teachers needed to learn how to engage students in learning beginning with their very first experience in the classroom."[1] This book describes and documents those remarkable years from a variety of voices and perspectives, including those of Dr. Hall, teachers, administrators, funders, paraprofessionals, and staff developers.

Our staff developers, all experienced educators, met Newark's teachers where they were pedagogically, showed respect for the work and challenges facing them, and assured them that Bank Street was there to learn with them, to share that learning and to support their efforts. The first year was spent developing relationships and building trust, observing in classrooms, furnishing classrooms with age-appropriate furniture and materials, introducing trips outside the schools to museums and the airport, and, overall, discovering the rich resources available within their own community.

Prior to Bank Street's intervention, teachers did not venture from the classrooms, due to fear of the neighborhoods. By the second year, according to one evaluation, Newark's teachers were using the Bank Street language about development but weren't "doing it" in their classrooms. However, by year three, "they were saying and doing it!" Teachers, leaders, and families were appreciating the excitement about their learning, the children's engagement in their lessons, and about the caring, democratic communities being created in Newark's classrooms with Bank Street's support. Change does indeed take time; there are few quick fixes in education and school reform.

Our thirteen years of building relationships, managing the inevitable challenges while effecting change in Newark's public schools, were wonderful, positive, and productive years. Special thanks go to the incredible Bank Street staff, including Carol Lippman, Margot Hammond, and Lynne Einbender, and to Newark's Marva Banks, who graciously shared her room with Bank Street staff developers. The tangible outcomes for Newark's teachers and their children were all accomplished with less than $2 million annually during the early years. We could have done even more for the children, their teachers, and the community with just a quarter of the millions spent by Zuckerberg and others in Newark, with their unimpressive results.[2]

One of my most unforgettable and remarkable collaborations occurred over three years and three trips to Panola County, Mississippi. In early spring 2009, I received a phone call from my friend and colleague Dr. Lee Anne Bell, professor and director of Barnard College's Education Program. Lee had just ended a telephone conversation inviting her to come to Batesville, Mississippi, to hear and to film a remarkable story. The Black students, now adults, who had integrated the public schools in Batesville, 1969–1971, had received invitations, for the very first time, to their fortieth high school reunion. The caller, Cheryl Johnson, had found Lee's Storytelling for Social Justice project on the internet, liked what she read, and decided to call her. Lee then invited me to join her on this adventure. Having heard many stories about how African Americans were treated in Mississippi, I was initially hesitant to give a positive response. But, as Lee talked more about the story, we both saw the potential for a unique and special experience.

Moreover, Cheryl had told Lee about a film that she had seen depicting school desegregation in Clinton, Tennessee, and she hoped to also document the Batesville story. It so happened that I had seen that same film on our Bank Street Long Trip to Knoxville and Nashville in 2005. We had stopped in Clinton, where we had a remarkable discussion with Vice-Mayor Jerry Shattuck, city manager Steve Jones, school director Dr. Jerry Woods, and Rev. Alan Jones about their peaceful school integration experience. Within a few minutes of listening to Lee, I was in on this unexpected opportunity.

In June 2009 Lee and I interviewed thirteen African American adults on a Saturday morning in a Baptist Church Hall in Batesville. These former classmates described their individual childhood experiences in leaving their supportive Black school, Pattan Hall High School, and entering the white school, where they were treated very badly. Even the teachers ignored them by teaching directly to the white students and ignoring the Black students, even when their hands were raised. Only one teacher, Ms. Anderson, defended them. While she always made them feel welcome, they felt "isolated, lonely, and disconnected." According to one individual, "we learned to tolerate stuff and to work independently." Surprisingly, this conversation had never occurred among them before, and as students they had not shared these feelings with each other.

They also noted that the white schools were not eager to enroll Black students and used many devious strategies to keep them out. Among the strategies was that you could be admitted only if your school did not offer a subject that you wanted or needed. Cheryl told the white school that she wanted to study Latin and so was admitted. In general, the Black students felt that no one prepared them for integration, and that they had no tools to deal with the negative experiences they faced on a daily basis, for example, someone "leaving a live coon in a paper bag'" in a Black classmate's locker.

Lee was invited to attend the reunion party that night at the country club. She reported back that the event was enjoyable and that both groups of classmates appeared quite happy to see each other. In meeting the white classmates, Lee inquired whether they might be interested in sharing their experiences with school integration. They said yes, and so our team, including the videographer, returned to Batesville in 2010 and interviewed almost the same number of white adults. Without knowing what we had already heard, these adults confirmed everything that we had learned from their former Black classmates.

They stated that they did not treat the Black students well and actually were quite mean to them. On the football team, Marshall, who became a successful businessman, received excessive physical punishment, and the students were called many negative names. One white male stated that in the South, children listened to their parents. His parents had told him that Blacks couldn't learn like white children, yet here was this group of very smart Black students. It was confusing to him and very much "like the destruction of the Santa Claus myth." Another individual stated that she was competing with Cheryl in history; however, she never spoke to her. Another person recalled staples being thrown in a Black girl's hair, which we had heard from the Black classmate. A few individuals said they knew it was wrong to treat their Black classmates so badly but couldn't do anything to stop the behavior, because they would have been ostracized. At the end of both individual sessions, each group said they would love to come together.

In 2011, the third year, we returned to Batesville. Lee brought the two groups together, an invaluable experience in seeing these adults now greeting each other like long-lost friends. We all met in their former high school on this trip. In the joint interview, following a tour of the school during which their memories came alive, they reflected on the past, shared feelings, told stories, and discussed the reality of the cultural climate of that period. There were powerful moments. Among them was one white classmate's comment that "Cheryl was my stiffest competition for grades." This astounded Cheryl, who commented, "I didn't know Charman thought I was smart."

Another moment was when a white classmate, now a lawyer—and from his earlier exchanges, a very thoughtful individual—apologized to his Black classmates for his and his peers' negative behaviors toward them during their school integration experience. Unexpectedly, one of the most outspoken Black adults thanked him, adding that it really meant something for her to hear his apology even though she had initially thought an apology would mean nothing to her.

As I listened to the classmates tell their stories, I was fascinated by the process of their remembering. For the Black adults, the memories of those long-ago experiences were very much alive, and were often quite painful in the retelling; for their white classmates, they had to try to recall events from that period, which required "going back in time with a group of people." The white students' experiences were not personally painful, and with limited or no knowledge of the Black experience, they did not carry the pain experienced by their Black classmates.

Over the three years, I recorded many comments from both groups that were especially meaningful to me, and which I felt might be used productively someday in telling their story, a transformative one. These are some of the statements or themes that I heard:

- When the opportunity for school integration arose, not everyone in the Black school chose to attend the white school in Panola County.
- Individuals on both sides said they were unprepared for integration in a society where roles were clearly defined and were never questioned; segregation was the rule.
- Many white students said they knew that bullying was occurring but didn't know what to do. They had no tools available to them.
- Black and white students lived separate realities: each saw two different things from one picture or one experience.
- "How we are molded is responsible for passivity and lack of awareness."
- Many Black parents didn't realize the impact (of integrating a school) on their children.
- For the Black graduates, there was no prom experience; on arrival at the prom, they were told that they would not be allowed inside by the white science teacher. (In the joint session, the white classmates said they were not aware of that situation. One male adult

said he knew because he had stepped outside to smoke and saw what had happened. He had never revealed that story but was astonished that his classmates had not noticed the absence of their Black classmates.)

- Several Black students agreed that one classmate (now a lawyer) was the brightest in her class but was derailed from being valedictorian because of her race.
- One white classmate who had moved from a small town to Batesville commented that "being a white student did not keep me from feeling invisible."
- Another white classmate noted that they were all adolescents and were struggling with their own identities and fitting in, which placed additional pressure on them.

Finally, we learned that all the Black graduates except one had left Batesville, had been successful in their careers following college, lived in different parts of the country, had never communicated with each other until the reunion, and many had now retired. Many of their white classmates remained in or around Batesville. Lee and I also had the pleasure of visiting Cheryl's family home and the home of two of her white classmates. One of them took us to see the University of Mississippi, and *The Panolian* office, the local newspaper and journal. While everyone we met was gracious and welcoming, our meetings with all the classmates were among the most enriching, truly cathartic, and memorable learning experiences ever, and I was extremely happy and grateful to have been there.

The DVD from the three-year footage is entitled *40 Years Later: Now Can We Talk?* Along with a teacher's guide, the DVD is available through Teachers College Press, NYC.

According to Prof. Jacqueline Jordan Irvine, Lee Anne Bell produced a "moving and powerful documentary that uses storytelling to expose as well as heal the racial divide in American society."

DIFFERENT APPROACHES, SIMILAR RESULTS

The key difference between my work at LaGuardia and at Bank Street took some time to identify. The programs developed in both places were aimed at underserved populations, to increase educational and career opportunities for all students. Both institutions were successful in providing those opportunities for students to think about or to accomplish their goals. I soon realized that the main difference was in Bank Street's clearly articulated developmental approach to working with children, youth, and adults, aptly named the developmental-interaction approach. This approach looks at the whole child and how he or she relates to peers, adults, and materials. My experience acknowledges that the developmental approach is effective across diverse communities with the additional perspectives from race theory, cultural and historical data and information, and reflection. Graduate students and teachers used their knowledge of child development and their observational skills to understand and build relationships with their students, as well as with other adults with whom they interacted, and to continually reflect on the effects of their interactions. We performed similar work at LaGuardia without defining a specific approach but using accumulated knowledge from the available social science research, and from our professional experiences and observations.

For me, Bank Street's approach to teaching and learning was compatible with social work, and I was delighted to read that Bank Street's founder, Lucy Sprague Mitchell, was initially heavily influenced by social worker Jane Addams, founder of Hull House in Chicago, and later by an educator, a nurse, and others such as John Dewey. This led to her embracing a holistic approach in understanding children and adults: one must look at the whole child or person.

The fact that the college focuses on developing healthy and informed thinkers and doers in society is not surprising given its progressive history. Mrs. Mitchell saw in schools an opportunity to build a better and more humane society and was determined to fulfill her dream. She began the Bureau of Educational Experiments in 1916, offering classes and workshops for teachers during this period of great social reform. The Long Trips played an important role in the curriculum. In 1950 the Bureau received approval from the New York State Board of Regents to offer degree programs as Bank Street College of Education. Since that time, its social agenda, embedded in its mission, has continued to influence and direct its programs and strategic plans.

My work in higher education for over forty-four years has been an incredible experience and journey. Both the kinds of programs and the kind of leader I became were heavily influenced by my social work background. I was also influenced by the progressive, collaborative, and socially conscious leaders and colleagues with whom I interacted. My experience in the social work field was important in developing empathy, patience, understanding, and the nonjudgmental attitude needed to be a good practitioner, and later, in my administrative and supervisory roles, to be a fair, compassionate and balanced leader, one whose aura, somehow, creates a sense of possibilities. Given the latter description, I concur with educator and author Carol B. Hillman that supervisors can act as change agents.

As a supervisor, my general approach was to develop trusting and respectful relationships, have clear goals and expectations for each staff member, support each individual's strengths, be a good listener, and provide feedback as needed, while simultaneously being aware of behaviors or attitudes that are idiosyncratic and could be challenging. I also encouraged my staff toward professional growth, to communicate with colleagues beyond our division, and to participate in conferences and other external meetings for their own professional and personal development. In addition, I have always made a conscious effort to reach out to and welcome new employees to Bank Street. Their responses were usually appreciative.

RETIREMENT FROM BANK STREET: WHAT'S NEXT?

Prior to my retirement from Bank Street College, I was honored to be recognized by the Pemberton Society in 2011 for "promoting the ideals of the Pemberton Society." In that same year, I was given a Civic Spirit Award by the Women's City Club of New York that was attended by my family and many friends. The convergence of these events in the same year caused me to reflect on my then-twenty-two years at the college, knowing that there was so much more work to be accomplished in education and the human services fields. Several discussions were held with my staff to prepare them for my retirement over a twelve-month period. A few senior staff decided to retire, but the majority intended to remain with their programs. I was also aware that there were other individuals to continue the division's work on my retirement.

Following conversations with Bank Street's chief academic officer, Dr. Jon Snyder, he ensured that all the programs within my division, except for one, would continue to exist at the college on my leaving. Dr. Snyder was an extraordinary and brilliant educator who cared deeply about social justice and consistently advocated for high-quality education as the norm for all children regardless of race, gender, or class. He was always supportive of the programs in my division, and I do believe that he saw them as fulfilling the mission of Bank Street's founder, Lucy Sprague Mitchell, to build a better and more humane society.

Upon my retirement in 2012, several events were organized by different groups throughout the college, which were delightful and celebratory. My years at Bank Street had expanded the college's connections to thousands of new and diverse populations through the DCE's wide range of programs, and I had been successful in working across divisions and with all staff throughout the college.

The week before my retirement, I received a phone call from Calvin Sims, former board chair of the Harlem Educational Activities Fund/HEAF, the college prep program. "Fern, as you know, HEAF's executive director has submitted her resignation. I have just had a conversation with the board's executive committee, and they have asked me to reach out to you. We would very much like you to be interim executive director."

Not expecting this request, I responded, "Calvin, I am looking forward to retiring next week and am not looking for more work."

Without a pause, Calvin continued, "Fern, we all agreed that given your background and experience, you are the ideal person to step in at this point. Besides, you know HEAF, the staff, and the mission."

We continued talking about the upcoming summer programs, the danger of losing grants if there were a hint of organizational instability, the need for staff supervision, and other issues. I knew in my heart that I could not refuse this request, so I promised Calvin to call him the next day.

I kept my promise, indicating that I had one stipulation: I would be the interim E.D. but would not accept a salary; this would be my contribution as a board member. I added that I would work three to four days weekly until the new CEO was hired. I began my new interim position the week following my retirement, built relationships with the staff, gained new insight about the organization, and served on the search committee. I was interim for six months. During that period, the stark differences between governance, the board's responsibility, and leadership were more apparent. I learned far more about the culture of the organization and the interactions among staff. Anyway, HEAF's staff and I worked collaboratively to ensure that the transition to new leadership was seamless and that the current programs continued to function to benefit students.

Mr. Rose, HEAF's founder, wished to show his appreciation for my willingness to assist HEAF during that challenging transition period and consulted Calvin. Although that was unnecessary, since I had benefited from another growth opportunity, I suggested to Calvin that if Mr. Rose desired, he could fund the five boards with which I was then involved. A few days before Christmas, Calvin called me at home, and in a voice full of mystery and veiled excitement, asked whether I had received my mail. Still talking to him, I hurried downstairs and sure enough, there was an envelope from Mr. Rose waiting for me. On opening the envelope, I discovered five checks, each one addressed to a nonprofit, for $10,000 each, for a total of $50,000! I could not contain my excitement. I thanked Calvin for his help, donned my winter coat, and felt like Santa Claus as I personally delivered a check to four very surprised and delighted executive directors. The fifth check was mailed to Wave Hill in the Bronx. At the end of that exciting day, I thought with great joy, "All's well that ends well."

ANOTHER ROLE FOR HIGHER EDUCATION

My years working at Bank Street College were productive, inspiring, fulfilling, fiscally challenging, and replete with opportunities to grow, lead, and innovate. As a division, we followed the trends in education, economic forecasting, and the emerging human and societal crises to address them through program development, and to respond to requests for professional development from schools, communities, cultural groups, and government agencies, often through strategic partnerships.

As a result, I saw the power of institutions of higher education to address inequities and to bring about positive changes in this society. In the sixties, as noted earlier, northern and some midwestern universities provided the access needed for African American teachers from the South to obtain graduate degrees. In 1987, during the crisis of homelessness, Bank Street's Dr. Janice Molnar conducted research on homeless families and the impact on children's development. She accomplished this work by visiting shelters and talking with families and staff. A crucial finding was that exposure of young children to supportive and enriched high-quality early childhood environments had a positive impact on their verbal and cognitive skills within a very short timeframe. Sharing these findings, documented in *Home Is Where the Heart Is*, with the provider agencies led to significant city policy changes, for example, in the Board of Education, a special unit was created to provide special support services to children who were homeless, living in shelters, and their families.

There are other examples of the positive impact on low-income students, marginalized adults, and communities in need when colleges, schools, and communities come together to solve educational, economic, or other societal challenges: Trinity College in Hartford designed a neighborhood initiative, the Learning Corridor, near its campus that included a pre-K–5 and middle and high schools, to address the educational and societal problems in the surrounding low-income community; Bard College has its prison initiatives that provide higher education and career opportunities for incarcerated inmates; Clemson University supports its Emerging Scholars summer program to change the trajectory for low-income students through a rigorous academic program; Bank Street has its Liberty Leads Program, where underserved African American and Latinx youth from NYC underserved communities develop as learners, and over 90 percent enroll in colleges and universities; Clark Atlanta University's Environmental Justice Resource Center is a partner with the Deep South Center for Environmental Justice and other agencies in implementing minority worker training programs in several southern cities; the Caribbean Maritime University in Jamaica is a partner with the American Caribbean Maritime Foundation, a nonprofit that raises money for student scholarships so that lack of funds will hinder neither their graduation nor their goal to work within the maritime industry; and Dr. Lee Bell's DVD reflecting her reconciliation and healing work in bringing Black and white classmates who experienced school integration together in Panola County, Mississippi.

My hope is that the partnerships among colleges, public schools, nonprofit community-based programs, funders, and communities will increase. These partnerships can be transformative for the participants involved. A few years ago, the president of Columbia University raised a critical question: "How do we connect the enormously valuable intellectual work of the university to have the greatest possible impact on the problems of our time?" Well, higher education institutions have the capacity to bring the partners within their communities together to begin a conversation focused on identifying mutually desirable goals. When colleges are true partners with schools, and teachers and community leaders feel respected as equal contributors, more often than not, the positive impact is evidenced over time; the schools, students, communities, and colleges will all benefit from working together to build a more informed, economically sustainable, and humane society.

I have remained on several boards to support the important work they do to improve life for people and communities, and for board members to keep learning about new and emerging needs, and supporting effective and humane approaches to address these needs. As nonprofit boards, they are committed to raising the aspirations, access, and opportunities for underserved youth, especially Black and Latinx youth and adults of all ages. So while my community volunteer work continues, I will also continue to share my knowledge and experience, serve as a connector of people and resources, and, wherever I can, advocate for, and tell stories that transport, children, youth, and adults to new places, heighten their imaginations, and improve their lives and career trajectories.

Reflecting on the myriad of opportunities and experiences offered to me over those years and the extraordinary support that I have received in both my personal and professional undertakings, I remain ever so grateful to those individuals, progressive leaders, and role models, who took a chance on me, even when I didn't necessarily see the next step. I now try to do the same thing for the many individuals who contact me for advice or information.

Nevertheless, my backstory will always be linked to growing up in Jamaica, the wealth of available role models, the influence of the Jamaican culture on my socialization and positive sense of self, and the many influencing memories of family, friends, and schooling there that have served as the foundation for my inspiring educational journey in America. I call on the many poems learned in my youth whenever I need to remind myself of the goodness of the human spirit, the joy in giving and receiving, and the importance of believing in oneself. My sisters and I now travel back to Jamaica each year to keep connected to and share memories of our growing-up experiences in that wonderful, rich, colorful, and vibrant yet complex island culture, described by journalist and author Peter Abrahams as "Jamaica, an Island Mosaic."

•   •   •

On May 23, 2018, six years after my retirement, Bank Street surprised me with the special Ida Carp Award "for outstanding dedication to Bank Street

College and its mission." Most moving for me was to be honored along with six alumni at the Annual Alumni Association Awards, a marvelous and personally inspiring evening and event. Soon after that event, I was invited by President Shael Polakow-Suransky to become a trustee, again, at Bank Street College. I accepted his invitation with pleasure and again serve on six boards.

ACKNOWLEDGMENTS

I have many individuals to thank for their contribution to the existence of this work. When I mentioned to a few friends that I had started to write about my educational journey, beginning with my early education as a child and youth in Jamaica during the forties and fifties, they all encouraged me to keep writing. A few Jamaicans said that they had few or no memories of their school days, so they would be interested in reading about my memories. This revelation surprised me, since my memories were so vivid.

For stimulating my interest in writing, I extend special thanks to Sandy Watson, who many years ago invited me to participate in my first writing workshop in Tarrytown, and to Dr. Richard Lieberman for choosing to interview me as an immigrant from Jamaica for his fourth- and eleventh-grade curricula on "A Nation of Immigrants." The idea of sharing my story with a broader audience grew out of that interview, which lasted several hours.

I welcomed the encouragement received from Anthony Nordoff, Gene Gollogly, and Josh Marwell, who were brave enough to read the first rough manuscript, which I knew was nowhere near ready; I needed feedback to proceed. Lisa McMurtray from the University Press of Mississippi, Alex Moore, retired acquisition editor from S.C., and Faith Childs, literary agent, were all extremely helpful and encouraging after reading the manuscript; they guided me to rethink its structure, reorganize the chronology of events, further develop specific content, and to move more of me as both learner and teacher into the narrative. My friend Victoria Horsford was always there providing me with encouraging words, and a book on writing one's story.

In my immediate family, I am grateful to sons Yussuf, Javaid, and Nafees, who kept me laughing with their witty selves and who challenged me to rethink and reshape some of my ideas. Javaid offered ways to shape my stories to draw in the reader, while Nafees raised interesting questions about his and his brothers' names that I hadn't thought about, helped me to have more confidence in using the special features on my computer, and was available for my frequent calls for assistance. I am grateful to both Javaid and Nafees for the important role they played during the entire process. Many thanks go to Gillian, my daughter-in-law, who early in the writing process offered much appreciated technology and other helpful assistance. My sisters Hope and Phillippa were also early readers, offering support and hearty laughs as we recalled, from different perspectives, our youth in Jamaica; I checked with them frequently to verify some aspects of Jamaican life, while niece Tanya Yasmin provided encouragement, good humor, and helpful comments, and best of all, introduced me to using Google Docs!

Finally, special thanks to my husband, Ismail, for his unending support and quiet patience as he watched me at work over many years. While he has been a devoted husband, friend, father, and grandfather, Ismail has also been an inspiration to me, and I credit him for challenging me in so many positive ways. He is always there for me, and as I worked on this manuscript he would quietly remind me, with his usual global perspective, to include the Indian, Chinese, and Jewish people who were also significant contributors to Jamaican culture; and that they were.

My wholehearted thanks to all of you, family, friends, colleagues, and others whose names I may not have mentioned, who believed that I could write a story that captured your interest and attention. And from all your responses and encouragement, I was energized to improve on the narrative. Hopefully, there is a connection for each reader, whether it's a new perspective on Jamaica's social and artistic achievements, history of slavery, diverse cultures, my experiences in higher education, the Long Trips as a continuing education activity, African American historical and cultural experiences, or my listening and learning about school integration in Panola County, Mississippi.

In documenting my journey, I discovered two areas that enlarged my knowledge base and were personally satisfying: researching Jamaica's remarkable early history of resistance to slavery and oppression, and its growth in becoming a democracy within a short period; and increasing my awareness of, and knowledge about, African Americans' constant struggle to survive, obtain equity and equality, and prosper despite rigid social, educational, and political structures designed to exclude them.

My special thanks and appreciation are extended to my former Bank Street staff and directors, who provided high-quality professional development activities for teachers and school leaders and other adults, and created supportive learning environments for children and youth: Eileen Wasow, David Penberg, Lesley Koplow, Davia Brown Franklyn, Judith Gold, Farhad Asghar, Richard Rivera, Maureen Hornung, Marnie Ponce, Maria Benejan, Carol Lippman, Adrianne Kamsler, Margot Hammond, Ken Jewell, Steven Antonelli, Joy Ellebane, Toni Porter, Arlene Uss, Maddy Centeno, and Kate Baldus. Special thanks are conveyed to Elva Berger, Dana Hamilton, Merrill Lee Fuchs, and Thelma Wallace for their ongoing and loyal support of the Division of Continuing Education and me.

NOTES

Chapter 1: Growing Up in Rural Jamaica

1. Aaron Mair genealogy search. According to Aaron's research, the Mairs' history began with Alexander Mair's arrival in Jamaica from the town of Turriff, N.E. Scotland, in the mid-late 1700s. He married Helen, "a free black woman," and together they had eight "mulatto children," one of whom was Alexander Gordon (1790–1838). Alexander Gordon married Ann McKenzie, "both persons of colour & free conditions." Of their seven children, son William Alexander is the father of William Rufus Mair (my grandfather). My grandfather is the fourth-generation Mair. ("Mulatto," rarely used today, indicates that one parent is black and the other is white).

2. Haberdasheries were stores carrying sewing items, along with cotton goods, fabric, boots, shoes, and other items for sale, similar to a general store.

3. First Year, the first of three local exams taken during the senior year of elementary school, providing access for the local people to aspire to white-collar jobs in the post office, Jamaica Railway, teaching, and nursing.

4. Darwin Porter and Danforth Prince, *Frommer's Jamaica*, 1st ed. (Foster City, CA: IDG Worldwide), 197.

5. Erna Brodber, an XLCR classmate and sociologist, tells "stories outside of published history to point out the whitewashing and distortion of Black history through religion and colonialism" (*Myal*, endpaper). *Myal* describes in vivid and familiar Jamaican metaphors, poetry, and language, the power of obeah as experienced in Grove Town, a village in one of Jamaica's parishes.

Chapter 2: Living and Learning in Kingston

1. Basil K. Bryan, *The Jamaicans, Children of God in the Promised Land* (Denver: Outskirts Press, 2014), 508.

Chapter 3: Cultural, Educational, and Religious Experiences: Cultural, Educational, and Religious Experiences

1. Michael Hughes, "Reid, Victor Stafford," in *A Companion to West Indian Literature*, (New York: Collins, 1979), 103.

2. Leonard E. Barrett, *The Rastafarians* (London: Heinemann, 1977), 6.

3. Bryan, *The Jamaicans*, 317.

4. The fact that one may have siblings beyond one's immediate family is a common reality on the island; families handle the "discovery" or knowledge each in their own unique way. Some families are accepting of the "newly discovered" siblings; others not so much, remaining distant.

5. Peter Abrahams, *Jamaica, an Island Mosaic* (London: Her Majesty's Stationery Office, 1957), 139.

6. Madeline Kerr, *Personality and Conflict in Jamaica* (Birkenhead, Great Britain: Willmer Brothers & Haram, 1963), ix.

7. Kerr, *Personality and Conflict in Jamaica*.

CHAPTER 4: HIGH SCHOOL: MY EXCELSIOR YEARS

1. A. Wesley Powell, *The Excelsior-EXED Story: The Methodist Church in the Caribbean and the Americas* (Jamaica: Stephensons Litho Press, 1989), 15.

2. Powell, *Excelsior-EXED Story*, 16.

3. Philip Sherlock and Hazel Bennett, *The Story of the Jamaican People* (Kingston: Ian Randle; and Princeton, NJ: Markus Wiener, 1998), 405.

4. Abrahams, *Jamaica, an Island Mosaic*, 121.

CHAPTER 5: REFLECTIONS ON JAMAICAN LIFE

1. Powell, *Excelsior-EXED Story*, 69–70. "Evon Blake, a journalist and publisher of a magazine known as *New Day* [drew] to our attention the absence of black Jamaicans in our banks and other financial institutions." The change strategy was to be a test case, so he contacted Mr. Powell for "a candidate of black complexion who would break the colour barrier for the first time."

2. Abrahams, *Jamaica, an Island Mosaic*, 167.

3. After Emancipation in 1838, and to increase the ratio between whites and blacks, indentured workers were recruited from Scotland, England, Ireland, and Germany. Many also arrived as punishment for criminal acts. They were unwilling or unable to do the strenuous labour required, so the white establishment brought in Chinese and Indians as indentured labourers. These groups were predominantly men who soon developed relationships with Jamaican (black) women, thereby expanding the existing groups of mixed-race Jamaicans.

4. Abrahams, *Jamaica, an Island Mosaic*, 47–51.

5. Abrahams, *Jamaica, an Island Mosaic*, 50.

6. Sherlock and Bennett, *Story of the Jamaican People*, 4.

7. Kerr, *Personality and Conflict in Jamaica*, 101.

8. Sherlock and Bennett, *Story of the Jamaican People*, 293.

9. Philip Sherlock, *Keeping Company with Jamaica* (New York: Macmillan, 1989), 120.

10. Sherlock and Bennett, *Story of the Jamaican People*, 61.

Chapter 6: Becoming a Civil Servant

1. Sherlock and Bennett, *Story of the Jamaican People*, 272–80.
2. Sherlock and Bennett, *Story of the Jamaican People*, 273.

Chapter 7: The Letter of Invitation

1. Abrahams, *Jamaica, an Island Mosaic*, 242.

Chapter 8: Coming to America: Chicago to New York City

1. Vanessa Siddle Walker, *Their Highest Potential* (Chapel Hill: University of North Carolina Press, 1996), 151.
2. Mission statement, African Diaspora Consortium brochure, available from the ADC.

Chapter 10: NYU Graduate School of Social Work

1. Bellevue Hospital is a teaching hospital, the oldest public hospital in the United States, and is now known as the Bellevue Hospital Center. Its executive director promises "a deep commitment to providing the highest-quality care to all New Yorkers, and to delivering healthcare to every patient with dignity, cultural sensitivity and compassion." Excerpt from his letter in the Bellevue Hospital Patient Guide, page 3.

Chapter 11: Returning to Work in NYC

1. The Jack and Jill Club of America, a membership organization, is "dedicated to nurturing future African American leaders by strengthening children through leadership development, volunteer service, philanthropic giving and civic duty." Mission statement from The Jack and Jill Club of America.

Chapter 13: Raising Our Family in New York City

1. Javaid Khan, *MOHAMMAD ISMAIL KHAN, Our National Treasure*, (self-pub., Shutterfly).
2. Quotes are from a reference letter written by Gary Comstack, Department of Sociology, Wesleyan University, January 15, 1996.

Chapter 15: Bank Street College

1. Albion is a medium-security level facility for female inmates, offering a variety of programs to help incarcerated individuals to redirect their lives and become productive, law-abiding members of society. The facility is located in upstate New York, quite a distance from New York City.

CHAPTER 16: THE LONG TRIPS

1. Bank Street College, *Street Scenes*, Fall/Winter, 1998, p. 4.

2. The Sankofa Circle at Bank Street College was founded by Lucia Jack (now deceased), to create a community of likeminded adults who believed in "looking to the past to inform the future," the meaning of the Adinkra Sankofa symbol.

3. Suzanne Landau and Jean Fisher, *Yinka Shonibare: Double Dress* (Jerusalem: Israel Museum, 2002).

4. The August 6, 2019, issue of *Carib News* noted that a memorandum of agreement was signed as "part of a program of reparative justice that will see the establishment of a joint Glasgow-Caribbean Centre for Development Research."

5. Arlene Uss, "Testimonials," *Teaching Four-Year-Olds, A Personal Journey*, Carol B. Hillman (Lincoln: Exchange Press, 2010), 8.

CHAPTER 17: CONNECTIONS AND PARTNERSHIPS WITH NONPROFITS

1. Stevens Institute of Technology, *Savvy Cyber Professor*, Design and Development Institute, June 4, 2003.

2. Joyce Antler, *Lucy Sprague Mitchell* (New Haven: Yale University Press, 1987), 327.

CHAPTER 18: A MOMENT FOR REFLECTION

1. Jonathan G. Silin and Carol Lipman, *Putting the Children First: The Changing Face of Newark's Public Schools* (New York: Teachers College Press, 2003), 55.

2. Joe Nocera, "Zuckerberg's Expensive Lesson," *New York Times*, September 8, 2015, OpEd.

BIBLIOGRAPHY

Abrahams, Peter. *Jamaica, an Island Mosaic*. London: Her Majesty's Stationery Office, 1957.

Antler, Joyce. *Lucy Sprague Mitchell*. New Haven: Yale University Press, 1987.

Bank Street College. *Street Scenes*. Fall/Winter, 1998.

Bell, Lee Ann, executive producer, and Markie Hancock, director. *40 Years Later: Now Can We Talk?* DVD and discussion guide. New York: Teachers College Press, Columbia University, 2011.

Brodber, Erna. *MYAL*. Long Grove, IL: Waveland Press, 2014.

Dillard University. "Deep South Center for Environmental Justice: Worker Training Program." New Orleans.

Elrod, G. Franklin. *Career Education for Special Needs Individuals: Learning, Earning, Contributing*. Columbia: Dance Graphics, 1989.

Frommer's. *Jamaica*. Foster City, CA: IDG Books Worldwide, 2000.

Gibran, Kahlil. *The Prophet*. New York: Alfred A. Knopf, 1964.

Gleaner Company. *Geography and History of Jamaica*. 24th rev. ed. Kingston: Gleaner, 1995.

Goldtree, Reena N. "New Directions in Caribbean History." *American Historian*, May 2018.

Hughes, Michael. "Reid, Victor Stafford." In *A Companion to West Indian Literature*. New York: Collins, 1979.

Irvine, Jacqueline Jordan. Review of *40 Years Later: Now Can We Talk?*, 2013, Zinn Education Project, https://www.zinnedproject.org/materials/40-years-later-now-can-we-talk.

Kerr, Madeline. *Personality and Conflict in Jamaica*. Birkenhead, Great Britain, William Brothers & Haram, 1963.

Landau, Suzanne, and Jean Fisher. *Yinka Shonibare: Double Dress*. Jerusalem: Israel Museum, 2002.

Millett, Catherine M. *Investing in High Potential Underrepresented Youth: The I-LEAD College Outreach Program Is Paying Dividends*. Princeton, NJ: ETS, 2004.

New York University. *Notebook*. Special issue, 1960.

New York University Bulletin. General Information. June 27, 1960.

Powell, A. Wesley. *The Excelsior-EXED Story*. Jamaica: Stephensons Litho Press, 1989.

Sherlock, Philip, and Hazel Bennett. *The Story of the Jamaican People*. Kingston: Ian Randle; Princeton, NJ: Markus Wiener, 1998.

Siddle Walker, Vanessa. *Their Highest Potential*. Chapel Hill: University of North Carolina Press, 1996.

Silin, Jonathan G., and Carol Lippman. *Putting the Children First: The Changing Face of Newark's Public Schools.* New York: Teachers College Press, 2003.

RECOMMENDED FOR FURTHER READING ON JAMAICA

Bernal, Margaret Reckford. *Island Reliquaries: Voices from a Jamaican Past.* Kingston: Arts Jamaica, 2013.

Bishop, Jacqueline. *My Mother Who Is Me: Life Stories from Jamaican Women in New York.* Trenton, NJ: Africa World Press, 2006.

Bryan, Basil K. *The Jamaicans: Children of God in the Promised Land.* Denver: Outskirts Press, 2013.

Meikle, George. *In Praise of Jamaica.* Toronto: George Meikle, 2011.

ABOUT THE AUTHOR

Fern June Khan formerly served as dean of the Division of Continuing Education at Bank Street College and as associate dean for La Guardia Community College's Division of Adult and Continuing Education. She is board president of the Partnership for After School Education/PASE and serves on the boards of several nonprofits in New York.

Printed in the United States
by Baker & Taylor Publisher Services